LOST ROAD COURSES

- Riverside International Raceway
- Ontario Motor Speedway
- Bridgehampton Raceway
- Green Valley Raceway
- Edmonton International Speedway
- And Many More

MARTIN RUDOW

CarTech®

CarTech®, Inc.
6118 Main Street, North Branch, MN 55056
Phone: 651-277-1200 or 800-551-4754
Fax: 651-277-1203
www.cartechbooks.com

© 2016 by Martin Rudow

All rights reserved. No part of this publication may be reproduced or utilized in any form or by any means, electronic or mechanical, including photocopying, recording, or by any information storage and retrieval system, without prior permission from the Publisher. All text, photographs, and artwork are the property of the Author unless otherwise noted or credited.

The information in this work is true and complete to the best of our knowledge. However, all information is presented without any guarantee on the part of the Author or Publisher, who also disclaim any liability incurred in connection with the use of the information and any implied warranties of merchantability or fit-ness for a particular purpose. Readers are responsible for taking suitable and appropriate safety measures when performing any of the operations or activities described in this work.

All trademarks, trade names, model names and numbers, and other product designations referred to herein are the property of their respective owners and are used solely for identification purposes. This work is a publication of CarTech, Inc., and has not been licensed, approved, sponsored, or endorsed by any other person or entity. The Publisher is not associated with any product, service, or vendor mentioned in this book, and does not endorse the products or services of any vendor mentioned in this book.

Edit by Paul Johnson
Layout by Monica Seiberlich

ISBN 978-1-61325-772-2
Item No. CT549P

Library of Congress Cataloging-in-Publication Data Available

Written, edited, printed, and designed in the U.S.A.

Front Cover: Bridgehampton, located near Sag Harbor, New York, opened in 1957 and was one of the first permanent road courses in the United States. It hosted Can-Am, NASCAR Grand National, and World Sportscar Championship among other races. Stirling Moss called it America's most challenging track. The Chevron Bridge still stands on the course, but the track remains idle. (Photo Courtesy Judy Rudow) Inset: Jim Hall in the Chaparral 2G negotiates the many daunting twists and turns on the course. (Photo Courtesy Pete Lyons)

Front Flap:
A bemused crowd sees 1955 Grand Prix Race winner Sherwood Johnston shake hands with car owner Briggs Cunningham. (Photo Courtesy Gus Iacozili Collection)

Frontispiece: Dan Gurney earned the title as The King of Riverside. Gurney dominated at the track, winning five Grand Nationals and two Rex Mays 300s. He proved he was a versatile and talented driver year after year and was always very fast in whatever he drove at Riverside. (Photo Courtesy Allen Kuhn, vintage-sportscar-photos.com)

Title Page: A few Lotus cars, a couple of specials, a Bandini, an Abarth, even a Formula Junior get the starter's flag for an early 1960s small-bore modified race at Continental Divide Raceway. From the top of the hill, you could see the entire course. (Photo Courtesy Castle Rock Museum)

Contents Page:
The starting field crests a hill at Bridgehampton for the 1964 GT Double 500. Joe Buzzetta (30) and Gary Wuesthoff won in their Porsche 904. Others on the first row are Treischman/Young in an Elva-Ford and Rosendale/Alderman in a Genie-Alfa. At this stage in the track's history, the Chevron Bridge had not yet been built. (Photo Courtesy Robert Bohl)

Back Cover Photos

Top: The starting grid for the 1962 Pipeline 200 event. From front to back, #96 Dan Gurney (Lotus 18), #6 Roger Penske (2.5-liter Cooper), #77 Bob Schroeder (deTomaso Iris), #45 Bob Donner (Porsche RS-61), #16 Chuck Cassell (Porsche RS-60), #47 Harry Washburn (Porsche 550), and #36 Bob Hurt (Ferrari TR). (Photo Courtesy Willem Oosthoek Collection)

Bottom: This great study is of Bruce McLaren winning the 1967 Can-Am at Riverside in one of his fabulously successful cars. (Photo Courtesy Riverside Automobile Museum)

Author note: Some of the vintage photos in this book are of lower quality. They have been included because of their importance to telling the story.

Table of Contents

6	Preface	
7	Acknowledgments	
8	Introduction	
10	Chapter 1	**Augusta International Speedway/Raceway** The Legend of Alligator Hollow
18	Chapter 2	**Bridgehampton Raceway** America's Daunting Road Course
30	Chapter 3	**Continental Divide Raceway** Racing in the Rocky Mountains
42	Chapter 4	**Edmonton International Speedway** Racing's Far Northern Outpost
52	Chapter 5	**Green Valley Raceway** The Little Road Course of the Lone Star State
60	Chapter 6	**Greenwood Roadway** A Track Paved with Passion
68	Chapter 7	**Hilltop Raceway** Still Standing After All These Years
74	Chapter 8	**Marlboro Motor Raceway** The Grand Lady of the East
86	Chapter 9	**Meadowdale International Raceway** The Midwest Monster
98	Chapter 10	**Bahamas Speed Weeks** Party Central for the Racing Set
108	Chapter 11	**Ontario Motor Speedway** Where Hollywood Glitter Meets Motor Racing
116	Chapter 12	**Riverside International Raceway** Multi-Faceted Jewel in the Desert
132	Chapter 13	**Roosevelt Raceway** Too Good for Its Own Good
140	Chapter 14	**Stardust International Raceway** Dust and Drama in the Desert
148	Chapter 15	**War Bonnet Raceway Park** The Future Recreation, Vacation and Racing Destination
156	Chapter 16	**Watkins Glen** A Road Course History Not Forgotten
164	Chapter 17	**Westwood Motorsports Park** Wet, Wicked and Twisty
174	Epilogue	

Dedication

To the men and women whose dreams propelled
them to build the racetracks in this book.

Preface

During the summer of 2014, I was offered a unique opportunity. CarTech, one of the country's leading automotive publishers, was looking for an author. They were planning a book that would cover the racing history of abandoned racetracks around the continent. These were tracks that had been built specifically for racing, were no longer operating, and in many cases had been totally lost.

As an amateur historian who had been a big racing fan back in the heyday of so many of these tracks, it was an ideal project for my interests and abilities. After agreeing on the project, I decided that an in-person look at what was left of these old tracks would be an essential part of the background for the book. Accordingly, my wife and I left in early April 2015 in our trusty Rialta Motorhome and took an 8,400-mile trip around the country in a little over five weeks, going from one track site to the next, and we visited all the track sites profiled in this book with the exceptions of Edmonton and Nassau.

Walking the grounds of the old tracks or at least their sites, visiting with people who had raced at the tracks, and researching background material in person at local libraries and museums was a fascinating part of this project. Thanks to the Internet it is possible to conduct a lot of research without even leaving your office, but I felt and still feel that a personal touch is vitally important to the integrity of a project such as this. Along the way we met many great people who were eager to share their memories and memorabilia of racing days at nearby tracks. We also ran out of gas in Colorado . . . were stranded in the mud at the bottom of Hilltop Raceways . . . and, fittingly, even got stuck in roadside sand at Bridgehampton.

The trip and the months that followed in which I rounded up the photographs, programs, magazine articles, and stories have been both rewarding and fulfilling, and again I have been helped by the contributions of many generous people. Some were glad to help out of enthusiasm for the project, others rightfully requested and received compensation for the use of their photographs and research. I am grateful for all their assistance, and hope that this book reflects the passion that they, and I, have for those great days of racing.

— Martin Rudow

Acknowledgments

The photographers who loaned or leased their photographs for use in this book are credited in the photo captions. I am grateful to all of them, but in particular I thank the following people and institutions that provided use of their photos: Tom Johnston, Doug Dyar, Terry O'Neil, Douglas Mesney, Henry Jones, Bill Sadler, Brian Sinfield, Pat Bryan, Brent Martin, Ken Jones, Robert Raymond, Cliff Reuter, Jerry Melton, John Randall, and Dave Nicholas. Institutions that graciously lent me the use of their archives and photos from those archives at no cost include Bill Green and others at the International Motor Racing Research Center, Pat Flynn of the Riverside Automobile Museum, the Las Vegas Tourism Bureau, and the Castle Rock Historical Society. Thanks to all of you for your generosity.

Others received compensation for the use of their photos. Their dedication to keeping racing memories alive is beyond the price they charge. They include Pete Lyons, Dale Von Trebra, the Nassau County Department of Parks, Recreation & Museums, Photo Archives Center; the Henry Ford Museum Photo Archive, John McCollister, Ron Shaw, Ron Nelson of www.classicvintagemotorsports, and the Willem Oosthoek Collection.

Some individuals provided substantial contributions to the book through research and making material available to use. They include Mike Martin, whose own USRRC book remains the definitive record for that great series; Bill Green and others at IMMR; Peter Klebnikov, Mike Matune, Pat Flynn, and the Riverside Museum; the Nassau Country Museum; Steve Lloyd. Martin Spetz made scans from his extensive program collection available to me. My primary proofreader, also a volunteer, is Phil Edwards.

My sincere apologies to anyone who deserves to be included in this list but was inadvertently left out. I appreciate all the efforts of those who contributed to this special volume on the history of lost racetracks in North America.

INTRODUCTION

The 1950s and 1960s were an amazing time in the history of motorsports. Fueled by a passion of the variety of cars, large and small, both foreign and domestic, that were available, many men and a few women too wanted to test these cars and their own driving abilities to the fullest. Road racing began on public roads in places such as Watkins Glen and Bridgehampton in New York state and Pebble Beach and Golden Gate Park in California. After World War II, servicemen returned to America with a newfound interest in the grand European tradition of road racing. But there were few road course tracks in the country to hold races for sports cars and other open wheel classes. During the 1950s and 1960s, a number of new road course facilities opened in the United States to fill a need for amateur racers.

Racing on Runways

General Curtis LeMay allowed the widespread use of partially decommissioned Air Force facilities for road racing. It was a way to boost troop morale and show the usefulness of the bases to nearby residents. Country airports soon followed suit. The result was a period of delirious growth in sports car racing, which saw fields of more than 200 cars develop almost overnight as the 1950s hit mid-decade. The Sports Car Club of America (SCCA) led the way by sanctioning and conducting races throughout the country; in Canada local road racing enthusiasts formed their own groups. Photos of cars racing on flat concrete surfaces with hangars and other airport buildings in the background remain an iconic image of mid-1950s sports car racing.

Purpose-Built Racetracks

In just a few more years, as airport courses were less available or proved to have their own limitations, the need for purpose-built road courses became apparent. Airport courses proved to be usable into the late 1960s in unusual places, such as Nassau in the Bahamas. But in most places, purpose-built courses were the destination of choice for amateur road racers. And not just amateur weekend racers.

There was money to be made in racing by the 1960s, thanks to the professional racing opportunities first offered by the United States Auto Club (USAC) and those sanctioned by new rules from the SCCA. Fueled mainly by passion but also by the welcome reality that you could at least pay your expenses from race winnings, more professional teams and manufacturers became involved. They in turn supported the need for tracks with better safety features and other improvements to be more friendly to the spectators, whose presence was necessary to pay for the whole thing in the first place.

Courses such as Watkins Glen were vital to the economy of the town they were built around. Riverside, Ontario, and other similar tracks took advantage of the car-crazy culture of Southern California. In Canada, the stiff-upper-lipped British influence led racers to build Westwood, a course near Vancouver. It was impressive that these racers essentially built the track themselves and carved it out of the wilderness. Ambitious entrepreneurs with big hearts and rather small pocketbooks built independent road courses, and surprisingly enough these tracks often attracted some of the biggest racing names of the day.

Top Drivers Attract Big Crowds

Many fondly remember this as the golden era of American road racing. Automotive technology was improving by leaps and bounds in engine development, chassis design, and aerodynamics. Legendary drivers, such as Mario Andretti, A. J. Foyt, Al Unser, Dan Gurney, Parnelli Jones, and many others, raced and won races in four or five different types of race cars, including Can-Am, Formula 1, Indy Car, Sports Car, Trans-Am, and stock cars. Bruce McLaren, Jim Clark, John Surtees, Denny Hulme, and a long list of other foreign drivers arrived on American shores to compete in these top race series and made history on these classic road courses.

At that time, there were very few specialists, and many drivers demonstrated amazing versatility in driving radically different equipment. Teams such as Lance Reventlow's Scarabs, Jim Hall's Chaparrals, and Carroll Shelby's Cobras, as well as imported cars like McLaren, soon were competing with the cars and drivers of established manufacturers like Ferrari and Porsche. American-powered specials joined in and these cars competed in races that drew fans numbering in the tens of thousands. Can-Am, Trans-Am, the United States Road Racing Championship (USRRC), USAC Indycars, and Formula racing grew in popularity through the 1960s, and we thought it would never stop.

Many of the tracks covered in this book hosted the top professional racing series of the decade. Edmonton held Trans-Am, Can-Am, and Formula Atlantic races. Riverside attracted nearly every series and even started one of its own, the International Race of Champions. Even lesser-known tracks, such as Augusta and Greenwood, held national races, such as USRRC events. Some of the tracks that could attract top drivers and teams for one or two years, though, began to fail as the competition for top teams and spectator interest became too fierce.

Then, just as rapidly as it had grown, the popularity of road racing began to wane. With a grassroots oval racing system supporting it, National Association for Stock Car Auto Racing (NASCAR) stock car racing on oval speedways gained popularity because, in no small part, the casual fan easily understood and appreciated this form of racing. The safety concerns raised through a series of disastrous road racing wrecks came together in the early 1970s and dampened the enthusiasm for that form of racing. The tracks that had never really been financially stable were hit by declining interest. Many faded away and closed. Commercial interests quickly swallowed up those that had been holding out against development and today almost nothing concrete remains of them. Others just became empty and abandoned and even exist in some form today. All are part of a fabulous, colorful history that saw passion, epic race battles, spectacular cars, and mayhem played out in those specially built facilities that are remembered here.

In Conclusion

In writing this book, I delved deep into the history of each track to reveal the unvarnished story and uncover what made each track unique. In the process, I have covered the track's establishment, major races, decline, and closure. In the process, I have gathered previously unpublished photographs that show these tracks as they appeared during their time of operation, and I have also acquired photos of most of the road course properties as they stand today. But I have provided a comprehensive racing and track history, more than a business history of financing and track construction, although that is part of it, too. I hope you enjoy this retrospective into the golden era of road racing, the likes of which we shall not see again.

Augusta International Speedway/Raceway

THE LEGEND OF ALLIGATOR HOLLOW

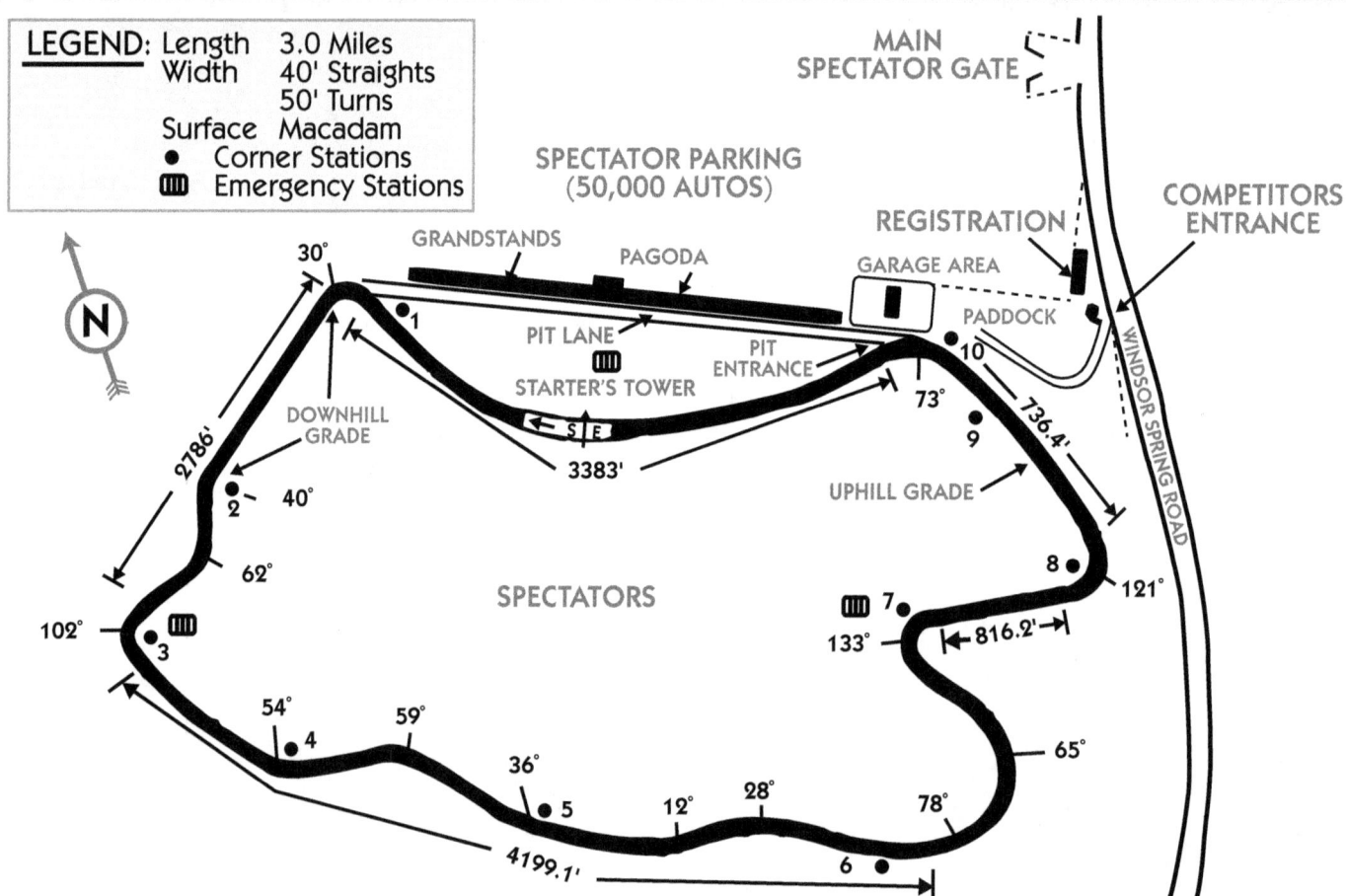

This facility and track map shows all of the details of this 3-mile road course. The United States Auto Club (USAC) stocker cars and the USRRC race shared the track. (Illustration Courtesy Henry Jones Collection)

Race fans of the Deep South embraced grassroots dirt-track oval racing and raised stock car racing to new heights. Conversely, the region eventually gravitated to the European tradition of road racing. This was true in the early 1960s when Augusta International Speedway was built and remains true today.

Augusta has the honor of having had more racetracks than any other city in Georgia, all ovals of various lengths and surfaces. But only Augusta Speedway/Raceway offered a true road course as well. Augusta Speedway/Raceway was intended to be a major motor sports complex, even including hydroplane boat racing, so naturally road racing had to be included. There was not much doubt, though, that drag racing and, especially, oval car racing were to be its main sources of income. Still, race management looked at recently built tracks such as Riverside and Elkhart Lake and saw the big road racing crowds those facilities drew. Could it be done in Georgia as well? If effort and money spent were measures, the answer had to be yes, then and now. So did it work? History provides the answer.

CHAPTER 1

Augusta, Georgia
1962–1969

Facility 3-mile road circuit, half-mile oval (dirt and paved), quarter-mile dragstrip, kart, micro-midget ovals
Principal Events USRRC, NASCAR Grand Nationals
Current Status County park; some of the old course remains

Drivers line up for the start of the 1964 Augusta USRRC Manufacturers' race. On the front row, from left to right, are the Cobras of Graham Shaw, Dave MacDonald, and eventual winner Ken Miles. The too-far-away grandstands can be seen in the background. (Photo Courtesy the Henry Ford)

Ground was broken for the new Augusta International Speedway during the summer of 1959. Enough stock for the original goal of $840,000 had been sold to get the whole project underway. The stated goal of President Brunson and the rest of the Speedway's investors was to build nothing less than the finest motorsports complex on the continent and they certainly proceeded with that plan in mind. The original oval drag/complex was quite spectacular. Seven metal grandstands (leased from a Florida company) were located along pit lane. The entrance area was part of a 500-foot-long, 20-foot-high wall next to the Augusta International Speedway Complex that ran along the nearest access street. Along the top over the entrance ran 5-foot-high concrete letters: "Augusta International Speedway — Where The Masters Race" (an oblique reference to Augusta's most famous sporting event). But, as one fan remembers, once you were inside, the track was "a real dustbowl ... you came home from a day at the track with your clothes caked with red Georgia clay."

The centerpiece of the facility was to be a 2-mile oval, which would have catapulted the complex into the top level of National Association for Stock Car Auto Racing (NASCAR) events. But it was never built. Financing was just too tight for such a major undertaking. However, the half-mile track that was built was still good enough to attract many of the biggest names in stock car racing. Brunson, the man thought to be the driving force behind the whole project, died at about this time, and Marshall Spray, the original secretary/treasurer of the corporation, became the most visible face of the complex.

A 200-lap, 100-mile event on the original half-mile dirt oval was the first race at the facility, and it was held on June 19, 1962. Only 16 cars started the race that saw top stocker Joe Weatherly start on the pole position and drive his Bud Moore–owned Pontiac to victory over Ned Jarrett.

Joe repeated the performance and won on July 17, 1962, over Richard Petty. Fred Lorenzen took home the win over Petty on September 13, the last race of 1962. They were big names in stock car racing and are still remembered today. Augusta had no trouble attracting top talent. One of the top drivers of the day, Glenn "Fireball" Roberts, was on the board of directors for the track and even helped design parts of it. His death following a racing accident in mid-1964 was a real blow. Many feel that with his leadership the track could have stabilized and grown. Maybe it would still be around today. But we will never know.

In April 1963, a crowd of 4,000 saw Ned Jarrett take his Ford to the victory lane over Richard Petty in the main stock car race of the year. Weekly oval and drag races were going on as well and they continued through the life of the track.

Marshall Spray is selling local officials on the potential of the proposed Augusta Speedway complex. (Photo Courtesy Augusta Museum of History)

1963: The Short Life of the Road Course

The road course, which was known as the Augusta International Raceway, part of the Speedway complex, was constructed during the summer of 1963 and was baptized that fall at the Augusta 510. Although certainly a road course, and a good one, it was designed primarily for stock car racing. All of its 21 turns were banked to some extent; the most severe was the first turn, which was at 40 degrees. Not what sports car drivers were used to.

The track itself was 3 miles long and 45 feet wide. Unlike many other road/oval/dragstrip complexes, the road course was completely separate from the drag straight and main grandstands, something that was probably a mistake for drawing spectators. Still, perhaps, it all could have worked if the facility had had more time to build a reputation, but track management needed a fast return on their investment; their enthusiasm had gotten the better of them and they had expanded the Augusta Speedway/Raceway too rapidly.

This aerial photo shows the extent of the Augusta complex. The oval tracks, a long way off, the dragstrip, and the golf course greens are clearly visible. The road course grandstands, still being built as this photo was taken, proved to be too far away from the action on the course. Today, this area has been completely developed. (Photo Courtesy Henry Jones)

Micro midgets had their own oval at Augusta, far from the road course. (Photo Courtesy the Augusta International Raceway Preservation Society)

The famed and feared Alligator Hollow is shown as it currently appears. This shot was taken looking down from the edge of the old course. (Photo Courtesy Judy Rudow)

The facilities for the road course portion of the complex track included a 15,000-square-foot garage area (50 x 300 feet) with two restrooms and showers. The track could hold 100,000 spectators, including bleacher seats for 20,000. However, the grandstands and bleachers were built far from the track. You had a heck of a view of the pits but far less of the action on the track.

The track elevation change was 120 feet. The highest point was at the pit exit and the lowest point was on the "backstretch" where spring-fed infield lakes drained into Spirit Creek just outside the track. It was the fastest part of the road course; cars carried a lot of speed into the tricky area. Top stock car racer Joe Weatherly called this part of the track "Alligator Hollow." The turn at Alligator Hollow was banked with a 20-foot drop on the outside; a small lake was on the inside. The edge of the track at this point was only 5 feet from the lake, which was not shallow. A car going into it might sink very quickly. Alligator Hollow was such a perfect name for a portion of a track in the Deep South. "Skunk Hollow" might have been even better, but I'll take Alligator Hollow.

The Augusta 510 was the first event held on the road course. It was run on November 17, 1963, with a noon start time and a 5:00 pm end time. The race actually covered 417 miles (671 km) because of the time limit. It was run counter-clockwise, as was the United States Road Racing Championship (USRRC) race held the next year.

The pole sitter was Fred Lorenzen with a qualifying speed of 89.545. He ran only 12 laps before engine failure forced him to retire. Lorenzen, Fireball Roberts, and sports car star Dave MacDonald were teammates for the Augusta 510.

Veteran NASCAR drivers respected MacDonald. The slight young man from California could drive anything, they said. In addition, his familiarity with shifting for corners gave him an extra advantage over other drivers who were used to ovals. Roberts won overall and MacDonald's 2nd-place finish gave Holman-Moody's Fords the top two spots. A total of 36 cars started the race and 16 finished. The event lasted for 4 hours and 50 minutes and the average speed was 86.32 mph. Ten lead changes took place during the event, and Richard Petty led the most laps (56). The total purse for the event was a guaranteed $50,620. The expected turnout (and the base used for calculating the purse) was 75,000 fans, but only 15,000 actually attended. From a driver's point of view, one disturbing factor emerged from the weekend: The surface was very abrasive. Tire wear was going to be a problem for the track. As was money. The track management lost a lot of money on this event.

1964: USRRC Race at Augusta

Bringing the USRRC series to the course for the 1964 season was a real coup for the track's management and seemed to signal the depth of their commitment to road racing at the circuit. When General Manager Marshall Spray announced the upcoming USRRC event, he stated, "We've finally gotten to the top of the ladder in sanction," and promised that the management would pursue similar big-time road racing events in the future. A purse of $10,000 was offered.

The March 1 race was the first of the season for the USRRC. As usual, the plan was to run two races on Sunday: the Manufacturers' Championship and the Drivers' Championship. Unlike the situation at two of the other USRRC tracks that year, enough of both groups of cars showed up for the Augusta event to make decent fields for the two separate races.

Later in the year at Greenwood and Road America, they ran both groups in one race to make a decent-size field. Two

This is a look at Alligator Hollow during the USRRC race. Poor weather hampered spectator turnout, which was just 8,000, far fewer than expected. (Photo by Joe Cawley, Courtesy Henry Jones)

separate 156-mile races, starting 2½ hours apart, gave drivers, including Dave MacDonald and Ken Miles, the opportunity to race in both. Their Manufacturers' Race was run in Shelby team Cobras; the Drivers' race with MacDonald in a Shelby team King Cobra and Miles back again in the "regular" Cobra ... But I'm getting ahead of myself.

The presence of the Shelby Cobra team was enough to spark the interest of even the most die-hard oval racing stock fan. After all, Shelby was a southern boy and his cars were really (much) glorified hot rods. The Shelby team was coming off an impressive 1963 season that saw its Cobras win both the SCCA "A" production and the USRRC GT Championship.

The Atlanta region of the SCCA provided the road course volunteer expertise for the weekend, and overall, drivers were pleased with the course and the facilities. The Shelby team was the only one entering cars in the Manufacturers' Race, although other Cobras were in the hands of privateers. Shelby was making the cars available to selected drivers and was not eager to have his own cars obviously outclass those of the customers. But outclass them they did, in the hands of MacDonald and Miles. Better cars almost assuredly; better drivers beyond a doubt. These two drivers were as good as anyone in the country during those years, and MacDonald had the advantage of having raced on the course during the previous fall. They were, quite literally, an unbeatable combination.

After letting clients' cars lead the first few laps, MacDonald and Miles took over and won handily. A spin by MacDonald and a resulting stall in the sand that surrounded the course gave the race to Miles. MacDonald was able to get out of the sand trap and finish a comfortable 2nd. In addition to the Cobras, Stingrays, and Porsches, a lowly Volvo P-1800 and a Bug Eye Sprite also raced and finished. Eighteen cars in all; not really a satisfactory turnout in the eyes of most observers.

In the Drivers' Championship race, the Cobras ran at the front again. The King-variety Cobras of Dave MacDonald and Bob Holbert finished 1st and 3rd. Jim Hall thrilled the crowd with a spectacular drive to a 2nd-place finish. Hall was driving one of his own Chaparral IIs and was actually quickest both in qualifying and in the race itself. He sat on the pole with a 1:47.2 while the best MacDonald could do in his blue King Cobra was a 1:48.2 to share the front row. Other notable cars in the field included Elva-Porsches (Charlie Hayes and Chuck Dietrich), a Ferrari 250LM (Buck Fulp), and assorted Porsches and Corvettes. A field of 27 cars assembled for the race.

The garages at the track were not exotic, but competitors were out of the sun and rain. Team Shelby Cobras await their handlers in the garage area prior to USRRC qualifying. (Photo by Joe Cawley, Courtesy Henry Jones)

USRRC practice makes for strange bedfellows as Jim Hall's Chaparral cuts under the much slower Morgan 4+4 of T. J. Kelly. The banking that was built into almost every Augusta turn is clearly evident. (Photo Courtesy the Henry Ford)

George Koehne's Genie-Ford (#93) won fifth overall in the USRRC Drivers' Race, Roger Heftier's Elva Mk7-BMW came in dead last, but he finished. The grandstands look close to the action here but the actual course was much farther away. (Photos by Joe Cawley, Courtesy Henry Jones)

At the start, Hall's tires slipped in some gasoline that had sloshed out of his tank, probably due to the slant on the road at the start/finish line, and several cars passed him. He was a considerable distance behind early leaders MacDonald and Holbert when he finally got going again. He then spent most of the race working his way through the pack. Track announcer Chris Economaki whipped the crowd of 8,000 into a frenzy as the white Chaparral closed in on the leading King Cobras.

On the 35th of the 56-lap race, Hall passed Holbert for 2nd place. From then on he steadily narrowed MacDonald's lead from 18 to 3.4 seconds going into the last lap, at which point Hall spun off at Turn 3 and ran out of time to challenge for the lead again. MacDonald finally won by 26.8 seconds with Holbert a distant 3rd. MacDonald's average speed was 97.653 mph, a much faster time than had been recorded by any of the numerous stock cars that had raced on the track the previous fall. He claimed a purse of $1,500 for his efforts.

Alligator Hollow claimed one victim that day when Chuck Dietrich, driving an Elva-Porsche, went over the bank and dropped 20 feet before landing upright on all four wheels. He was unhurt but his car was out of the race. Overall, the circuit was deemed fast. Dangerous, too, but not overly so. Reporter Brock Yates called it an "unforgiving circuit."

The 8,000 spectators had to be pleased. The only drawback was the placement of the main straightaway and the main grandstands to watch it: 200 long yards separated them, making for a viewing experience that was far from intimate.

If the 8,000 USRRC spectators were pleased, track management definitely was not. Again, they lost a bundle on a road race. They never really had the financing to match their dreams, and this road race loss hurt them. Harold Peden, whose company had graded and paved the road course, was, by necessity, paid in stock and became the default owner of the entire facility. Facing the need for major course repairs and safety enhancements after less than one year of racing on the circuit, Peden and the other stock holders decided, for the time being at least, to schedule no more road events at the facility.

In fact, that was pretty much it for road racing at Augusta, professional or otherwise. From then on the road course was allowed to deteriorate. Spectators at other motorsport events at the track occasionally drove around it, sometimes to their sorrow because it was not a safe place for amateur high-speed driving. Local sports car enthusiasts used the parking lot for gymkhanas and autocross events, but they were never allowed to use the road course.

The old Devin-Chev of Wilbur Morgan chugs out of the pits ahead of race winner Dave MacDonald's King Cobra for the start of the USRRC Drivers' Race. The Devin made just four laps. (Photo Courtesy the Henry Ford)

The old long backstretch beckoned unofficial racing for years after the course officially closed. The trees have grown up since then. (Photo Courtesy Judy Rudow)

Much of the old road course still exists. This section of the old Turn 1 now leads to the complex of sports fields that is part of Diamond Lakes Regional Park. (Photo Courtesy Judy Rudow)

The track did not survive the times, but an exquisite memorial stands in its place. Augusta has the best memorial to the racing of yesteryear at its race complex of all the places I visited. (Photo Courtesy Judy Rudow)

Racing at the noted Southern track drew to a close. When it was all over for the Augusta International Raceway complex, it was simply auctioned off to the highest bidder. (Photo Courtesy Henry Jones)

The 1964 season saw another major change when the oval was paved with asphalt and stock car racing went on. The largest Augusta Speedway crowd ever (14,000) saw the largest field ever (30) take the green flag on November 1, 1964. The race also received the title Jaycee 300; the race was increased to 300 laps over the previous 200. Darel Dieringer won the event in a Bud Moore–prepared Mercury. A good turnout, but, overall, local fans were not pleased to see the oval paved. Dirt tracking was their preferred form of motor racing.

1965: More Oval Racing

Top names on the stock car racing circuit continued to show up for oval racing at Augusta. On August 15, 1965, Dick Hutcherson (Ford) won a 200-lap event with a 2.75-second lead over David Pearson. On November 14 of that same year, Richard Petty, still in a Plymouth, took home a victory in the Georgia Cracker 300.

In those days the wild and crazy Curtis Turner used to land his plane at Augusta for his races on the oval, just a few feet away from the track. When taking off he would "buzz" the oval, to everyone's delight.

1969: The Last Season

On March 16, 1969, David Pearson (Ford) won the first of two events during the last season of racing at the track. He won over Richard Petty (now in a Ford) with Bobby Isaac (Dodge) finishing 3rd after starting on the pole with a record lap of 86.901 mph. On October 19, 1969, a field of 29 cars took the green flag at the track for the last time. The 4,500 that attended the race only saw two lead changes between Bobby Isaac and Richard Petty, back in the same cars. The entire race went caution free. The race time was only 1:16:12 and the average speed was 78.74 mph (126.72 km/h). Bobby Isaac won for the second time at the track.

Today: Diamond Lakes Regional Park Complex

Forty-five years later people around Augusta still speculate about why the track was closed. "Political corruption" is heard. NASCAR's support was suspect. Reportedly, they really wanted the Bristol track to succeed rather than Augusta. A more rational conclusion is that the track simply never drew the kind of spectator support it needed. Initially, management spent money to build a major facility and bring in top talent, but the spectator support just was not there. Toward the end, the track's third owner ran up more bills than he could pay. Finally the facility was auctioned off and the county took ownership, with no interest in continuing racing at the facility.

The remains of the track were unsecured for years. People drove around the oval as well as the road course to relive old memories or to create new memories. But the death of a young motorcyclist on the old course led to it being closed to such shenanigans. First, holes were punched into the oval's surface so no one could drive it, and then the county gradually took advantage of the cleared land to build the Diamond Lakes Regional Park complex. Similar to the way Augusta Speedway was envisioned in the beginning as a multi-use motorsports facility, Diamond Lakes Regional Park is a multi-use recreational facility that supports all kinds of sporting events, from baseball to soccer to golf.

Today, traces of the former 3-mile road circuit are the only remnants of the complex and the course is being developed into new parts of the Diamond Lakes Park. In large part thanks to the efforts of Henry Jones, an Augusta resident who has great memories of racing at the complex, a memorial to the track and the men who raced there was erected next to the park headquarters building.

As surrounding residential streets were being built, Jones and others convinced the developers to remember the course further by naming roads after some of the drivers who raced there. Street names include Dave MacDonald Drive, Ken Miles Drive, Glenn Roberts Drive, Frank Warren Drive, T. J. Kelly Drive, Weldon Adams Drive, and Ted Tidwell Lane. The main entrance to the Manchester subdivision and the circle is Dave MacDonald Drive. Because Dave had the most laps at the road course, he received this honor.

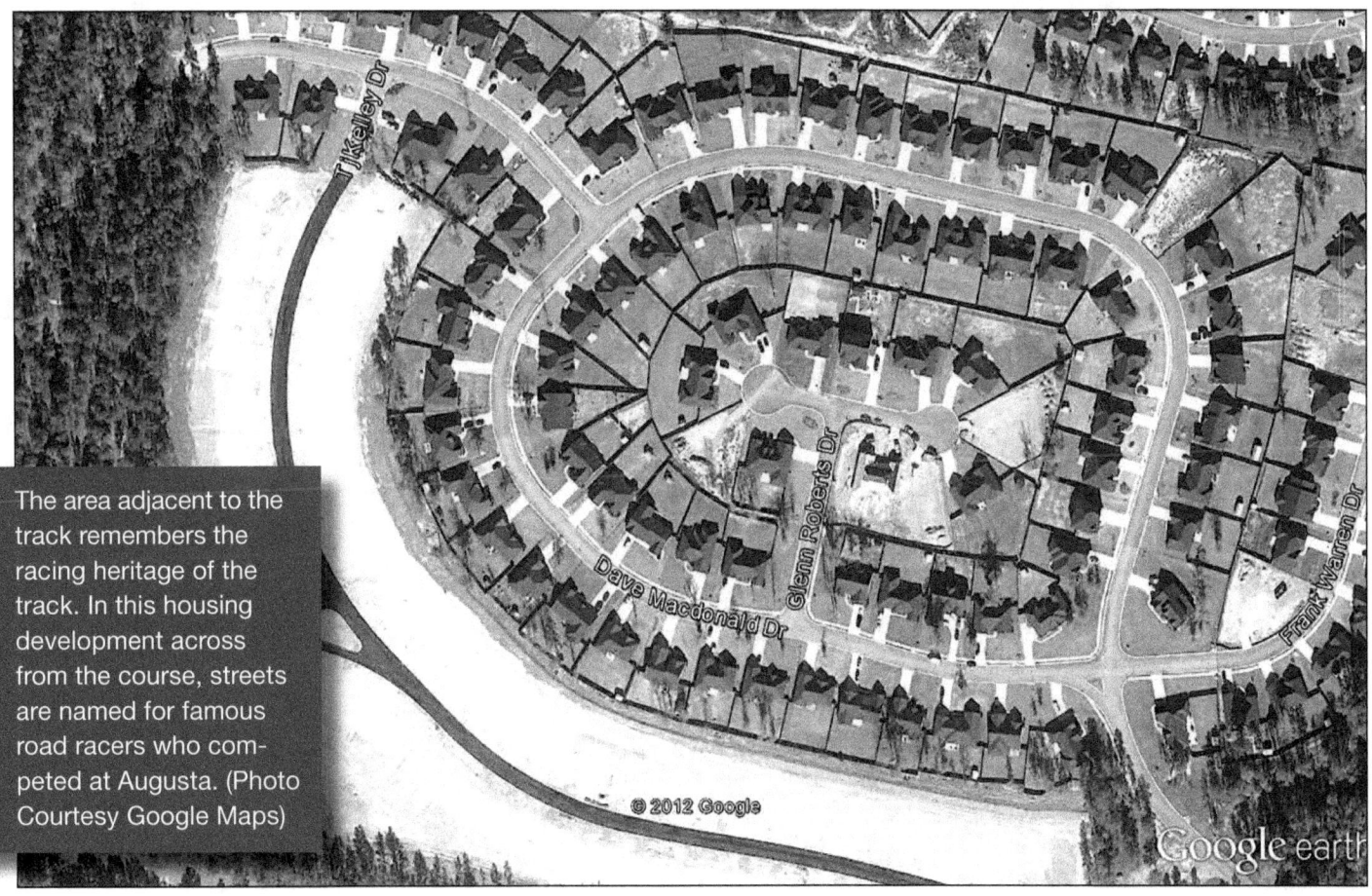

The area adjacent to the track remembers the racing heritage of the track. In this housing development across from the course, streets are named for famous road racers who competed at Augusta. (Photo Courtesy Google Maps)

BRIDGEHAMPTON RACEWAY

AMERICA'S DAUNTING ROAD COURSE

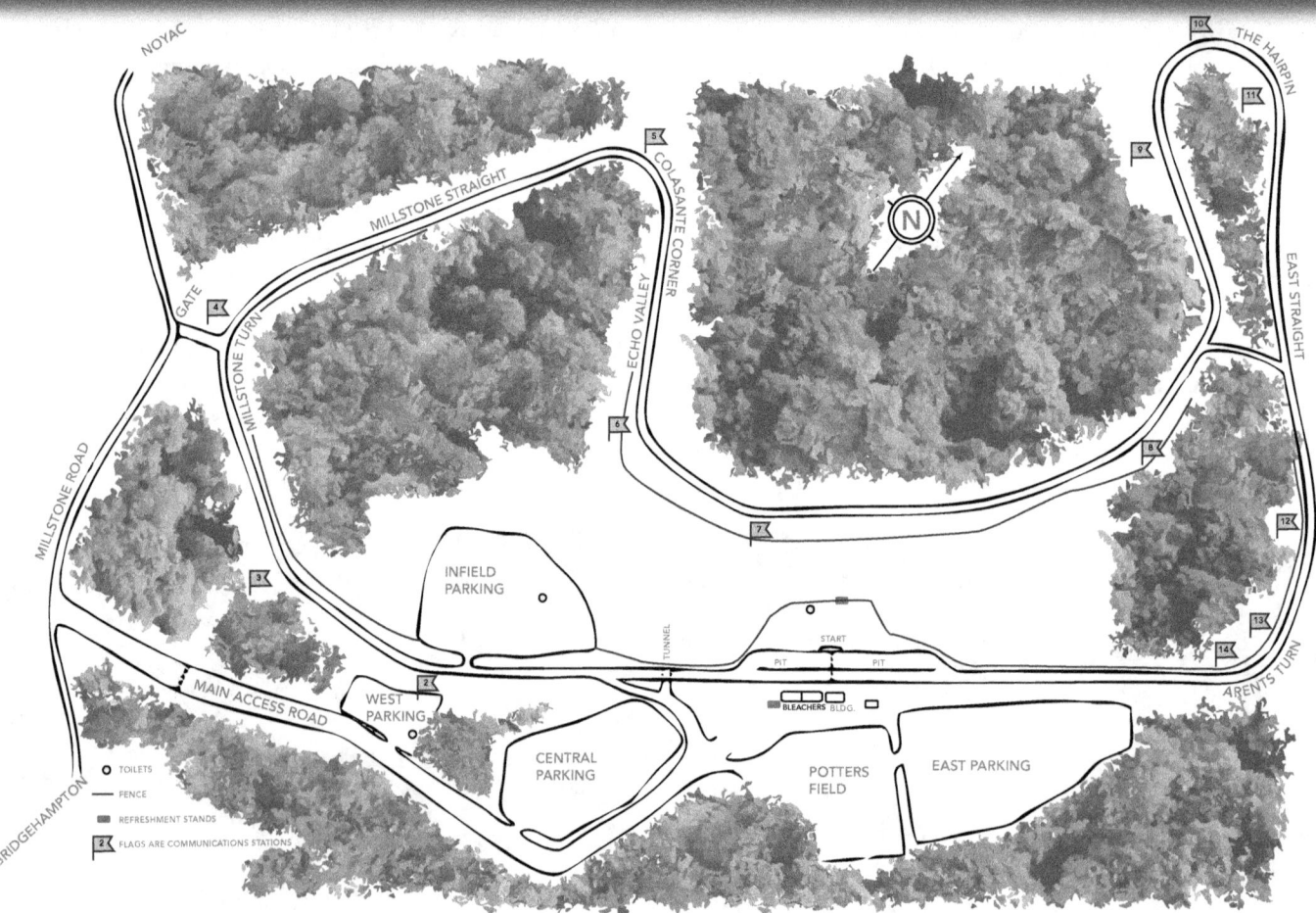

The Bridgehampton course map. The little numbered flags are the turn numbers, not golf course holes. The clubhouse now occupies the "Potters Field" space. (Illustration Courtesy Martin Spetz Program Collection)

Racing at Bridgehampton was many things. It was exciting, naturally, and as colorful as any other course. Challenging? Even Stirling Moss called it one of the most challenging courses in the world. Its unique location overlooking beautiful Peconic Bay gave it a stunning backdrop and the big-time racing it brought to the tip of Long Island makes it one of the most memorable courses, too.

The race course at Bridgehampton lived and eventually died in a region that had extensive racing history. Road racing in the then-remote potato farming village of Bridgehampton had started on public roads in 1915 and lasted until the 1920s.

In 1949, J. Bruce Stevenson, a World War II flying ace and president of the local MG Car Club, revived racing in the little town. Like most other road races of the day, it was to be held on public roads. Why not? If it had been good enough in 1915, it would be good enough now!

The course that Stevenson and his principal backer, local businessman B. J. Corrigan, came up with was roughly rectangular in shape, 4 miles around with a humpback bridge, and long straightaways that skirted the ocean. It was all on concrete road surfaces. Notably, it was located partially in neighborhoods and city streets just south of Bridgehampton, the

CHAPTER 2

Bridgehampton, Long Island
New York
1957–1999

Facility 2.85 miles, 13 turns, asphalt, 3,100-foot straightaway
Principal Events USRRC, Can-Am, Trans-Am, FIA, NASCAR
Current Status Golf course

Wasting no time at the 1969 Can-Am, Bruce and Denny are in the lead. Eventual 3rd-place finisher Jo Siffert drives Porsche #0, five rows back. (Photo Courtesy Douglas Mesney)

middle and least prosperous of the three Long Island Hamptons. That road course survives nearly unchanged today, and the Bridgehampton Museum honors this legacy with annual rallies on the local roads. In 1949 Bridgehampton hosted America's second road race of the postwar era (Watkins Glen had hosted the first). It was a hit. The number of people who showed up is debatable, but it was perhaps upwards of 30,000. Regardless of the actual number, it was a boon to the town's prestige and economy.

A great mix of pre- and postwar cars, including three Bugattis and the first Ferrari imported into the United States (by Briggs Cunningham), entered the races. An 8C 2600 Alfa won the first feature in the hands of George Huntoon.

Racing on the course was immediately popular and drew drivers and spectators from all over New England, despite an approach consisting of two-lane roads and long traffic backups. Celebrities, such as Dave Garroway and George Montgomery, were honorary guests and Briggs Cunningham, as was to become the norm, came with a stable of exotic imported cars, including that Ferrari. Walt Hansgen made the first race of his accomplished and ultimately tragic career in 1951, driving a Jaguar XK-120. As with Watkins Glen, though, racing soon outgrew the round-the-houses course. And, as with Watkins Glen, the point was made dramatically.

Preliminaries for the 1953 event saw the course's first flip, and a fatal one at that. Bob Wilder, a successful local driver in an Allard J2X, lost control coming off the humpback bridge and suffered a fatal crash. The bridge survives today virtually unchanged on Bridge Lane. City fathers and race officials nervously let the weekend's racing continue, but during the Sunday final some of the huge and hard-to-control crowd of 50,000 surged across the fragile snow fencing and several of them were hurt when a Jaguar rolled into them. A brilliant race between Phil Walters (OSCA) and Bill Spear (4.1 Ferrari) had to be called on the spot. Also called off, for all intents and purposes, was racing on Bridgehampton's city streets. The New York legislature later made it official: no more racing on their state's public roads.

1957: Bridgehampton Opens with a Bang

The new Bridgehampton course had a soft opening in August 1957 with a drivers' school. The track then hosted a wide variety of events, even a soapbox derby and a foot race. NASCAR failed to make it there, but SCCA club racing, followed by national and international racing, attracted decent crowds. Bridgehampton opened in 1957, along with a number of other prominent road courses, including Laguna Seca, Lime Rock, and Virginia International. Opening weekend for Bridgehampton was on two absolutely glorious early fall days, September 28 and 29. The recently plowed-up sand was a pristine white, the sky was blue, and the newly laid asphalt cut a colorful dark path through the white dunes.

Winning a Bridgehampton race was a big deal in 1951, and it earned Tom Cole and his Allard a cover shot. (Photo Courtesy Mike Martin Collection)

That first race had 139 entries, and reports said that spectator cars were parked as far as a mile away. Estimated attendance was a promising 30,000, although it was likely much more; many people entered without going through the ticket booth. Walt Hansgen won the main event in a D-Jaguar. This was the first of eight-straight feature races that the fearless Hansgen won in SCCA events at the track, all in cars that were part of the Briggs Cunningham team. Hansgen should be remembered as the King of Bridgehampton, not just for his wins there but also for being the first to master Turn 1 flat out.

Unlike some other courses supposedly bordered with sand (Riverside and Stardust come to mind) Bridgehampton's track border really *was* sand, not pebbles and small rocks as were the other two courses. The sand could help you stop quickly when you went off in a straight line, but it also could catch a turning wheel and send you end-over-end in a heartbeat, as happened all too often. The sand could also become airborne quickly and create a nasty sandstorm when strong winds blew, as they did frequently on the hilltop. This was hell on motorcycle racers.

Only a few grandstands ever graced the track, and they were small, wooden, and old. Most spectators stood in the sand behind snow fencing or sat on the dunes. Many other great viewing spots were scattered around the dunes and grandstands.

1958: SCCA Returns

The start of the 1958 season showed the early instability of the track's finances, as there was uncertainty over whether an SCCA National would be held, despite the previous year's good turnout. In the end, fans were rewarded with a good day of racing that saw the Cunningham team show up again with Walt Hansgen and Briggs Cunningham firmly established as masters of the track. Hansgen won and set a new lap record of 1:52 in a Cunningham D-Jaguar. George Constantine, who had so many memorable races with Hansgen in the late 1950s, came in 2nd in an Aston-Martin DBR-2.

A 100-mile NASCAR event, reportedly the first Grand National held on a non-oval road course, was held that year, and attracted the big names in stock car racing, including Lee Petty, Junior Johnson, and Buck Baker. It was quite a show. Jack Smith won in a Chevrolet. As was the case with the big crowd the year before, ticket gates could not handle the traffic and thousands of people simply strolled in through the woods and watched the races for free while track management began sinking under debt. The Cunningham team showed up again for the next year's SCCA race. Hansgen, this time in a Jaguar-powered Lister, again beat Constantine in the DBR-2, which was now running a larger engine. A crowd of 8,000 was reported, but it was hard to estimate crowds at courses such as Bridgehampton because spectators were scattered instead of concentrated in grandstands. A few local businessmen banded together to help run Bridgehampton pro bono and reduce track debt as well as provide some basic amenities.

1960 and 1961 Seasons

For several years, the SCCA Nationals were the top events at Bridgehampton. The 1960 race saw Hansgen win again, his

This driver has an off-track excursion at Echo Valley. The soft sand at Bridgehampton was forgiving but was a consistent concern. If you were caught in it, you'd lose traction and your race was over. (Photo Courtesy Robert Bohl)

The BRRC is Created

In 1954 B. J. Corrigan, other local businessmen, and wealthy weekenders got together to form the Bridgehampton Road Race Corporation (BRRC) to develop a safer, closed-circuit course in the wooded hills 4 miles north of town. The group purchased "woodlots" from dozens of old farms, and ended up with a spectacular 560-acre parcel. Two Grumman Aircraft engineers came up with the design for a challenging course and, with the $300,000 the BRRC had raised, surveying, grading, and paving commenced. Fund-raising went on in many forms, including selling shares at $5 a pop to passersby at the Candy Kitchen, which still exists on Bridgehampton's main street.

Ground level fund-raising was successful enough to open the track, but Bridgehampton was always a bare-bones operation and never tapped into the funding to reach its huge potential: a world-class racetrack only 100 miles from Times Square! But unlike other racetracks with similar woes that had to close, Bridgehampton stuck it out for more than 40 years, admittedly gearing down as time wore on. And it attracted some of the world's best racing drivers and the world's fastest cars to the big-time international racing series that were held at the track, especially in the 1960s.

The pits were built inside the track, something that became an annoyance to drivers needing to leave quickly for a parts run or any other reason. One particular high point among the few amenities the track had to offer was The Circuit Club, a rich guys' party hangout built across from the pit area that was not really that fancy but still, almost by default, attracted the big-money boys and even celebrities such as Paul Newman and Truman Capote. During initial construction, funding was so short that bulldozer operators kept quitting because they were not being paid. At least one operator sued and was paid in shares, which he then gave to his lawyer as payment. Track ownership began to gradually move away from racing people and locals.

Here's a contemporary write-up by Peter Klebnikov on the Bridgehamptonraceway.com website.

"The layout featured a jaw-dropping 180-degree view of Long Island's North Fork, Shelter Island, Sag Harbor, and the sailboats on Peconic Bay. The circuit had four vertical elevation changes totaling 130 feet and eight distinct corners, including a banked hairpin curve around a hillock at the lowest point of the course. A flat-out straightaway nearly three-quarters of a mile long suddenly disappears into a hair-raising decreasing-radius downhill curve, known as Millstone Turn. More than one international star has called this steep decline, which is blind and taken flat out in most race cars, the most difficult turn in racing. Sam Posey, for one, said that sailing off the abyss in a sports racer was like 'flying into an air pocket' in a plane."

Racing legend Stirling Moss called "The Bridge," as it was immediately nicknamed, "the most challenging course in the United States."

It was exciting but dangerous and this is why racing moved out of the town of Bridgehampton. Briggs Cunningham (#16), Charles Moran (#12), and Robert Yung (#19), all in Ferraris, power out of Bridge Lane onto Ocean Road during a 1952 race. (Photo Courtesy Pete Lyons/petelyons.com)

Formula 1 legend Stirling Moss has a chat at Bridgehampton, which he called America's most challenging track. Moss had retired from full-time racing in 1962 and was on hand to drive the pace car for the 1965 USRRC race. (Photo Courtesy Robert Raymond)

fourth win in a row at The Bridge, but the first without Jaguar power. The Cunningham team had gone to Maserati, and Walt drove a beautiful 2.9-liter Tipo 61 to victory. A rather small field that included a Ferrari California competed in an eight-race schedule.

The SCCA regional races in late May 1960 saw Hansgen win in both the Formula Junior (Cooper) and feature (Tipo 61) races. The Vanderbilt Cup race had been revived the year before at its old Roosevelt Raceway site on Long Island; it moved to Bridgehampton in 1961. In 1960 (as in earlier races), it was a race for Formula Juniors, and for once, Hansgen did not get all the wins; he finished 3rd in a Cooper-Fiat-OSCA hybrid from the Cunningham stable. Peter Ryan, whose flame burned brightly but briefly in the early 1960s, won in a Lotus 20. Hansgen did manage to win that year's featured SCCA National race, though, in a Tipo 63 Maserati.

A particular renegade driver added drama to both days. He showed up in a Corvette, drove like hell in the big-bore production race, was black-flagged, and then refused to pull off. After he finished, his license was suspended but he was not sent home, which was a mistake. He showed up the next day and snuck onto the track for the feature. He roared off again, passing almost everyone and scaring them with horrendous, fast driving. The whole field was black-flagged, the race stopped, and the offender arrested by local police (and I don't mean track police) before the race was restarted without him.

The pebbles that underlay the Bridgehampton sand unexpectedly became the short-time savior of the track. In the fall of 1961, a construction company bought ten years' worth of the gravel, and that cash allowed annoying debts to be paid off and provided enough funds to keep the track going for several years. But soon after this welcome announcement came the word that everyone who arrived at Bridgehampton in any capacity (entrant, pit worker, press, and friends) was to be charged a $2.00 daily pass. Much grumbling ensued; remember, that's about $20 in today's money. The tradition of freeloaders only vaguely associated with some race car or the other getting in for free had gotten out of control. Track management decided to limit the numbers with this change and raise some needed revenue at the same time.

Even so, for years to come many people claimed that the Bridgehampton pits were the most crowded of any big-time racetrack. At Bridgehampton, as at other tracks at the time, fans enjoyed a level of access to drivers and cars that is unthinkable in today's racing world. For that $2 paddock pass in the 1960s, you could listen in on world champions such as Denny Hulme or John Surtees decoding the handling of their cars with their chief mechanic, see Stirling Moss flirting with a race queen, or be part of the banter between teammates.

1962: The Double 400

In 1962 a glamorous new event arrived that tested the limits of fabulous drivers such as Hansgen: the Double 400. It was the track's first international race, offering FIA Grand Touring cars Manufacturers' points. The Double 400 drew unique sponsorship from the *New York Daily Mirror*, along with its means to publicize the event.

Also unique, for these parts anyway, was the two-day format that allowed drivers to race 400 km for GT1 and GT2 cars (up to 2 liters) on Saturday and 400 more for GT III (over 2 liters and FIA/SCCA modifieds over 1 liter) on Sunday. Chevron jumped in to help with co-sponsorship and the track was able to hold the highest ticket price to just $2.00, even for admission to the fabulous clubhouse where you could buy high-priced cocktails.

Legendary Mexican driver Pedro Rodríguez, who never missed a professional Bridgehampton race if he was in the country, was there with a 4-liter Ferrari supplied by Luigi Chinetti; he easily won the prototype class. Ferrari 250GTs went 1-2 in Saturday's GT race, where the real race was between Walt Hansgen in a lightweight E-type Jaguar and Dick Thompson in a Sting Ray. Hansgen beat Thompson when the Corvette broke down shortly before the finish. Rodríguez set a new course record of 1:49.6. Saturday's GT 1 and 2 races were good too; Hansgen was there in a Fiat-Abarth, but Bob Holbert won a close one in a 1.6-liter Porsche-Abarth.

The September race weekend was the most all-around successful at the facility to date with a record field and reported record *paid* attendance of 15,000.

Perhaps buoyed by the big turnout for the previous season's 400s, over the winter the track management installed a much-needed tunnel between the paddock and the outside world. No longer would racers needing a quick run for a part be stuck inside until the races were over and it was too late.

Apparently, the change did not affect the Cunningham team and Walt Hansgen, who had probably brought along everything they could possibly need anyway. He won the SCCA National for the mind-boggling eighth-straight time. His tactic was simple and it kept working. He got the jump on everyone at the start, took the downhill sweeping right-hander flat out, and never let anyone pass. It helped of course to have the hottest machinery underneath you, and Briggs Cunningham saw to that. That particular weekend is remembered for its great weather.

That summer saw a NASCAR invasion of the track for a 100-mile Grand National, held in conjunction with the interclub races. Richard Petty won in a Plymouth with a fast lap of 1:56.8, compared to the sports car track record of 1:49.2 (Rodríguez the year before). The race was made more interesting by the promise of a total eclipse of the sun on Saturday, which, in

Check out the fabulous field for the 1963 Double 400 GT race. Front row: Shelby Cobras, with (from left), Ken Miles, Dan Gurney, and Bob Holbert. Following them are the lightweight E-Jags of Walt Hansgen and Briggs Cunningham. The Cobras of Gurney and Miles finished 1-2. (Photo Courtesy the Henry Ford)

the end, did not darken the track. A good turnout of stockers was on hand, including Lee Petty, Fred Lorenzen, Marvin Panch, and Fireball Roberts. Of course, it was really a preliminary to the big event of the year, a return of the Double 400.

1963: The Double 500

In 1963, the Double 400 became a Double 500, with a lineup similar to the previous year's race. The GT cars ran 500 km on Saturday while prototypes did 500 km on Sunday. A fabulous GT field included Briggs Cunningham's E-type team led by Walt Hansgen and Carroll Shelby's awe-inspiring Cobra team of Bob Holbert, Ken Miles, and Dan Gurney. Hansgen, of course, was not awed in his lightweight E-type, and led the Cobras, for a while at least, before Gurney and Miles finished 1-2 with Hansgen 3rd. The next day Hansgen prevailed with a Buick-engined Cooper over Pedro Rodríguez in the Le Mans–winning 3-liter NART Ferrari. More than 14,000 fans were there to see the Hansgen car stagger home with various ailments with Rodríguez closing fast and turning in a new lap record of 1:47.2.

1964: Grand National is Back

Walt Hansgen did not win the next year's SCCA race, but it was because he was not even there. He was off chasing bigger fish on the international scene. In his place, Tom O'Brien piloted a V-8 2-liter Dino Ferrari to the feature win. A Cobra beat Bob Grossman, a veteran of the course, in big-bore production. Grossman's skill, course familiarity, and his Ferrari could no longer keep pace with Shelby's snakes, which, with their awesome power, were the ultimate weapon on the long straights of The Bridge.

The Grand National race was back in 1964. Evidently the stockers had been popular enough to warrant their return. After some sports car prelims, Bill Wade, a lesser-known name, won in a Mercury. Walt Hansgen was there, too, in a Ford, coming in 3rd. The crowds were impressed by the fender-banging style of the NASCAR drivers as they twisted around the road course. The stockers did not have much experience with road courses and delighted the crowd by plowing through the sand as they "straightened" turns and tore up safety tires. "At one point you could see six different dust clouds around the track," recalls one spectator. "It was grand mayhem."

Another unusual feature of Bridgehampton is that, up until the end, it didn't have much in the way of ARMCO barriers. When the heavy, iron-like stock cars, Corvettes, and Cobras went off into the woods, spectators could see how far they went by watching the trees bend.

At the Double 500 that year all eyes were on Cobra and Ferrari as the two were locked in an FIA Manufacturers' battle, and Shelby entered no fewer than six 289s at Bridgehampton. They finished 1, 2, 3, 4, 5, 6; that's right, a complete sweep after Ferrari had focused its efforts instead on a European race the same weekend. Walt Hansgen was the big winner again in the prototype class, again over the Ferrari-equipped Pedro. This time, Walt drove a Scarab owned by John Mecom. Hansgen showed his mastery of the course by passing Pedro on the inside of Turn 1. He took the lead, which he never lost, and set a new lap record of 1:44.6 in the process.

1965: Arrival of the Big Races

The second half of the 1960s saw Bridgehampton hold its share of big national series: USRRC, Can-Am, and Trans-Am. It started in 1965 when the annual mid-May SCCA National was replaced by the USRRC. The Chaparrals were the attention-getting cars of the 1965 USRRC series, and their sleek white bodies looked great against the blue skies, blue water, and white sands of Bridgehampton.

Only veteran Bridgehampton racer George Wintersteen was able to make it close for a while in his Cooper Monaco/

Stock cars raced wheel to wheel at Bridgehampton. The starting field lines up for this 1964 Grand National race. NASCAR champions Richard Petty (#43) and David Pearson (#6) reside on the front row. Petty finished 13th and Pearson finished 8th. Driver Billy Wade won in a Mercury (#1). (Photo Courtesy Robert Bohl)

In the 1964 GT Double 500, Joe Buzzetta (#30) and Gary Wuesthoff won in their Porsche 904. Others on the first row are Treischman/Young in an Elva-Ford and Rosendale/Alderman in a Genie-Alfa. The field crests and runs down the hill. The famous Chevron Bridge has not yet been built. (Photo Courtesy Robert Bohl)

Chev. In the end, Jim Hall and his teammate Hap Sharp had little trouble making it a 1-2 finish for the white cars from Texas. Hall also set a new lap record, a very impressive 1:38.8 that broke the previous record by three seconds. It was a great field of 38 starters (combined Manufacturers' and Drivers' Races). Track management had designated the race for the Vanderbilt Cup, as were the next four USRRC races (over the following four years) at the track. About 12,000 spectators saw Hall win the trophy.

The 1965 Double 500 mid-September weekend saw Hap Sharp back at the track in a new 2C Chaparral, and again he won the feature race. He beat Pedro Rodríguez's 4.4-liter Ferrari after early leader Walt Hansgen broke down in a Lola T70. It was the first time Hansgen was beaten in a feature race at Bridgehampton. (Early the next year, the popular and talented Hansgen lost his life testing one of the potent but erratic Ford GT-40s). The first GT car was Bob Johnson's 289 Cobra. The race marked the road course debut of promising young driver Mario Andretti. Here's what a clearly nervous Mario said before the race: "This is really a tricky course. I'll have to be very, very careful!"

1966: Best Yet

The 1966 season was heralded as the best yet for the track. The USRRC was back, as was an SCCA National, the stock cars, and then the inaugural Can-Am race in September (the Doubles were gone). In the USRRC race, Jerry Grant finally had a big win in Dan Gurney's Lola. The fast but inconsistent driver had consistently qualified fast in USRRC events but failed to finish. This time, he did both. But it was tricky; the week before the race saw very heavy rains and the track was often under water or covered with wet sand. Grant completed his qualifying session between rainstorms; he ran a 1:39.2 and beat a strong field of 33 cars for the win.

Spectators loved Bridgehampton for its dizzying turns and elevation changes. Drivers loved it, too, although some were nonplussed by the lack of amenities. Arriving for practice at the Grand National that summer, NASCAR star David Pearson looked around the sand dunes and drawled: "This here is the end of the earth and that ain't no shit." Then he went on to win the race.

The brand-new Can-Am series came to Bridgehampton that year, and Dan Gurney was the winner in a Lola T70 Ford. For the popular Gurney, it was his only win at the track and the only time Ford power won a Can-Am race. Gurney barely held off New Zealand ace Chris Amon in a McLaren in the closing laps, and staggered exhausted out of his car at the end.

The race was also notable for the international debut of winged sports cars. The Chaparral 2Es of Jim Hall and Phil Hill showed up with rear-mounted wings and created an enormous stir throughout the motorsports world.

1967: A Wet Year

The summertime SCCA events in 1967 were wet races at the track, and the weather kept fans away. But in May the USRRC went off without rain and featured a fierce battle for the lead between George Follmer and local boy Mark Donohue. Donohue took the checkered flag. At that time, he was establishing himself as top USRRC dog in his Lola T70-Chevy. Longtime pro Masten Gregory showed that he still had it by coming in 2nd in a McLaren M1-C, despite two laps missed while being stuck in the sand. Mike Goth was 3rd in a Lola with a frightening amount of the left front fender missing after an on-course crunch.

Spectators on the hillside enjoy the great view at Colasante Corner as cars stream by in the 1967 USRRC. Spectator control at Bridgehampton was never adequate. (Photo Courtesy Douglas Mesney)

Turns 1 and 2, shown here in the 1967 Can-Am, are today's entrance roads to the golf course. Lothar Motschenbacher (McLaren) leads Sam Posey (Caldwell) and a small pack. (Photo Courtesy Peter Klebnikov)

Spectators take advantage of the high dune hillsides to view the Can-Am cars of Bob Nagel (McKee, #24) and John Surtees (Lola, #7). (Photo Courtesy Douglas Mesney)

Mario Andretti powers out of the final turn in this shot from the 1967 Can-Am in the Honker-Ford, which was sponsored by Paul Newman. He went on to finish 8th while Denny Hulme and Bruce McLaren finished 1-2. (Photo Courtesy Robert Raymond)

Bruce Jennings deserves mention here; the longtime top East Coast production car ace was in a Porsche Carrera 6 prototype and took top under-2-liter honors.

The Can-Am that year was another stop in the Bruce and Denny show, as Hulme took 1st with McLaren right behind him. Hulme was very fast on the course, breaking the old lap record with a fine 1:29.65, the first time under 1:30 for anyone. For the race, which started late Sunday afternoon on September 17, the weather was perfect. The immaculate McLarens thoroughly dominated Can-Am and most cars could not challenge them for outright victory. However, behind them the race for 3rd was hot with George Follmer finally prevailing in a Lola Mk 2.

The fast, narrow, and bumpy course could make Can-Am racing pretty wild. In this sequence from the 1967 race, Skip Barber (McLaren-Elva, #14) spins in front of Mario Andretti (Honker, #17) in Turn 1 while Bruce McLaren motors on. Next, Bill Eve (Lola T70, #76) adroitly slides inside both Barber and Andretti. (Photo Courtesy Douglas Mesney)

Indy 500 stars such as Roger McCluskey (#12) came to try their luck at Bridgehampton in 1967, but a drop in oil pressure in a Pacesetter Homers Lola T70-Chevy took him out of the race. (Photo Courtesy Douglas Mesney)

Werner Frank (Porsche 908) was the first U-2 car home in the 1968 USRRC as he was at a couple of USRRC events that year. Spectators were very close to the action here in the final turn! (Photo Courtesy Douglas Mesney)

1968: Track Facilities Upgrade

Despite its chronic financial problems, the track management was able to make some upgrades for the 1968 season. Paving went on for the Turns 7 and 8 back straight, which Donohue described as the roughest, most challenging part of the course, as well as for the pits and the main track access road. The Circuit Club was also enhanced. How fancy it had become is subject to opinion, but standards for such things were generally lower in the 1960s than they are today. One thing is for sure: The after-race party scene at the Circuit Club was plenty rowdy for many years with drivers, mechanics, and spectators mixing it up at the bar.

Skip Scott won the USRRC when Mark Donohue, who had been having things his own way in that final season for the series, broke a halfshaft and spun wildly off course. Carl Haas owned both Scott's and Chuck Parsons' cars, and tried to arrange a dead heat, but Scott, who had been a bridesmaid for too long, would have none of it. The weekend was wet except for the USRRC event itself. Preliminary events on Friday and Saturday had to contend with rain and fog that at times obscured the course and caused delays. But, as the locals said, Bridgehampton was surrounded by water, and being there at times resembled being out on a boat in the ocean.

No one knew it, but that was the last time the USRRC raced at Bridgehampton for the Vanderbilt Cup. The series closed down at the end of the year in favor of the much grander Can-Am. Waiting in the wings, too, was the exciting new Trans-Am series, making its first stop at Bridgehampton. Mark Donohue, who was taking over for Walt Hansgen as master of the track, won with ridiculous ease in his Penske-prepared Camaro. Another Penske Camaro was 3rd, in the hands of Sam Posey. George Follmer managed to split the two Penske Camaros with his AMC Javelin.

Front row for the 1968 USRRC. Neither Mark Donohue (McLaren M6A, #6) nor Lothar Motschenbacher (McLaren M6B, #11) finished, but Skip Scott (#26, barely showing just behind) eked out a win in a Lola T70. (Photo Courtesy Robert Raymond)

A sparse crowd was on hand to see a field of only 17 cars, but even a small crowd can present problems when some of them become too rowdy. Two spectators managed to drive their cars onto the track and had a race of their own. But this stunt had a potentially tragic outcome: They hit a course worker on a motor scooter head-on. All survived, but the worker went to the hospital, and the (very) amateur racers to jail. Donohue's win gave Camaro a big lead in the Trans-Am season points race.

Hopes for an exciting Can-Am race were rewarded with a race on September 15 that was a slam-bang affair that more than a few observers called "the greatest ever" Can-Am race. The race took its toll on finishers, but not before providing a lot of thrills. It did not look that way at the start, when the Bruce and Denny show started again, but this was not to be their day.

In practice and qualifying sessions, Hulme, despite driving on a surface described as "tremendously rough," broke the lap record (his own) with a 1:27.69. The McLarens started out in the lead but both had to retire, a very un-McLaren-like performance. Jim Hall led the field in a Chaparral for an electrifying five laps; at times less than a second separated the first four cars. Eventually, Mark Donohue hung in there for the win in his Penske McLaren M6B. Behind Donohue, Hall showed that his big-engined Chaparral would soon be ready to challenge anyone in Can-Am, and that pretty much meant anyone in the world.

On the first lap of the exciting 1968 Can-Am, Denny Hulme (#5) thunders up the back straight followed by Peter Revson (#52). Neither finished and Mark Donohue (#6) earned the win this time. (Photo Courtesy Douglas Mesney)

1969: Spectacular Can-Am

In the spring of 1969, Bridgehampton again hosted the Trans-Am gang. By this time, the series had grown into a knockdown, drag-out fight among the Detroit automakers, and the racing was tremendous. Parnelli Jones and George Follmer were driving Bud Moore's Mustangs; Carroll Shelby's Mustang team and the Camaros of Roger Penske were also there to battle it out. Mark Donohue looked ready to pilot one of those Camaros to victory again, but Donohue, after a blow-up in qualifying, had to start at the back of the pack. Despite a heroic drive through the field, that handicap was too much for him to overcome. George Follmer earned the win.

Despite the big-bucks image, many Can-Am teams had modest car transporters. Bob Nagel towed his Can-Am Lola T70 to and from the track on this flatbed trailer. (Photo Courtesy Robert Raymond)

In the 1969 Can-Am, Bruce (#4) and Denny (#5) in their McLarens pulled away from the very powerful cars behind them as they started their second lap. Hulme won and McLaren took 2nd while Jo Siffert in a Porsche 917 nabbed 3rd. (Photo Courtesy Peter Klebnikov)

1969 Can-Am. Chuck Parsons hit a course marker, borrowed Peter Revson's nose section (they were driving identical Lolas) and soldiered on to 7th place. (Photo Courtesy Douglas Mesney)

Bridgehampton and the New York SCCA had an interesting idea that summer that did not pay off: run a half-national the weekend of the Trans-Am race, and the other half with a Formula Continental Championship scheduled for the following weekend. But the Continental Championship was moved to Lime Rock after a hurricane ravaged the track.

Definitely the big spectator event that year was the Can-Am race, with 26,000 fans coming out to see, as Denny Hulme put it, "us [the McLaren team] get beaten." If that is indeed why they came, they were disappointed because the Bruce and Denny show went right on truckin'. Bruce set a blistering new lap record in qualifying, too; 1:24.62 or 121.76 mph. Yes, Bridgehampton was fast.

The crowd was obviously cheering the loudest for the Ferrari Grand Prix driver Chris Amon in a Ferrari 612, who seemed to have the only chance to break up the McLaren team. Jim Hall, who had temporarily quit racing because of injuries, was on hand with a John Surtees–driven McLaren M12 that served as a spare car to the Chaparral. The car did well to qualify 4th. Chris Amon qualified his Ferrari 3rd.

Bruce and Denny did a psych job on the competition when the entire team took the afternoon off on Saturday qualifying to go waterskiing in Peconic Bay, leaving Amon and the rest risking their lives to match their times. Talk about confidence!

During the race, the two Kiwis played with the field for a while before pulling away and establishing large leads, with Hulme eventually winning. Swiss Grand Prix star Jo Siffert brought a factory Porsche 917 Spyder home in 3rd, the highest finish that year for the car. Although the car was heavy and underpowered, the showing was good enough to persuade Porsche to return to (and eventually dominate) the Can-Am. It was a 1960s event through and through. The race was delayed when the Hell's Angels showed up and insisted on serving as "crowd control" officers, or else they'd trash the place.

1970: The Last Big-League Event

The 1970 season saw the last big-league road racing at Bridgehampton. The June 1970 Trans-Am race was held in

Can-Am racer Dick Jones seems to be pointing toward the end as the track begins to fade from memory. (Photo Courtesy Douglas Mesney)

On the first lap of the 1970 Trans-Am, Swede Savage in a Plymouth AAR 'Cuda leads a pack through Echo Valley. Transmission problems knocked him out of the race. (Photo Courtesy the Henry Ford)

a driving rainstorm and saw a Roger Penske–entered Mark Donohue win again, this time in a Sunoco-sponsored Javelin. The race was notable in that Donohue showed some very aggressive driving. After Swede Savage's Plymouth Barracuda, which had led easily, had to stop with mechanical woes, Donohue put a lead of more than two laps on the rest of the field.

About 13,000 people showed up for this one and they seemed pleased with the race despite the rain. However, the track officials were less pleased. For safety, the SCCA ordered them to make some changes to the sand dune run-off areas around the track at 2:00 am the night before the race.

The rainstorm that plagued the Trans-Am was part of a network of severe storms that hit the area that summer. And it did more than wash away competitors' hopes; it also washed away part of the track. It was all too much for the cash-poor management to fix, and a scheduled Can-Am race was canceled. That spelled the end of big-time professional racing at The Bridge. The only other major race held at the track was a 1971 International Motor Sports Association (IMSA) event, won by Peter Gregg in a Porsche 914-6.

However, for more than 25 years thereafter, amateur car, motorcycle, and motocross racers reveled in the challenges of Bridgehampton. As Buddy Pugliese, a promoter who put on Club Ford events at the track for many years, said, "Anyone who was lucky enough to turn in a good lap at Bridgehampton had one helluva ride."

Just about all of the club racing at the facility was a treat for thousands of drivers over the years. But tragedy was also part of the Bridgehampton experience. During the 1973 Vanderbilt Cup finale, now an SCCA regional, a 911RS tried to pass a competitor on the straightaway, crossed up somehow, and hit the Chevron Bridge abutment. The driver, a promising competitor reportedly thoroughly enjoying himself, later succumbed to his injuries.

Today: A Private Golf Course

Zoning changes in the late 1970s created a land rush around the track and soon complaints about the racetrack

The famous bridge that once witnessed mighty engines now sees only golfers' cars and service vehicles. It has been kept as a highly visible reminder of Bridgehampton's great racing days. (Photo Courtesy Judy Rudow)

noise from weekenders wanting a peaceful getaway from New York City became a real threat to Bridgehampton's existence. Noise regulations and a minuscule budget combined to limit the track's scheduling to smaller-bore amateur races and motorcycle events. The magic of the days of International 500s, Trans-Am, USRRC, and Can-Am racing were gone.

Slippery realtors sold housing parcels near the track with the assurance that the track would be going out of business soon. When it did not, the new property owners were furious. In 1981, a local developer proposed to plaster the hilltop with condos, and a group of local racing enthusiasts called Friends of Bridgehampton was formed. In an unusual scenario, the racers joined environmentalists, who despised housing developments even more than racetracks, and together they torpedoed the proposal.

In 1982, an angel appeared in the form of Robert Rubin, a Wall Street trader and serious car enthusiast whose prize possession was a Ferrari 250 GTO. He acquired shares from the original holders and eventually gained control of the track. Rubin and the Friends of Bridgehampton tried to keep the track alive and envisioned holding a vintage weekend at the track that would rival the Monterey gatherings. But even pleas from actor/racer Paul Newman could not dissuade town officials from turning an increasingly blind eye to the tourist benefits and publicity that a return to big-time racing and vintage events could bring to the area.

Town politicians did not grant the needed permits to hold such events. In desperation, Rubin decided to develop the facility as a luxury public golf course. Interestingly, many local residents preferred occasional racing to the threat of pollution and continual disturbance from a public golf course and came in droves to town board meetings in favor of the track. However, the politicians ignored public opinion and approved the golf course. The final flag fell in the spring of 1997 and today a golf course sits on the old track's ground.

The legendary Chevron Bridge, the main straight, and the Millstone Turn still survive. Fairway access paths follow the track contours, but otherwise it is difficult to find a trace of the once mighty Bridgehampton race course among the grassy golf greens and underbrush. Rubin still owns the land and because he tried to keep racing alive at The Bridge for as long as possible, it is hard not to wish him well.

As for the fabled Bridgehampton race course, much of it lies buried under the fairways. That makes The Bridge a true ghost course.

The start/finish line and pits at Bridgehampton today. The big tree is opposite the pits' exit lane. The front straightaway still has the original thick and resilient paving. Grumman engineers designed it to aircraft runway standards. (Photo Courtesy Judy Rudow)

The Millstone Turn looking toward the entrance of Millstone Straight. (Photo Courtesy Judy Rudow)

Only golf carts and errant golfers are seen coming out of Echo Valley today. (Photo Courtesy Judy Rudow)

Continental Divide Raceway

RACING IN THE ROCKY MOUNTAINS

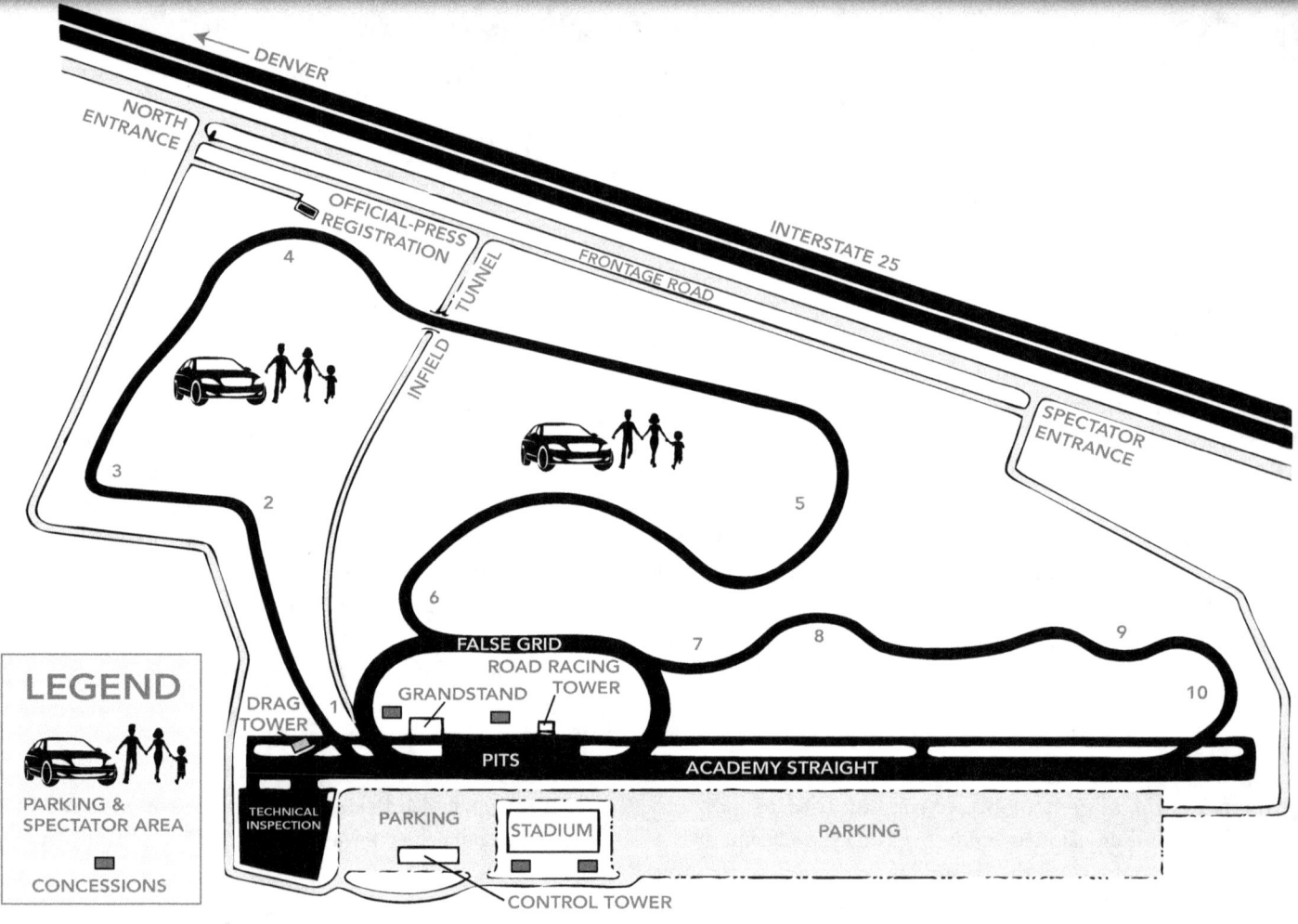

A more detailed look at the track from an early race program. Races were run clockwise and the turns are numbered to reflect that. The "Stadium" was actually a section of bleachers built into the hillside. (Illustration Courtesy Martin Spetz)

When you visit the location of the Continental Divide Raceway (CDR) today, you immediately see traces of an old road going through the tall grass that covers the site. Another road is next to a grassy hillside. I thought this was going to be an abandoned course that is easy to photograph and explore, with so much of it remaining in plain sight.

Wrong. First of all, a high wire fence cordons off the entire site with very official "No Trespassing" signs on the only visible access gate. And even if you did get in, the road courses you see are not remnants of the old Continental Divide track at all. Far from it. They are what remain of the aborted housing project that was once planned to rise on the track's site.

Castle Rock, Colorado, is 25 miles south of Denver, at the base of the huge flat-topped rock formation that gave it its name. Today Castle Rock is in the middle of a fast-growing metropolitan sprawl that is quickly wiping away the traces of the old prairies and foothills that used to define the area. When the raceway was opened in 1959, Castle Rock was a sleepy town of 1,100, just off the main highway from Denver

30   Lost Road Courses

CHAPTER 3

Castle Rock, Colorado
1959–1983

Facility 2.7 miles, 10 turns, oval, dragstrip
Principal Events SCCA Nationals, USRRC, Trans-Am, USAC sports and Indy cars, Winston West stock cars
Current Status Undeveloped private property

What a field for the 1960 Continental International at the Continental Divide Raceway! Front to back, Loyal Katske and Jim Hall (Birdcage Maseratis), Hap Sharp (Cooper-Maserati), Carroll Shelby (Scarab), followed by Bob Donner in an RSK, and a 3-liter Ferrari driven by Russ Cowles. In this race, Shelby nabbed the win. (Photo Courtesy Castle Rock Museum)

Wall-sized photo of the track from its early days shows how it was plunked down in the middle of nowhere. Although it looks flat in this photo, the course had some mild elevation changes. The hillside grandstands were located right across from the main paddock area on the inside of the oval. (Photo Courtesy Castle Rock Museum)

Chapter 3: Continental Divide Raceway 31

to points south. The racetrack was on an empty prairie 3 miles south of downtown Castle Rock.

The location was originally planned for a sports complex to be known as the International Columbine Sports Center. The complex was to host Denver's major professional sports, present and future. A 4-mile racing oval was even planned. These plans fell through before anything was actually built, and the location became a motorsport venue after a hillclimb was staged in 1957 on a dirt road running through the property.

The Colorado Motor Raceway, Inc. assumed responsibility for developing the location as a racetrack in 1958. The new group initially raised money via a stock offering and then sold a majority share to Sid Langsam, a Denver millionaire and sports car enthusiast. Operating as Continental Divide Raceways, Inc., Langsam built the raceway to accommodate "almost anything that runs on wheels." This included stock cars, sports cars, motorcycles, and dragsters. Langsam had raced a little, but most of the other initial owners and officers of Colorado Motor Raceway, Inc. came from non-racing backgrounds.

When it opened in 1959 at a construction cost of $750,000, CDR had many great features for both drivers and spectators. Its road course was 2.8 miles long, and included a 0.5-mile banked oval and a dragstrip. It offered a minimum 30-foot width, a paved pit area, ample run-off areas, and a smooth asphalt surface. Spectators parked for free, and the parking area held up to 30,000 cars. The entire course was visible from a banked seating area on a hillside right above the start/finish line. This ability to view the entire course from one location was unique and very special in racing. An interesting element was that the course was 6,500 feet above sea level, the highest road race course in the country. What effect would that altitude and resulting thin air have on cars' performance? No one was really sure.

1959: Racing Begins at CDR

The first road race at the new course was held on August 9, 1959. A regional SCCA race, it was dominated by Bob Donner of Colorado Springs, who was the owner of a nearby radio station. Donner, who was a top contender at CDR for many years, won the feature and another race in his Porsche RSK.

Another race held on November 15 attracted more attention simply for its novelty. It featured compact cars in a six-hour enduro. Sanctioned by the Denver Sports Car Club, the event was the first opportunity in the nation for such cars as Falcons and Corvairs to race against one another in a race just for them. A Rambler driven by Indy pilot Johnny Mauro and midget ace Tommy Rice held the lead most of the day and won easily over a Volkswagen Beetle. It was hardly an exciting or prestigious field but was an interesting outcome nonetheless.

Write-ups of the race mentioned the great viewing opportunities for spectators, but did not say how many took advantage of the opportunity to watch a six-hour enduro for smaller cars.

Whatever they were driving, drivers found the course challenging and interesting. The 3,500-foot pit straight was followed by a fast, blind, downhill reverse-camber turn. Speed varied between 80 and 120 mph through the turn, and drivers were immediately confronted by another similar turn. The rest of the course was made up of quick turns involving hard braking and quick acceleration, but the consensus was that Turn 1 and Turn 2 would separate the men from the boys, and for that matter, the women from the girls. Denise McCluggage was an early contestant at the track.

1960: More Races

The 1960 season saw a more vigorous schedule. The racetrack's management was not going to be shy about attracting all kinds of racing and racing fans. Events were scheduled for sports cars, dragsters, motorcycles, and midgets. All-night economy runs and more events just for compact cars were also on tap.

Jim Hall made one of his early stops that season at CDR's Mother's Day races, the event that initiated the season there. Hall showed up in a brand-new Maserati Birdcage that drew everyone's attention. On the track, Danny Collins smacked Hall's spinning car head-on with his Corvette and knocked Hall out of Sunday's feature. Collins recovered and took 2nd overall to Charlie Lyons in a Porsche Spyder. Collins reported that the back sections of CDR had more like 15 turns rather than the 10 advertised. Hall had better luck at the track through the years.

It's a testing-only day for the Scarab formula cars in the Meister Brauser team pits at a 1960 USAC CDR race. They came along with the team's two Scarab sports cars that went 1-2 in the feature, the formula cars not being eligible to run. (Photo Courtesy Castle Rock Museum)

Several drivers raced Maserati Tipo 61s in the track's early days. Loyal Katske drove this one, but DNF'ed in this late August USAC race. (Photo Courtesy Castle Rock Museum)

Top USAC driver Rodger Ward created a stir when he drove a Porsche RS at the 1960 Colorado International at CDR, but unfamiliar with course and car, he finished only 10th. (Photo Courtesy Castle Rock Museum)

On the weekend of June 25–26, 1960, Continental Raceway went big time when the USAC/FIA Internationale was staged at the track. President Sid Langsam had even bigger plans. In the event program he announced that they were going after nothing less than the U.S. Grand Prix the following year. But first they had to make it through the Internationale.

Interesting classes were set up. Saturday was amateur day; Sunday's races featured purses of up to $1,000 for the first car over the line in a Formula Junior feature. Amateur racers could compete in these professional races but not accept prize money. Two other races shared the bill with the Juniors, all classes running together divided by the slowest and fastest cars. Fastest of the weekend was none other than Carroll Shelby, who was nearing the end of his driving career. (Of course, it wasn't the end of his racing career.)

Shelby drove a Meister Brauser team (so-named to promote Meister Brau beer) Scarab and dominated a very good field that saw another Scarab (which came in 2nd), three Tipo 61 Maseratis, three Porsche RSKs, and four Ferraris (one with Chevy power). Other drivers included USAC oval veteran Rodger Ward, in a Leader Card RSK, who placed 10th. Shelby set a lap record that stood for a while: 2:08.32.

The Formula Junior purse was won by top formula ace Steve Wendt, who beat Hall for the checkered flag. Both were in Elva-DKWs. It was Colorado hot for Sunday's races, but Saturday's amateur events ended up being held in a late-afternoon downpour. When you were behind in your schedule, as was the case Saturday, you faced the constant threat of a late-afternoon Eastern Rockies thunderstorm for which the area was well known.

An interesting contrast to the USAC event, with all its big names, was the SCCA National held three weeks after the USAC event. After the conclusion of that weekend, the consensus was that the SCCA event was more interesting because of the close racing throughout the classes, even if the cars were not as spectacular. Porsches took the first five places, led by Bob Holbert's RSK. Jim Hall again had problems, this time in a 5.7-liter Maserati that was the fastest car out there but suffered from tire pressure woes. Hap Sharp entertained the crowd when his Cooper-Maserati burst into flames in the pit area only a few laps into the feature after some homemade oil lines ruptured. Again, a late afternoon shower hampered one of the companion races.

The sports car season finished with a Labor Day weekend race in which the Scarab Meister Brauser team of Augie Pabst

Corvettes in the hands of eventual winner Bob Johnson and 2nd-placer Danny Collins tool around Turn 1 in front of the half-full stands for a B Production race at the 1960 Colorado International. (Photo Courtesy Castle Rock Museum)

Chapter 3: Continental Divide Raceway 33

and Harry Heuer dominated the feature. Pabst actually covered the one-hour distance at a faster average pace than Carroll Shelby had maintained earlier in the year. For a change, Jim Hall actually finished the race, taking 4th in a Porsche RS-60. Not a bad field for an SCCA regional race.

1961: Politics Interfere

A stellar season looked to be on tap for 1961. After a regional race on June 11, which saw the first use of a 1.3-mile "course within a course" for a Formula Junior race, the stage was set for the first big road race of the season: the Colorado Speed Week, highlighted by a USAC 200-miler. But politics got in the way; the SCCA and the USAC were locked in a battle for the heart and soul of American road racing. The SCCA was trying to hold onto racing by amateurs only, while the USAC was attracting top stars by paying prize money. Drivers were banished by the SCCA for accepting prize money, and others feared to participate in USAC events and face the same sanction even if they took no money.

Road racing looked to be in perilous shape. This was the background for the circuit's biggest race of the year: the second Continental Divide USAC weekend, July 1–2.

The somewhat odd cover for that year's event program shows a couple of race queens from the previous year's USAC race looking on as Carroll Shelby, in bib-overalls, spits tobacco juice from the victory stand. Inside, though, the program enthusiastically promoted the weekend's events as well as the track's upcoming October participation in the USAC's first International Auto Racing Month. Beginning on September 24 in Italy and ending at Laguna Seca on October 22, the new series promised to attract the world's best drivers and include races at Riverside and Watkins Glen. Heady company indeed for the young track in the mountains!

The effects of the USAC-SCCA conflict were evident in the starting field of the USAC July race. The SCCA had

Bob Donner, who lived and owned a radio station near the track, was a top Porsche contender and frequent supporter of the CDR track in the early 1960s. (Photo Courtesy Castle Rock Museum)

refused to sanction the event. As a result, the field for the $7,500 USAC race was small and not impressive. According to *Competition Press*, "The under-2-liter field was good, full of name drivers and good machines. The over-2-liter field started fair and ended pitiful."

Race day saw two 100-mile heats. The day had its drama as Alex Sargent took exception to another driver's line through one of the turns that resulted in his Birdcage being bent out of the race. Sargent pulled up next to the other car when both retired to the pits and each took a few roundhouse swings at the other.

After several other less dramatic retirements, Ken Miles emerged victorious overall in a Porsche RS-61. Miles also won the under-2-liter division and took home a good percentage of the event's $7,500 purse.

The quality of the field was so poor that the track announcer actually apologized for it during pre-race commentary. A little more than 10,000 spectators had arrived expecting what the program and pre-race publicity had promised. The Colorado region of the SCCA provided workers for the event. When questioned about why they were working at an SCCA-disapproved event, one worker replied, "They can do what

Augie Pabst drove to victory in the beautiful Meister-Brauser Scarab at the July 1960 CDR race. (Photo Courtesy Castle Rock Museum)

Jim Hall was a frequent competitor at CDR in all kinds of cars. Here he smoothly tools a Birdcage Maserati around Turn 6. His luck was bad at this 1960 Mother's Day event when he was knocked out of the race after being hit by an errant Corvette. (Photo Courtesy Castle Rock Museum)

they want to drivers. But they better not fool around with workers. Drivers they can do without, workers they can't."

With this event behind them, everyone (drivers, workers, and spectators) looked forward to the rest of the road racing season at CDR, climaxed by that big USAC event in October. But then everything came to a screeching halt.

Road Racing Suspended

Hard on the heels of the Colorado Speed Week 200, track president Sid Langsam announced the suspension of any further road racing at the circuit. Langsam cited the ongoing squabbles between the SCCA and USAC. In particular, the SCCA's failure to grant them "open" status for the USAC events had made it impossible to attract the kind of fields they needed for the event's success. It was just two years since the track had opened with such promise; now Langsam bitterly said that the sanctioning bodies involved were more a hindrance than a help to the success of the track.

Langsam wrote a scathing letter to the SCCA national office stating that its lack of cooperation with its own local regions had led to his actions. He hinted at possible legal action and stated that the SCCA's rulings had already severely affected the quality of the field for the July 1 weekend.

The SCCA was backpedaling hard and in early August granted sanction for the October 1 event at the track. It made no difference, replied Langsam; there would be no road racing at CDR for the rest of the year. Ray Lavely, the track's general manager, was let go. But lo and behold, despite everything, there was another road race at CDR that year.

With no road course available for hundreds if not thousands of miles, there was pressure on the SCCA's Colorado region to do something for its members. Because the region had been so supportive through the track's short existence, Langsam relented and allowed it to hold a non-spectator regional race on October 14 and 15. A 10-race program was staged with the hillside devoid of spectators and no local media coverage, pre- or post-, of any sort. Local driver Don Ives won the feature in a Porsche RSK. Special mention went to race chairman John Dilatush, who performed heroic feats in that capacity and also won two races in his Crosley Special.

So ended a tumultuous 1961 season, a year perhaps more notable for what happened off the track than on the track.

1962: The First Go

When 1962 rolled around, the track announced three road race dates, including one in September, when they hoped to pull off something really big. The others were regional SCCA affairs, fitting since the local SCCA region had come through again and raised $10,000 from members to lease the track for those three dates.

The "First Go" event under the SCCA's lease program was held June 2 and 3 and drew only a sparse crowd. The few who attended enjoyed a decent show as a new Formula Junior lap record was set by Chuck Hall in an Elva: 2:10.3, which compared favorably with Carroll Shelby's course record of 2:08.32.

The season lurched along with another small event in July. This one saw "grudge matches" that featured two cars on the track at a time, racing against each other. The reaction from the small group of spectators to this type of racing was mixed.

The third race of the short 1962 season was the most interesting. A Bonneville land speed car provided some excitement

The starter's flag goes up for a few Lotus cars, a couple of specials, a Bandini, an Abarth, even a Formula Junior at an early 1960s small-bore modified race. From the top of the hill you could see the entire course. (Photo Courtesy Castle Rock Museum)

Continental Divide Raceway was certainly situated in a rural area. And the mostly undeveloped landscape east of the track forms a backdrop for this early-1960s big-bore race. Today the area is filled with freeways and strip malls. (Photo Courtesy Castle Rock Museum)

Ferrari 335S, chassis 0700, raced with the Von Neumann team before it was purchased by Seattle's Ed Purvis (in car) who brought it to CDR for the 1960 USAC event. With Skip Hudson driving, they took third overall. (Photo Courtesy Castle Rock Museum)

for the opening of the day. This vehicle, which was not designed for high-speed turns, failed to stop at the end of its straightaway demo run. It flipped end-over-end several times and fortunately driver Tommy Thompson was not injured. After that start, everything else was a bit anticlimactic, but Hap Sharp won two races in a 2.7 Cooper Monaco. Jim Hall won Formula Junior races in his Brabham and actually led Sharp for a while in the feature.

1963: Promotion Pays Off

The highlight of 1963 at the track was the USRRC event in mid-August. But before that, the track tried an oddball jalopy/stock event on the road course in early July that saw the Modifieds barely able to match the times of a stock MG. It pulled a crowd of 3,800, most of whom, observers felt, were sports car racing fans anyway. Speaking of MGs, the local MG Car Club held a club event on the track, but other than the USRRC race, that was about it for sports cars on the track that year. Yet that USRRC event almost made up for the lack of anything else.

Ten thousand fans saw a great race between Augie Pabst (Scarab) and Bob Holbert (Cobra) that was not decided until the last lap. As was frequently the case in USRRC events, the

A huge crowd assembled to watch the first lap of the 1963 Continental Divide Race sees a top field led by Harry Heuer's Chaparral, Jerry Grant's Lotus 19, and Don Wester's Porsche TS-61. Eventual winner Augie Pabst in the Scarab is already passing other drivers at Turn 2. (Photo Courtesy the Henry Cadler Collection, Douglas County History Research Center, Douglas County Libraries)

The Chaparrals were expected to win at the 1965 USRRC, and the #65 of Hap Sharp accomplished the feat. Jerry Grant is hidden behind Sharp; Jim Hall is in the #66 Chaparral, and Augie Pabst (McLaren/Olds) is behind them on the pace lap. (Photo Courtesy Ron Shaw)

Jerry Bruihl (#41) in his Lotus 23 Special had a sensational 1965 USRRC under-2-liter season, coming in 4th overall in the final standings. Here he leads Don Skogmo, Genie; Ed Leslie, Webster Special; and Skip Scott, Cobra. (Photo Courtesy Ron Shaw)

A rain shadow engulfs the track while the 1965 USRRC race stays hot as Chaparrals try to move past Jerry Grant. (Photo Courtesy Ron Shaw)

Drivers' and Manufacturers' Championship races were combined to make an exciting and good-sized field of 33. Pabst was away last when his engine stalled and he had to work his way through the pack gradually in the 64-lap race. Meanwhile, Harry Heuer in a Chaparral had a big lead before pulling off the course on lap 43. Pabst passed Holbert in Turn 5 and held the lead to the checkered.

The big crowd that enjoyed the race so much was lured partially through the efforts of Stirling Moss, who arrived days before the event and did a great job of promoting it, particularly in Denver. He was gracious at the track, too, signing autographs for 90 minutes during lunch breaks and calling the course one of the most challenging on the continent.

1964: Not Much Excitement

Despite the artistic and commercial success of the USRRC race, none was scheduled for 1964. The season did not provide much for road racing fans, just a couple of spottily-attended divisional races, with one notable exception: the Continental 250, a USAC stock car race held on June 28. Parnelli Jones took 1st place that day in a Bill Stroppe–owned Mercury and claimed the $3,925 winner's purse. Jones built a huge lead and won by over three minutes despite sliding off the course and taking long pit stops. The stellar field included frequent sports car winner at the track Augie Pabst, as well as Lloyd Ruby, Norm Nelson, and Troy Ruttman. About 11,000 fans were out for this one on a day that saw showers and sun breaks in equal measure. By contrast, a later SCCA race drew only 1,482 fans to see a 105-car field of little known cars and drivers.

1965: Regional Activity

Things looked up a little in 1965 when the first annual Colorado Grand Prix was announced. The SCCA now offered an open-wheel group that included Juniors, Formula Vees, and everything else without fenders, divided into three groups by displacement: Formula A, 1,600 to 3,000 cc;

Roger Penske watches Mark Donohue storm by en route to an 8th place finish at the 1967 CDR Trans-Am race. Jerry Titus won this one in a Mustang. (Photo Courtesy Ron Shaw)

Formula B, 1,101 to 12,600 cc; and Formula C, up to 1,100 cc. No superchargers allowed.

Big things were expected for the Formula, which later morphed into the popular F5000 Continental series. It was big enough that track management and the Colorado SCCA region scheduled the event and gave it that illustrious Grand Prix name. They were rewarded by a very good event on May 16, 1965, which saw a dramatic late-race duel for the lead between Hap Sharp, who always seemed to show up for races at the track, and Earl Jones.

Sharp was driving an ex-Brabham 2.5 Cooper, Jones a 1600 Brabham. In Saturday practice, Sharp shattered the course record with a 2:04.1 lap. Twenty-eight cars lined up for Sunday's feature, lured by the $3,000 purse. Sharp took the lead and held it all the way, but Jones came very close to him over the last few laps and ended up just one second behind. The 7,000 spectators must have gone home satisfied.

A USAC stock car race scheduled for late June of that year was rained (and blown) out, and everyone was getting ready for the year's big event: August 15's USRRC race. The Chaparral team of Jim Hall and Hap Sharp, both by now very familiar with the track, were the sensation of the USRRC that year. George Follmer (Lotus-Porsche), Jerry Grant (Lola-Chevy), Jerry Titus (Elva-Porsche), and the rest mounted a challenge against Hall and Sharp.

The Chaparrals fought it out for the lead with Jerry Grant for several laps before Hall pulled into the pits on lap 27 and never got up to speed again. Sharp pulled away from Grant and finally won the 196-mile race in a dominating fashion. Follmer won the under-2-liter class, which was hotly contested that year in the USRRC. Grant, always good for at least one fast lap on any given weekend, had some consolation in setting a new lap record: a blistering 1:55.1.

During the race, a famous incident took place: Cobra driver Dan Gerber slid off the track all the way onto nearby Interstate 25, drove around on it to a side entrance gate, only to be denied entrance for lack of a spectator ticket! He was eventually able to get back into the race and took a commendable 13th overall.

An SCCA National that attracted only a local field closed out the 1965 year at CDR. The USRRC was scheduled to return to CDR the following year for another mid-August event, but it was canceled a few weeks before the scheduled date. The Colorado Racing Association could not or would not come up with required race fees.

1967: SCCA and USAC

The track had been kind of drifting along now for a few years, holding some big races, but more often the season consisted of exciting and fun regional races, but nothing to draw big crowds. Then for the 1967 season, management decided to make some big and welcome changes. A two-lane road was dug under the back straight that allowed spectator access to the infield viewing areas, Turn 4 was widened, and a 1,500-seat bleacher setup was installed inside Turn 1. In addition, volunteer SCCA workers installed more than 2 miles of snow fencing for better infield spectator control. All in all, a welcome renewed dedication to road racing.

The season began with the Colorado Grand Prix for the SCCA's Formula series, the first of the year. A Formula B car dominated the Sunday, June 14, 1967, feature as Gus Hutchinson won easily in his new Lotus-41-Ford. Saturday was dominated by an unwelcome snowstorm; 4 inches of the white stuff pretty much wiped out the practice sessions and preliminary races. It warmed up and was sunny for the start of things Sunday, but no doubt many spectators had already been scared off.

An accompanying closed-wheel race featured an attempt at Jerry Grant's lap record by Denver's Bud Morley in a USRRC McLaren-Chevy. Morley won the race and just missed the lap record by .2 second. At the two-thirds mark a snowstorm reappeared and dumped enough snow to slide a few drivers off the suddenly slippery course. The sun did come out again, and the track dried before the end. All racers were hampered by any off-course excursion, which was met by very wet and muddy grounds.

By the time the season's biggest race, Trans-Am, came around on August 27, drivers had figured out that the course's altitude robbed them of about 20 percent of their power. Not much could be done about that, but everyone tried to make adjustments. Jerry Titus won the race in his Terlingua

A storm brews over the mountain and it's an unwelcome sight to both drivers and spectators at CDR. This one dumped snow on race winner Bud Morley (McLaren Mk II, #4) and Tom King (Cooper) in this 1968 Colorado Grand Prix preliminary race. (Photo Courtesy Ron Shaw)

Mustang, citing his enjoyment of the "undulating, reverse-camber turns around the lower section." This time, the weather was beautiful for racing; the only clouds brought welcome cooling mid-afternoon, no snow or rain.

Trans-Am was famous for close racing, but this one was fairly dull for the 6,000 spectators, not a very good crowd anyway for a major stop in the series. Continental's increasingly bad surface had not improved since the track's inception, and it had a bad effect on tires.

1968: A Good Year

Even with the USRRC out of the picture and the track not able to come up with enough money to attract Can-Am racing, there were still some very serious events held at the track in 1968. Open-wheeled action in an SCCA Formula race, a USAC road race, and another stop on the Trans-Am circuit (rough track surface or no) made up the schedule. Regional SCCA racing was on tap, too, and of course drag racing went on every weekend.

The Colorado Grand Prix kicked it all off on May 26 with Dr. Lou Sell in an Eagle-Chevy winning over an SCCA pro formula car field that was still sorting itself out. This was the first race of the season for the ambitious new series that already had races scheduled all over the country. A good field of 36 cars started the race for A (F5000), B, and C Formula cars. Everyone connected with the series was relieved to see that the featured Formula A cars could stand up to a full road-course outing and that so many of them were running at the end, 19 in all. During qualifying Jerry Grant's old course record was shattered as eventual 2nd-place finisher Jerry Hansen recorded a 1:51.5 in his Lola-Chevy. What was claimed to be a record crowd for the track, 10,000 people, enjoyed warm and sunny weather.

As big as the SCCA race was, it merely set the stage for the USAC race a month later. This one, billed as the Rocky Mountain 150, attracted all the top Indy car drivers because the USAC was making a commitment to road racing.

The already-famous A. J. Foyt pulled out a win at the July 7 CDR race. Driving conservatively (by his standards), Foyt was able to outlast others in tough race conditions. Hot weather and tight turns were tough on the Indy cars. Foyt was delighted when the big crowd of 15,000 increased the purse. He was also delighted when the first turn at CDR was renamed "The Foyt Turn" as had been promised to the inaugural winner of the Rocky Mountain 150. Three USAC drivers broke the lap record in qualifying, with Ronnie Bucknum earning the record with a 1:49.57.

One other notable occurrence: It was the first time a turbine-powered car actually finished a USAC event. Art Pollard brought his STP car home in 5th place.

Once again, Trans-Am racing proved to be less popular at CDR than it was in other places, as a slim field showed up for the August 25. It was a chaotic weekend that saw protests, a threat to leave by some teams, and a disqualification. Mark Donohue had smooth sailing, however, as his Sunoco Camaro won by two laps over 2nd-placer Craig Fisher (Firebird). This was Donohue's year; he won for the ninth time in eleven 1968 season Trans-Am starts.

Locals finished the season at an SCCA National on September 28. It had been a good season for road racing at the circuit, and plans for the following year looked promising as well. But track management did not ask Trans-Am back; after an initial scheduling it was decided that the series was asking for more sanctioning money than they could afford.

1969: Tragedy on the Track

The SCCA was still at the track in 1969 with regionals and the Continental Series on June 8. The race was run in reverse direction, for some reason, and reports pegged it as the hardest-fought yet of the series. Rain fell (the first for a Continental race) and accidents marred the weekend's events. Tragically, the first fatalities occurred at the track that weekend.

Local racer Jim Mulhall lost control of his Indy car at 150 mph on a very wet track and slammed into the empty water barrels marking the course by the pit area. They were supposed to have been filled with water to act as safety barriers, which would certainly have affected what happened next. In the resulting chaos of flying parts and metal shards, Mulhall

In the 1969 F5000 race, Tony Adamowicz leads Jerry Hansen, Sam Posey, and George Eaton under a big sky. Adamowicz and Posey are in Eagles, the others in McLarens. Only Posey placed high, taking 2nd to winner Dick Simon. (Photo Courtesy Ron Shaw)

and a pit worker, Jack Barker, were hit by debris, and both succumbed to their injuries. Others were injured, too, but not as seriously.

Most experts on the track at Castle Rock declare this to be the beginning of the end for the track, as track President Sid Langsam was said to be devastated by the accident and the resulting loss of life. The downpour began halfway through the event and was so bad that the race was flagged after 28 of the planned 40 laps; Dick Simon won the race. Lack of emergency vehicles was cited as another reason for the cancellation, as all available ambulances were being used to move injured people to the nearest hospital.

Despite lingering shock over the terrible accident, racing went on as scheduled. A USAC Indy car race at the track was held on July 6, the Second Annual Rocky Mountain 150. A. J. Foyt, who had won the previous year and had a corner named after him, had to be happy again this year. A colorful portrait of Foyt graced the cover of the event program.

The race attracted a small but potent field headlined by names such as Gurney, Andretti, Unser, and Foyt. But Gordon Johncock took the win after some tight racing at the top. He complained afterward about the difficulty he had shifting on the 10-turn course, but still hung on for the win. A good crowd of 19,000 was on hand. Gurney had earlier lowered the track record in qualifying with a 1:45.8, the first racer to average over 90 mph on the circuit, and took 2nd in the final race, with A. J. 3rd.

As the summer wore on, a regional SCCA race in August saw every kind of weather imaginable except snow. In one long day, 90-degree heat, freezing cold, and heavy rains alternated with sun breaks as local driver C. B. Johnson won the feature easily in a McLaren. Johnson also won the final race that season, an SCCA National on Labor Day weekend. He beat fellow McLaren driver Bobby Aylward in the process. Entry fields were small for both these final races, well under 100 cars for each.

The Final Seasons

The third, and final, Rocky Mountain 150 was held on June 28, 1970. Drag racing was rolling along just fine, but road racing at the track had stalled. A hasty patch job resulted in a better surface just in time for the final road event at the track of any significance. The top USAC drivers of the day showed up, and Mario Andretti won convincingly as 100-degree heat sapped the strength of most men and machines. Al Unser set a new lap record and was the first man to dip under 1:45, with a 1:44.7 in qualifying. A long yellow flag during the race controversially let Andretti get right on Unser's tail after Unser had built up a large lead, and reportedly some passing went on under the caution flag as well.

When a driver won the Rocky Mountain 150 at CDR, the following year would feature them on the race program cover. Gordon Johncock won the 1969 event over Dan Gurney to win the honor for 1970. (Photo Courtesy Castle Rock Museum)

Drag racing and some minor club events continued at CDR, but Langsam closed the track early in 1973 when he was diagnosed with cancer. Among the final events of the 1972 season was an hour-long "spectacular" that included Evel Knievel successfully jumping a motorcycle over 10 parked cars.

The last road races at CDR were held in August 1982. Two smallish events, a Winston West Coors 200 stock car race and a regional sports car event rang down the curtain on the track.

With interest in motorsports of all types dwindling, the facility was sold to real estate developers in 1983. Still, planned development did not take place beyond the few roads set down as mentioned earlier, despite some gaudy brochures that showed the projected final look of housing on the site. The road race course was purposely torn up in the late 1980s so that there would be no more talk of reviving racing at Continental Divide. Today the entire site sits in the middle of a rapidly growing area awaiting the inevitable housing development that will surely take shape soon.

The hillside grandstands that once held thousands of fans and afforded great views of the track are lost today, as the site awaits the inevitable housing development. (Photo Courtesy Judy Rudow)

Edmonton International Speedway

RACING'S FAR NORTHERN OUTPOST

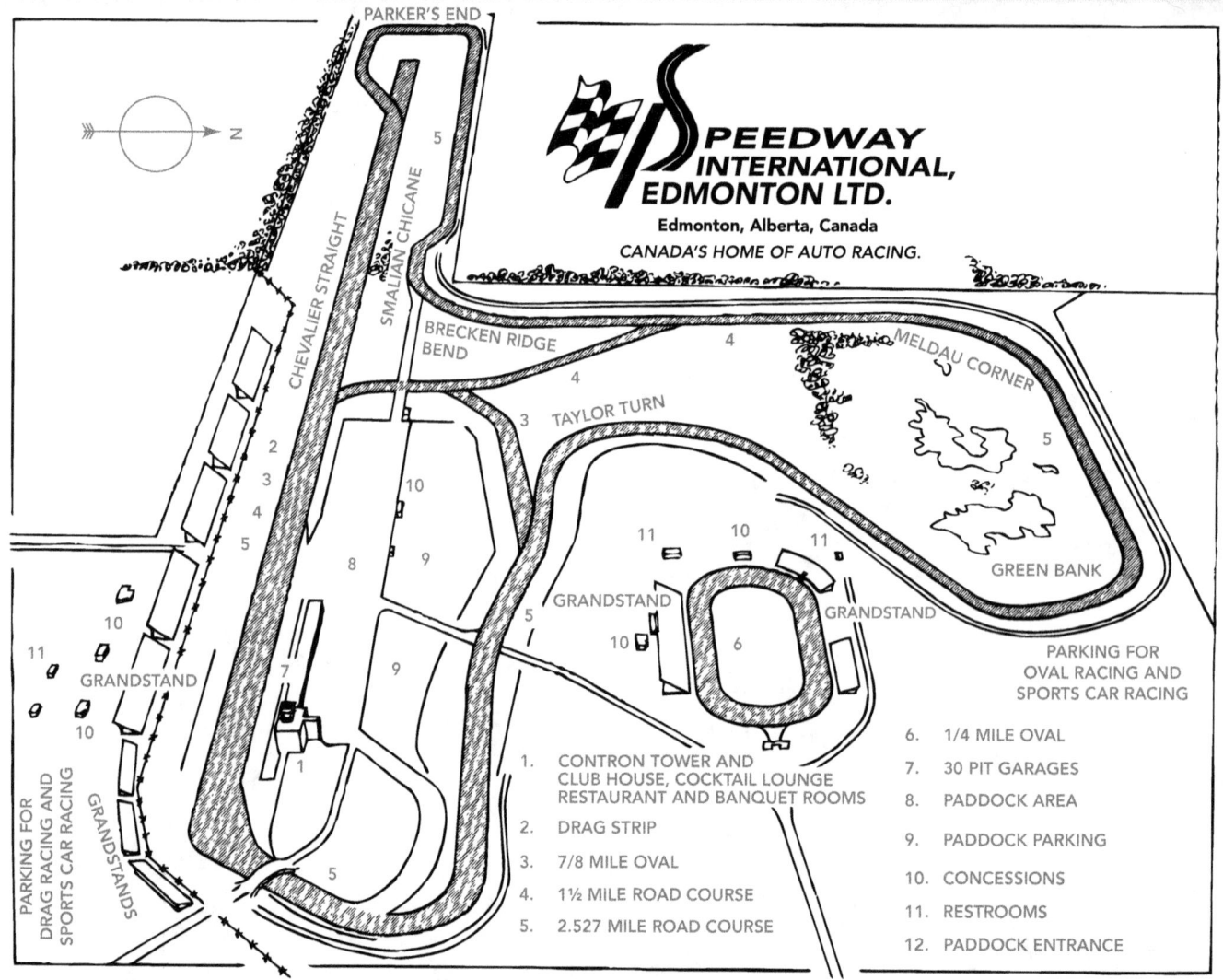

The course map shows the options for racing on the Edmonton course. (Illustration Courtesy Tom Johnston Collection)

During the 1960s, the city of Edmonton was thought of as a faraway little burg in the frigid Canadian wilds surrounded by inhospitable, flat, open prairies. Hold a Can-Am event there? You've got to be kidding!

Perceptions have changed. Today Edmonton is known as a fast-growing, prosperous city with growth fueled mainly by oil and natural gas production. And even back in those days it was, really, big enough to have a world-class racetrack that for a few years hosted some of the biggest names in road racing.

Oval racing had gone on in Edmonton for several years, primarily on the dirt-surfaced Breckenridge Oval. In 1952 Breckenridge was shortened to 1/2 mile and paved with asphalt by the four Booth brothers, early Canadian racing entrepreneurs. The new facility, renamed Speedway Park, had seating for 8,000 and did well for years as the leading oval racing facility in the area.

CHAPTER 4

Edmonton, Alberta, Canada
1968–1982

Facility	2.527 miles, 12 turns
Principal Events	Can-Am, Formula Atlantic, Trans-Am, Canadian Formula Atlantic
Current Status	Housing development and regional park; no trace of track remains

George Follmer and Peter Gregg keep their Mustangs ahead of Mark Donohue's Javelin in the 1971 Trans-Am. Donohue eventually moved by them, Follmer took 2nd, and Gregg was a DNF. (Photo Courtesy Edmonton Museum)

In 1967, the Booths decided to go all-out and build a facility that could attract the major players in motorsports. Led by general manager Reg Booth, a 1/4-mile dragstrip was opened with the full length of 4,350 feet. The following year, 1968, a road course (2.527 miles) was opened, twisty with one long straight and some slightly banked turns. A four-story control tower and administrative building was erected to handle all aspects of timing and scoring for drag and road racing. The oval remained as a separate facility partially circled by the road course. A paddock was put in next to the tower, 1/4 mile long and 500 feet wide with 30 permanent garages. The entire facility consisted of 211 acres, provided parking for 25,000 cars, and boasted 30,000 grandstand seats.

And it all was just 5 miles by a high-speed freeway from downtown Edmonton!

This photo from the very first weekend at Edmonton shows the diversity of those early days. This was a shakedown race to see if the track was ready for the upcoming Can-Am. (Photo Courtesy Tom Johnston)

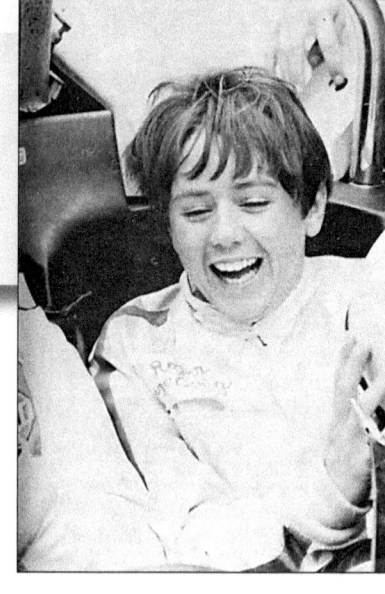

Canadian ski star Nancy Greene, after getting a high-speed lap around Edmonton with Bruce McLaren.

1968: Can-Am Gets Onboard

The track promoters jumped right in. The sports car racing scene had not been strong locally, so why bother to try to develop one when there was big-time racing available? This formula seemed to work right away as the track was able to land a late-September stop in the 1968 Can-Am series, the biggest and most prestigious branch of the sport in the late 1960s. Some people in the "lower 48" expressed concerns about the date. They wondered whether the ground would be frozen or drifting snow would block access to the track. The event was to be called the Klondike 200, which was not a reassuring name to those fearing cold and snow.

Preliminary to that big event, and to be sure everything would be ready for the ground-pounding Lolas and McLarens, the first race at the course was held on July 28. Dubbed the Alberta Cup, a regional Canadian Automobile Sports Clubs (CASC) event, it raised some eyebrows as teams towing to Edmonton were confronted with snowy roads and in some cases barely made it to the circuit on time. Would these, or even worse, be the conditions for the September 28–29 Can-Am race weekend?

Getting that 1968 Can-Am event was a major coup for the track management. It was the first time an event in the series, rapidly growing in prestige and popularity, had been held in Western Canada. As the group that put on major races in Canada, the Canadian Racing Drivers' Association was contracted to organize the event, and approved the fledgling course as being ready for an event of this caliber.

A Can-Am citizens committee made up of Edmonton businessmen was formed to promote and advertise the race, arrange a reception, and provide hospitality. The committee arranged garages off site for all Can-Am competitors, mostly in larger Edmonton car dealerships. When the committee ran out of car dealerships, some Can-Am competitors were given garage space in the city bus barns north of the track. General Motors brought in Canadian ski champ Nancy

The prairies stretch off into the distance behind the big crowd gathering for a late-1960s Can-Am event at Edmonton. (Photo Courtesy Edmonton Museum)

44   Lost Road Courses

A Lap at Edmonton Speedway

What was it like to drive the track that probably scared the wits out of Nancy Greene? A contemporary report describes it:

"From the start/finish line in front of the Player's Tower [the control tower], it's a drag race no matter what type of racing car you're in. For the most part, racers attempt to stay to the left-hand side of the track, finding the center and the right side a little bumpy. Down Chevalier Straight most racers start veering over to the right-hand side in the area of the Player's sign, so they can set up in top gear for the angle left at the end of the straight.

"Most drivers take the angle left at full throttle, and just before hitting Parker's End, they brake hard coming down from fifth to second, then accelerate slightly through the other part of Parker's End. Some competitors can get the car geared all the way back to the top gear before hitting the Smalian Chicane.

Chris Amon tried hard in his Ferrari to beat the McLarens, but at the 1969 Edmonton Can-Am race, he had to settle for 2nd behind Denny Hulme. Bruce McLaren was a DNF. (Photo Courtesy Brian Sinfield)

"Usually the drivers pick a line into the Chicane from the left side of the track for the first part of the Chicane, a right-angle turn backing off on the accelerator, then move over to the left side of the track, gear down to third, and take Breckenridge Bend. Out of Breckenridge Bend, into fourth gear, competitors accelerate to Meldau Corner, setting up on the far left of the track in preparation for the right-hand sweeping turn. Drifting left as they exit, it's next on to what has been described as the most treacherous part of the course.

"Divergent views exist regarding how to enter and motor through Green Bank; however, the most popular notion seems to be while in third gear dive down into the turn, and let the car drift high on the slight banking. As the car comes close to the top of the banked turn, brake hard, gear down to second, drive down and out of the turn, and set up for Taylor Turn on the right side of the track. Gear up to third in the short straight, and drop back to second before making a gentle arch through the banked turn.

"Most competitors attempt to use the banking of the turn for extra acceleration when coming out of Taylor Turn and quickly gear up to fourth gear prior to Turn 6, the Control Bridge. Setting up the far left of the track, drivers usually brake hard, drop into second gear, and make a sharp right turn before accelerating out under the Bridge. Then keeping to the left-hand side of the straight, it's on to lap two."

Even Dan Gurney (above) and Mark Donohue were no match for the factory McLarens at the 1968 Klondike 200. Gurney was a DNF; Donohue was 3rd behind Denny Hulme and Bruce McLaren. (Photo Courtesy Brian Sinfield)

Chapter 4: Edmonton International Speedway 45

Lolas abounded at the 1968 Klondike 200. From front to back, Ronnie Bucknam in a T70-Ford, unknown, Chuck Parsons and Skip Scott in T160-Chevs. Parsons led this group in, with a 5th overall. (Photo Courtesy Brian Sinfield)

Downtown Edmonton was really not that far away from Peter Revson (McLaren M20), the McLaren M8F of Hans Wiedmer, and the M8C of Tom Dutton in the 1972 Can-Am. They came in 6th, 14th, and 11th, respectively. (Photo Courtesy Brian Sinfield)

The Spirit of Edmonton, a game attempt by the local citizenry to be an even bigger part of the Can-Am world. They tried to promote their race to the rest of the world, but the car was not competitive. (Photo Courtesy Brian Sinfield)

Greene for the event and she arranged for a ride around the track with Bruce McLaren. After practice on Saturday Bruce took Nancy around the track and did a lap time good enough for 4th on the grid. Nancy's reaction to the experience: "Great," although in photos she looked more terrified than thrilled. To add even more glamour, Stirling Moss attended the event as the spokesman for the series sponsor, Johnson Wax.

Those were the Bruce and Denny Days of Can-Am, and the pair did not let anyone down, proving to be (by far) the fastest both in qualifying and on race day until Bruce had to retire. Denny Hulme was the winner in front of more than 41,000 fans, the largest crowd ever to see a motorsports event in Western Canada. By the way, there were several cases of severe *sunburn* over the weekend, so the worries about snow were misguided.

Drag racing, too, was popular at the facility, with top Northwest ace Jerry Ruth the regular headliner, as well as an occasional visit from Don Garlits and Don Prudhomme.

1969: Small Fields

In 1969 the Edmonton stop on the Can-Am circuit again was known as the Klondike 200. Scheduled to coincide with Edmonton's mid-July Klondike Days celebration, the event instantly became the highlight of the traditional week of festivities in Edmonton. Again, the town welcomed the racers in a big way, as they should have, especially in light of the fact that the series' headliners had to make a 2,000-mile tow to get there from the previous event at Watkins Glen. Evidently, many decided to stay home; just 17 cars finally lined up for the Can-Am feature on July 27. But those that did come put on quite a show.

Denny Hulme set a long-standing track record in qualifying that year with a 1:22.9, or 108.7 mph, in his McLaren M8-D. A rare breakdown sidelined Bruce McLaren and the seemingly inevitable Hulme/McLaren win. Chris Amon was second in a Ferrari. Locals were excited about Canadian George Eaton's 3rd-place finish in a McLaren Mk12. The event was also notable for the much-anticipated debut of Jim Hall's Chaparral 2H, even though it failed to make much of an impression on the track.

1970: The Spirit of Edmonton

Prestigious as it was, the Edmonton stop on the Can-Am series was not drawing as well as expected, although a claimed 44,000 fans was nothing to sneeze about. Also, the Canadian championship, known as the Gulf Canada Series, had drawn less than 500 fans for its June event. That series was an attempt to provide better opportunities for rising young formula car Canadian road racers. But despite these shaky crowds, Edmonton was proud of Speedway Park and the attention that its racing activities brought to their city. They were so proud that the city sponsored a McLaren M12 on the 1970 Can-Am circuit: *Spirit of Edmonton*. About 40,000 Edmonton citizens bought a share in the car.

The 1970 Klondike 200, again held as part of Klondike Days on July 26, was another runaway for McLaren cars, with Denny Hulme once again winning over new teammate Peter Gethin. Gethin was a late substitute for the team still trying to find a replacement driver after the death of Bruce McLaren just two months earlier. *Spirit of Edmonton* did not do too well, retiring early. A small field of 22 cars entered, with only 10 finishing.

Can-Am had to share the spotlight that year with the SCCA's L&M Continental Formula A series, which Ron Grable easily won in a Lola. The course again participated in the Canadian Gulf series. Eppie Weitzes showed up to support the Canadian series despite a Formula A championship points race that same weekend in Monterey, California. His sacrifice was rewarded with a win here in his McLaren M10B.

The Canadian series continued its rocky start. In the previous year the event at Edmonton had attracted only a dozen or so cars and a low spectator count. This year's event, held on the

The media ignores eventual last-place finisher Dick Hoffman in the #48 Camaro as race winner Mark Donohue pits in the 1971 Trans-Am race. (Photo Courtesy Edmonton Museum)

Eventual winners Jacques Couture and Dave McConnell keep their Jim Russell Racing Team green Lotus 69s ahead of the pack at the 1971 Player's Formula B race. They finished in that order. (Photo Courtesy Edmonton Museum)

Ron Grable taking 2nd place in the 1971 Lucerne 100 in a McLaren M10B. (Photo Courtesy Brian Sinfield)

shorter 1.5-mile version of the track, again attracted few spectators, barely more than 500. The writing was pretty much on the wall for what was a noble attempt to nurture Canadian road racing talent.

1971: Three Premier Events

For 1971 the Edmonton track was able to add another prestigious event: Trans-Am. The Can-Am race was shifted back to a September date, no longer a part of Klondike Days.

Held on June 20, the Trans-Am race featured the top entrants of the day and was sponsored by Player's Cigarettes, one of the top Canadian supporters of motorsports at the time. The series that year had started with a Javelin-Mustang duel for supremacy, with Mark Donohue and George Follmer leading their respective camps. A new series, the Player's Challenge for Formula B racing, kicked off the same day at Edmonton, making for a quality support race. A huge fire in Canadian Mustang driver John Hall's pits was the most notable occurrence as Mark Donohue's Penske Javelin won easily over George Follmer's Mustang despite nursing a sick engine home.

The Continental Cup, on August 1, resulted in an easy win for series leader David Hobbs, driving a McLaren that year. In addition to national sponsor L&M, Lucerne Milk signed on as local sponsor, providing an interesting contrast even in those less-health-conscious times.

The Can-Am races that year featured an attempt to dethrone Denny Hulme and whatever McLaren he was driving; the combination had won each of the previous editions of the Edmonton Can-Am race. Coming into the 1971 race, though, Hulme trailed his McLaren teammate Peter Revson in the seasonal point standings. Despite any efforts to the contrary, McLarens absolutely dominated the field that year, with Hulme winning over Revson. McLaren products took the first five places and 12 of the 17 finishers were in some type of McLaren-made car.

Except for the driver's name, this could just as well have been Denny Hulme's McLaren at the 1971 Can-Am race. Except that Denny won in an identical car while Peter Revson was a rare DNF. (Photo Courtesy Brent Martin)

1972: A Backwater Outpost?

All three series were back at Edmonton for the 1972 season, although some cracks were beginning to show in their popularity, smaller fields, and crowds.

The June 24 Continental race that year saw Hobbs again win easily over Alan Lader, former Class B champion who had moved up to F5000 and was in a McLaren M18-Chevy. Hobbs was driving a Lola T-300. The event had a more traditional local race sponsor, Molson Beer. An amusing sight was created by the sponsorship of Player's because series sponsor L&M could not advertise in Canada. Packs of Player's and their signage were rather clumsily placed over L&M whenever possible for the weekend, including on-track officials' shirts. A very paltry spectator turnout was noted.

Porsche's turbocharged 12-cylinder 917 was making a mockery out of McLaren's early dominance in the Can-Am series that year. Four-time Edmonton winner

The Porsche 917s in the hands of George Follmer and Mark Donohue were making a mockery of the 1972 Can-Am by the time the series arrived at Edmonton. (Photo Courtesy of Brian Sinfield)

Mark Donohue with two pretty Edmonton Speedway race queens after winning the 1972 Can-Am. (Photo Courtesy Brian Sinfield)

Mark Donohue again won the 1973 Edmonton Can-Am in a Porsche 917. By now, the series was fading in popularity but the Edmonton race still drew more than 20,000 spectators. (Photo Courtesy Brian Sinfield)

Bertil Roos won the 1975 Canadian Formula Atlantic race in this March 75B. (Photo Courtesy Tom Johnston)

Denny Hulme was definitely not the favorite going into the October 1 battle and in fact was lagging in season points in 3rd place behind the two Porsche aces George Follmer and Milt Minter. The race reports showed that Edmonton was not making a good impression on at least some of the motoring press. Edmonton and its race course were referred to more than once as a backwater outpost on the edge of the wilderness with not much for its citizens to do, but they still would not come out for car races, the ingrates. This time, though, they were wrong.

Despite some last-minute jitters, a respected town businessman guaranteed the track's expenses and a massive city-funded advertising promotion drew an excellent and enthusiastic crowd of more than 30,000, the largest in some time for a road race at the circuit. They saw an exciting race, too, as late in the going, Mark Donohue moved his Porsche ahead of Hulme, who by all accounts had driven a great race. The McLarens just could not match the speed of the Porsches and Hulme's streak of Can-Am wins at Edmonton was over.

The *Competition Press* race story reported that promotional attempts to lure people in and keep them happy once they were there loomed on the edge of ludicrous. A new track operator, Edmonton millionaire Tom Fox, was aboard and trying hard to bring the track back to financial health. Under his direction, the track offered a Corvette giveaway, a fly-over by a car-pulled kite, continuous performances by four rather obscure rock bands, an on-stage performance by some rather hastily recruited and unprepared drivers, and oversize model planes that buzzed the crowd both to their fright and delight.

As a side note, that year the track tried the same trick that had been a bonanza for some other circuits: staging a rock festival. They lined up acts including Joan Baez, the James Gang, Albert King, and Billy Preston for a three-day affair, but only about 3,000 people showed up and the promoters and the track took a bath. Bad idea.

1973: A Track in Decline

Despite Tom Fox's presence and the big Can-Am turnout the year before, not much of a road-racing schedule was announced for the 1973 season. Can-Am and Trans-Am were back, plus a national Road Race of (Canadian) Champions. Even fewer drag races were scheduled. The season started out with a Formula B race in early June nicely billed as part of the Players' Challenge Series for Canadian drivers. Unfortunately, it was not well attended.

A new field of cars and drivers attended the August 19, 1973, Trans-Am race. Transition was occurring after several early series favorites had moved on. In what became a very long day, John Greenwood won in a Corvette over the heavily favored Porsches. The race lasted more than four hours and was seen by only 5,000 people. For the teams, it was a far-flung race event and they were not excited about making the long tow to Edmonton only to be greeted by small crowds.

Another now-traditional fall date greeted the 1973 Molson Cup Can-Am. For that year, a 125-lap feature held after a 75-lap "qualifying feature" on Saturday decided the champion. Mark Donohue came in as a heavy favorite after showing time and time again that his Porsche 917/30 was the fastest car on the circuit and did not disappoint any of his fans, again winning with ease. Although Sunday's feature was called "boring" by some, Saturday's preliminary races had provided plenty of excitement with close qualifying races. Despite a good turnout of fans, it was the last year for truly major events at the road-racing portion of the circuit.

1976: Circuit Closing

The 1976 Player's Challenge series featured Formula Atlantic cars, and the mid-May event offered good prize money and drew many of the series' best. Canada's best was exemplified in Gilles Villeneuve and he won easily over the short 1.5-mile circuit, his fourth Formula Atlantic victory in a row in his March. It was then announced that the 1.5-mile circuit portion of the Edmonton Speedway facility was being closed to allow for a housing development. Drivers admitted that they would not miss the tight, bumpy course.

1977: More Formula Atlantic

Formula Atlantic continued to be the headliner for Edmonton's road racing circuit in 1977. Once again Villeneuve won over a highly competitive field that included Bobby Rahall and Keke Rosberg. Despite providing some very good close racing, the series was failing to draw the size of crowds it needed to sustain itself at tracks such as Edmonton. A long pause was taken between road events at Edmonton.

1981: The Jewel of the North's Last Hurrah

A return to heavy racing was promised for a 1981 weekend of Can-Am and Canadian Formula Atlantic races sponsored by Lethridge Brewery. After an absence of big-time road racing at the circuit for several years, the town and the track management went all-out to secure a spot on these two series' schedules. People who had not followed motor racing but remembered Edmonton's Can-Am years of the early 1970s were in for a shock when they arrived at the track for the August 15–16 race weekend.

Gone were McLarens, Chaparrals, and Porsche 917s. The cars running the series were now mostly re-bodied Lola F5000 cars with closed bodies and wheels. Carl Haas had supplied these almost exclusively for the series' first two years, but this year he was being challenged by other builders. Gone were Hulme, Donohue, and Revson. Geoff Brabham won over a quality field of new names that included Al Unser, Al Holbert, Teo Fabi, and Danny Sullivan. Quality but not quantity; only 11 cars were running at the end.

Can-Am shared the spotlight that weekend with Formula Atlantic cars that had last raced at Edmonton as Formula B.

Can-Am cars line up for the start of the 1981 Edmonton race. Can-Am shared the weekend with the FA cars, but it was not a big draw. (Photo Courtesy Brent Martin)

Canadian fans cheered on national favorite Gilles Villeneuve, who had won two championships in the intercontinental series and had been replaced by his equally talented son Jacques. Cars included Ralts, Marchs, and Lolas. A relatively unknown Canadian driver, Tim Coconis, won the race of his life over Rogelio Rodríguez and Jacques Villeneuve. Coconis and Rodríguez were driving Ralts, Villeneuve a March. Again only 11 cars were running at the finish. The spectator turnout for the weekend was disappointing but perhaps not surprising.

1982 Closure

The track closed in 1982 after the area was annexed by the City of Edmonton. Track owner Qualico Developments then demolished all the structures and converted the land to housing. The track was paved over or allowed to deteriorate. Nothing remains of the facility today, now that Edmonton is known as a truly international city.

Teo Fabi in a March 817 leads Danny Sullivan's Lola T-530 at the 1981 Can-Am race. Sullivan was eventually 2nd to Geoff Brabham; Fabi was 12th. (Photo Courtesy Brent Martin)

A park and housing development now cover the grounds of the old Edmonton track. (Photo Courtesy Roger MacMillan)

Chapter 4: Edmonton International Speedway

GREEN VALLEY RACEWAY

THE LITTLE ROAD COURSE OF THE LONE STAR STATE

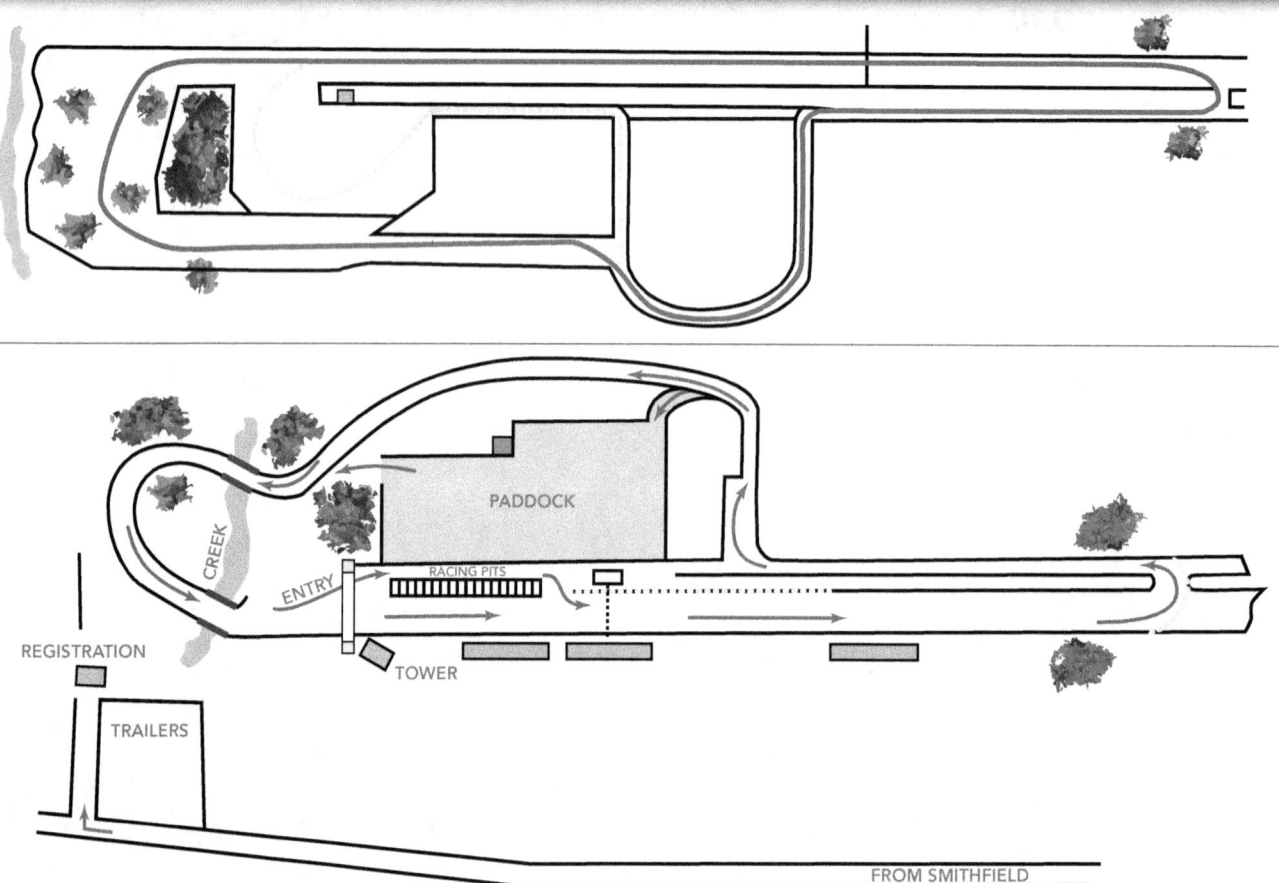

In 1963, when Green Valley Raceway opened, the road course was essentially composed of parking lots. Track officials set up the course using cones and fences. The road course configuration (top) was used for the first season. After that, the track layout was revised, and the new course (bottom) was used until the track closed in 1984. The new track extended across the creek (at the far left). Most races were staged on the new course, but smaller events were often run on the old course configuration. (Illustrations Courtesy Martin Spetz Program Collection)

When race fans around central Texas think of Green Valley, they think of it primarily as a dragstrip, and there's a good reason for that. The track hosted the biggest names in that sport both in American Hot Rod Association (AHRA) and National Hot Rod Association (NHRA) circles before and after it closed its road racing circuit.

Today, the former site of Green Valley is a densely packed housing development with little to remind anyone of the great racing, both in straight and twisty lines, that went on there.

Then, as now, the area around the site is known as West Richland with the town of Smithfield hosting the track. Located just a few miles from downtown Dallas, it promised to be a major attraction when it opened. Although road racing was never king in Texas, the popularity of drag racing there was as big as anywhere in the country.

Green Valley began as a dairy farm in the country owned by Bill and Dorothy McClure. The McClures had a vision that went beyond barns and cows, and in the late 1950s they

CHAPTER 5

Smithfield, Texas
1963–1984

Facility Course length varied between 1.6 and 2.1 miles, number of turns varied
Principal Events SCCA, NHRA, AHRA, Can-Am, Trans-Am, F5000
Current Status Housing development

Many Mustangs, a few Cougars, an AMC Javelin, and plenty of other cars bolt off the line at the 1967 Trans-Am event, the biggest race at Green Valley. Dan Gurney's winning Cougar is to the right. A good-sized crowd has shown up to see the action. (Jerry Melton Photo, Courtesy Cliff Reuter/etceterini.com)

converted a large flat portion of their farm into a 1/4-mile dragstrip. The surrounding area was indeed mostly a peaceful and scenic "green valley." When the McClures were ready to open in April 1960, they first approached the NHRA for sanction, but were surprised and disappointed to learn that the sanctioning body did not admit nitro dragsters. Because nitro power provided the most popular form of drag racing in those days, this was a blow to the McClures' hopes. Instead, they went to the AHRA and received a sanction from that group, which accepted nitro cars.

In the capable hands of promoter Ben Christ, the track thrived under the AHRA, attracting big crowds and top drag race teams from all over the South. Grandstands were erected and ample parking put in; the future looked bright. A summer routine was developed that lasted for years: local weekend evening drags and an AHRA feature event at the end of summer.

1961: Green Valley's Quasi Road Course

In 1961 a road course done on the cheap that incorporated the strip and its surrounding parking lots was put into use. However, Green Valley as a road race circuit never seemed to receive much respect. As a 1967 article stated, the original 1.6-mile course had been "Mickey Mouse'd out of seven-tenths of a mile dragstrip, a parallel return road, a couple of right-angle turns, and a swing around the pits. The return road was so close to the main dragstrip that you could easily throw a stone from one to the other." The whole thing was very tight and there were plenty of trees lining the course to make racing there more dangerous. It was obviously going to be a track favoring braking and handling over top speed. Just the kind of race course, local writer Bob Stonedale wrote in a 1959 *Competition Press* article, that the area did *not* need more of.

But the racers came anyway. Good ones, too.

Although much of the country was under snow, or at least under conditions too cold for racing, the promise of warm Texas weather drew more than 100 racers to the Polar Grand Prix, the inaugural event at Green Valley's road circuit. It was exciting for regional drivers who had only been able to race on airport courses in their area so far. The February 18 and 19, 1961, weekend drew 2,000 spectators on Saturday and 4,000 on Sunday. These crowd numbers were respectable even when compared to the track's dragstrip turnouts.

Jim Hall, who was beginning to make a name for himself even outside his native Texas, won the feature in a Porsche RSK over Delmo Johnson in an XK-SS/Chevy. Although Johnson's car was noticeably faster, the tight circuit proved to work in Hall's favor, just as Stonedale had predicted. Other than those two, it was a fairly average turnout of production and Formula Junior cars, with plenty of good racing going on both days.

Photos from the race show that the judicious placing of hay bales was still an unknown science in these parts; several cars smashed into them with a lot of damage to car bodies but fortunately none to drivers'. One hapless Triumph driver actually high-ended on the bales and he and his car had to be lifted off. The course was run clockwise and an abrupt right-hand hairpin greeted drivers coming to the end of the 3,700-foot dragstrip straightaway.

It never rains in Texas, but it did during this race in 1963. David Dooley (Jag XK-150) cuts inside of Jim Pease (AC Bristol). (Photo Courtesy Jerry Melton)

Harry Washburn was a frequent and successful racer at Green Valley in the early 1960s. In this photo, he drives his Cooper-Maserati. But he also raced a Lotus Super Seven that could beat the big Corvettes at the track as well as a Formula 1 Cooper. (Photo Courtesy Jerry Melton)

Delmo Johnson was one of the top big-iron drivers at Green Valley. Here, he leads Harry Washburn's Cooper F1. Washburn went on to win this 1964 SCCA Divisional feature. (Jerry Melton Photo, Courtesy Cliff Reuter/etceterini.com)

1962: Indeed a Road Course

The schedule featured more events for 1962, with regional and divisional SCCA races, beginning in February and ending in September. The Polar Grand Prix was the February race as usual. Alan Connell won the feature that day in a Birdcage Maserati-Ferrari, *despite* great power and average handling, a combination not always successful at Green Valley. Things were more normal (for this course) in the big-bore production race: Harry Washburn beat the AP Corvettes in a Lotus Super Seven. The reporter for this race remarked that Green Valley was indeed a "road course," with road hazards such as trees, signs, light posts, curbs, and ditches to prove it.

1963: Course Changes

The course was reconfigured enough at the end of the 1963 season to make it almost 2 miles long. From then on, different courses were used and the direction, clockwise or counterclockwise, was changed from one to the other often during a season. Because the course had basically been carved out of parking lots and access roads, it was easy to use one configuration or the other. All one really had to do was to put the pylons and hay bales somewhere else and, voilà, a new course was formed. The abrupt hairpin turn at the end of the main dragstrip straight was replaced on the longer course by a much more gradual sweeping right-hander that went a bit farther into the dragstrip's uphill run-off area.

The last race of that year saw the still-tight course with its many surrounding trees take a toll on the field as two cars ended up wrapped around trees. And speaking of "tolls," the starter was knocked down and then pinned under a spinning Lotus 18, and a wheel that went flying off the Ford Special when it hit a retaining wall totaled a flagman's Buick. After all this apparent carnage was cleared no one was hurt in any of these incidents.

Drag racing continued to reign supreme in Texas and there were only a few road races at Green Valley in 1963, 1964, and 1965 regional SCCA events. These events drew some top local drivers but rarely more than 100 cars or so, and crowds between 5,000 and 7,000.

The 1963 SCCA regional, held October 6, included the interesting variety of cars that showed up for events at the track in those days. A Jaguar 3.8 sedan and a Studebaker Hawk were among the 80 cars that tried their luck that day at Green Valley.

1964: One Highlight

Drivers such as local hero Delmo Johnson often won or at least placed well in these events, earning him at least a retrospective title as King of Green Valley.

An early September 1964 SCCA regional race Fall Roundup weekend shows this mastery. He was leading the feature until his Corvette Grand Sport had to retire with a split gas tank. Earlier in the day he had won three production races in a borrowed Renault and a combined formula and sports racer event with the Corvette. Drag racing safety standards proved to be valuable in that race for Jim Saunders, whose Kurtis-Chevy blew a clutch plate and skidded wildly down the main straight, bouncing off the dragstrip's guard rails before coming to a safe stop.

1965: The Weather Factor

The Polar Grand Prix continued to perk along, offering the usual unpredictable weather, and in 1965 saw the national racing debut of what became an iconic car: the Shelby GT350. No less a driver than Ken Miles was on hand to drive it, but it proved to be beatable. Charlie Barns, national G mod champion in a Merlyn, split two races with the GT350. Homer Rader in a Lotus 30 and Delmo Johnson in his ubiquitous Corvette GS beat both of them in the final. A crowd of 18,000 was reportedly on hand. If a true count, it shows the importance of scheduling dependable traditional race dates, and the wisdom of holding races on non-football weekends; this was Texas, remember.

In 1965 good Texas weather prevailed in the Sunburn Grand Prix, a ten-race affair that drew 4,500 fans. In this one, even with the enlarged track, small bores proved to be able to master their larger cousins as a Lotus 23B in the hands of Houston's Ken Leith won the feature over cars that included a Cobra, a Chaparral, and a Ferrari-Maserati. It was a preliminary to the course's longest race weekend of the year, the Pan American enduro sedan race, this time won by Minis up from Mexico, which placed 1-2. Bigger displacement cars, including a Barracuda, a Mustang, and a Valiant, were faster but spent more time in the pits as the hours wore on. The Pan American enduro race would be back with a more impressive field. At some point a race-prepped Mustang went into the little creek that meandered under part of the course and it was renamed Mustang Creek.

1966: Trans-Am Racing

In 1966 the McClures decided to devote all their energy to their dairy farm, which was still part of the property, and sold the racetrack to Ben Hielscher, another savvy promoter. He jumped on the popularity of Funny Cars and continued to draw good-size crowds for those events. The big grandstands lining the straight were often packed with fans.

Before the McClures totally left the scene they oversaw more modifications to the original road course for the 1966 sea-

This is a good view of the new spectator bridge to the infield and the grandstands. It was added for the 1965 season. (Jerry Melton Photo, Courtesy Cliff Reuter/etceterini.com)

Whichever direction they ran, Green Valley's long dragstrip straight led to an abrupt low-speed corner. (Jerry Melton photo, Courtesy Cliff Reuter, etceterini.com).

son. The track could now be run 2.1 miles long and races were run both clockwise and counterclockwise. Counterclockwise, the long dragstrip straightaway ended with an abrupt hairpin instead of the gentler first turns when run the other direction. Altogether, a faster course that local racer Bill Bagby still remembers as "not very challenging," but good for his torquey Triumph TR3. The new configuration was first used for the 1966 Polar Prix, which as usual was held in February.

At times the Texas weather lived up to its reputation and the early February Polar Prix's warm sunny days provided a welcome relief from the cold elsewhere. Other times it was chilly enough that Bagby remembers having to pit because his left hand was numb with cold. The facility offered other events as well as drag races: gymkhanas in its big parking lot, Karts (more than 200 in some events), and rally and race drivers' schools.

The Polar Prix, in some years known as the Southern Polar Prix, usually drew a good local crowd of racers. But the

Roger McCluskey helps out a fellow Vee driver whose car has broken down at the 1967 Polar Prix. (Photo Courtesy Jerry Melton)

Jerry Titus had several good races at Green Valley but always suffered from the heat as he shows in this photo from the 1967 Trans-Am, where he failed to finish. (Photo Courtesy Jerry Melton)

The 1967 Polar Prix had a great feature race field and a good spectator attendance, too. Joe Starkey (#51) and Bobby Aylward (#4) fought it out for first in their McLarens for most of the race before Starkey had to retire. (Jerry Melton Photo, Courtesy Cliff Reuter/etceterini.com)

1966 edition was a special race as big-name drivers Jerry Titus and Pedro Rodríguez fought it out in Shelby GT-350s. Rodríguez made a nifty move, drafting a fast Cobra down the dragstrip straight and taking advantage of the tight hairpin at the end to cut under Titus and eventually get the win in their race. Titus' hang-it-out style made a great contrast to the smooth, precise skills of Rodríguez.

About 12,000 fans, another great turnout, watched this one. Period photos show that a good portion of those 12,000 risked life and limb by standing just a few yards off the track, with absolutely no protection, not even the questionable hay bales, to have a close-up view of the action.

The Texas region of the SCCA again put on the Pan American 6-hour endurance race that year, this time as a national-points-counting Trans-Am event. Trans-Am was not yet that big, although it was rapidly drawing attention as that first season drew to a close.

They do things big in Texas, but this race drew mainly a motley collection of smaller sedans, including Volvos, Saabs, Renaults, and NSUs. Not the type of field that you would expect to attract Texas race fans, but a few bigger Mopar products and Mustangs were on hand, too. It rained during most of the 4 pm to 10 pm time slot for the race. Some factory support was evident, but no superstar drivers. Unless you want to count Horst Kwech, who teamed with Gaston Andrey to take 2nd overall in an Alfa GTA.

Mopar products were very competitive that year and might have won this race, but a pit stop near the end put the Barracuda of Charlie Rainville and Bob Johnson back in 3rd. Brad Booker and John McComb won overall in a privately entered Mustang while the "factory" Mustang finished far back. A Le Mans start, something that was already becoming a novelty by 1966, opened the endurance event.

1967: Gurney and Jones Dominate Trans-Am

On April 16, 1967, Trans-Am came to race again at the 1.6-mile Green Valley circuit, and it proved to be a pivotal event. Bud Moore drivers Dan Gurney and Parnelli Jones in Mercury Cougars were squarely in contention for the season title in the increasingly popular series. Green Valley was the first win for the manufacturer in the Trans-Am, and they made it 1-2 to boot. Gurney and Jones finished in that order in the Green Valley 300 (188 laps) after early leader Jerry Titus had to stop from heat exhaustion. Gurney and Jones made their factory sponsors even happier by crossing the finish line side-by-side, with Jones one lap down.

In an accident-free race 9,100 spectators were evidently not as uncomfortable in the 98-degree heat and 85-percent humidity as were drivers Titus and Gurney. Both admitted that problems with their cars' air circulation systems may have been as much to blame as the temperatures at the track, but it was plenty hot. Titus actually had to pit his Mustang and take a 3-minute ice bath after 40 laps before he retired. Fast-time-for-the-weekend honors went to Dr. Dick Thompson (Mustang) who turned a 1:11 flat, almost 80 mph.

The 9,100 spectators made a nice number, but the Trans-Am series was attracting bigger crowds elsewhere and this was near the Dallas area after all. A much bigger turnout had been anticipated.

Late in 1967, the SCCA informed the Texas region that they would not sanction another Trans-Am race at Green Valley. Irate Texas officials pointed out that their handling of the 1967 event had been well received, but SCCA Competition Director Jim Kaser simply stated that the track was no longer suitable for a national event of this magnitude. Protests fell on deaf SCCA ears, and there was not another big-time road race at the circuit for several years. But the track chugged along without the Trans-Am race.

1968: A New Track or Not?

The 1968 Polar GP was an SCCA National that year. It attracted 175 entries, showing the continuing interest in road racing, among local drivers at least. Bob Aylward had the fastest car in the area at that time, a McLaren M6B, but did not finish Sunday's national race. Spectators were entertained by the presence of TV star Dick Smothers, who did not impress with his driving ability, finishing far behind the leaders, but had a significant presence nonetheless.

Some type of trouble always seemed to plague the track; this time it was a very slippery course, and the turn workers had their oil flags out for the full length of each race. Heat again dogged the Sunburn SCCA Nationals in July 1968. Qualifying times were fast, and Bob Aylward set a new lap record of 1:06.6 in his McLaren. This big Chevy-powered car was able to overcome the handicaps of the tight turns and beat out a good field of Cobras and Lotus 23s to take the win. Good driving and the slightly longer course, when used, evened things out for the bigger cars.

Good news was reported in the November 2, 1968, issue of *Competition Press*: Green Valley was to be completely reconfigured, with the road course expanded to a full 3 miles. The track had been purchased by a California financial group led by financier

Hot local Mustang driver John McComb heads into a corner in the 1967 Trans-Am race. He finished in 17th place. (Photo Courtesy the Henry Ford)

The Green Valley road course was unglamorously carved out of the facility's parking lot, as illustrated in this shot of Dick Thompson in the 1967 Trans-Am, where he finished 3rd in a Mustang. (Photo Courtesy the Henry Ford)

"So this is why they call it *Mustang* Bridge!" Jerry Titus' practice Trans-Am Mustang joined one of many that met a sad end at the bridge. He did not crash in the race but also did not finish in the 1967 Trans-Am feature. (Photo Courtesy the Henry Ford)

Winner Dan Gurney and 2nd-place finisher Parnelli Jones after the scorching hot 1967 Trans-Am race. Both were driving factory-sponsored Mercurys. (Jerry Melton Photo, Courtesy Cliff Reuter/etceterini.com)

Bobby Aylward was a frequent winner at Green Valley; here he is in 1967 in a McLaren. (Photo Courtesy Jerry Melton)

Bob Marrill that was working with the present track manager, Ron Miller, to develop an unused portion of the property. No longer would the track consist of access roads and parking lot space. The dragstrip would still be used as the main straightaway but at its end cars would turn right and into the newly developed course, returning to the dragstrip for the next lap, clockwise. The old course would revert to a parking area only. NASCAR would be approached about running there and the building of a super-speedway was even discussed. Best of all, the course reconfigurations would be done by the next season, so the regular racing schedule would not be interrupted.

1969: Expansion Derailed

No mention was made of any new course when the 1969 season started, but an ominous note to those paying attention was sounded in the first *Competition Press* edition of that year. It reported that there was a new track manager and that the new course would be 2.6 rather than 3 miles. Changes this early in the new process? Optimistic notes were still sounded about the big-time future of the track, though.

The Polar Prix SCCA National races were held as usual in mid-February and Bob Aylward once again proved fastest, and this time his McLaren proved dependable enough to finish and win. A spectacular accident marred the race when a Mustang (Mustangs always seemed to have trouble at Green Valley) flipped end over end on the main straight, fortunately not hurting the driver.

Suddenly there was no more news out of Green Valley. Plans for track expansion quietly went away and, in fact, road racing ceased to be part of the track's activities. The national media took no particular notice of this; the track simply stopped appearing on race calendars. With Can-Am and Trans-Am soaring in popularity elsewhere and many tracks doing very well, Green Valley did not seem to matter outside its own area.

1974: Evel Knievel Tops the Bill

Through the 1970s and into the early 1980s, it seemed that track management and for that matter most spectators were no longer interested in road racing at the facility. Drag racing continued to be big, and then in 1974 the facility hosted an Evel Knievel motorcycle jump that was covered on *Wide World of Sports*. In the late 1970s as the road race circuit languished, track management switched its primarily drag allegiance to the NHRA. This helped a little with paying attendance for drags, but the facility was gradually deteriorating on many levels, and it was no longer attracting the big crowds of its heyday.

1984: Surprise Events

Then out of the blue both a Trans-Am and single-seater Can-Am race were scheduled for the same weekend in 1984. Don Walker, who had been the man behind the earlier, very successful Formula 1 race in Dallas, resurrected the track. Big concrete barriers were moved from the F1 race course in Dallas to Green Valley and the long-unused course surface was improved somewhat (but not enough). The race was run counterclockwise on the old 1.6-mile course, defined by the imported concrete barriers that made the course even more tight, unforgiving, and unattractive.

The days leading to the event, held on October 28, were not encouraging; rain fell in torrents and the track was muddy, slow, and slippery, even flooded in places. Construction went on night and day, only pausing for qualifying and practice sessions. The barriers were responsible for a lot of torn and missing fiberglass as the weekend went on. Can-Am qualifying saw a barrier-produced serious accident when Dick Guider's Marguey hydroplaned in deep water and hit several barriers. Guider survived but spent time in a local hospital with badly broken legs.

Race day, however, was beautiful, warm, and sunny. Even so, comments from the Trans-Am race, the Texas Challenge, were still not favorable. A typical remark: "The most ridiculous track I've seen in my life… the track was a real s***hole."

The trees that had not been overly dangerous during the slower days of the 1960s now were downright terrifying to drivers of fast Can-Am and Trans-Am cars. Wally Dallenbach Jr. stated that the trees should all be chainsawed down before any more laps were run on the track. There was talk that the race should be canceled. However, eventual Trans-Am race winner Willy T. Ribbs was complimentary about the course, although he made his comments with a certain irony.

Unfortunately, it was a rather mundane event when it did get going with few cars even finishing on the same lap. The sight of the big Trans-Am cars shooting through the narrow barrier-lined course at high speeds was exciting, though.

The Can-Am portion of the weekend was not much more competitive, Jim Crawford winning in a March 847/Chevy. None of the other finishing eight cars was on the same lap. In the end, the event was a financial failure and Walker did not try again. It was the end of road racing at the track.

1986: Closure

When the track totally ceased functioning in 1986 after Ben Hielscher's passing, its deterioration accelerated, although the land around it was not yet developed. In fact, it remained far enough out in the country that the track's buildings were allowed to stay in place and evidently were not even overrun by homeless squatters or gangs. But by the late 1990s, the surrounding neighborhoods had encroached upon the property and one portion after another was swallowed up, buildings and all, disappearing without a trace. The last remnants were of the dragstrip shutdown area and they were finally plowed under in 2015.

Today, only small portions of the parking lot, which served as part of the longer course configuration, and Mustang Bridge remain of the track, sad and lonely remnants of the area's best and most popular racing facility.

The author stands on the remains of the famous and once-feared Mustang Bridge. (Photo Courtesy Judy Rudow)

The last remnants of the Green Valley dragstrip had just been plowed under in April 2015. (Photo Courtesy Judy Rudow)

Greenwood Roadway

A TRACK PAVED WITH PASSION

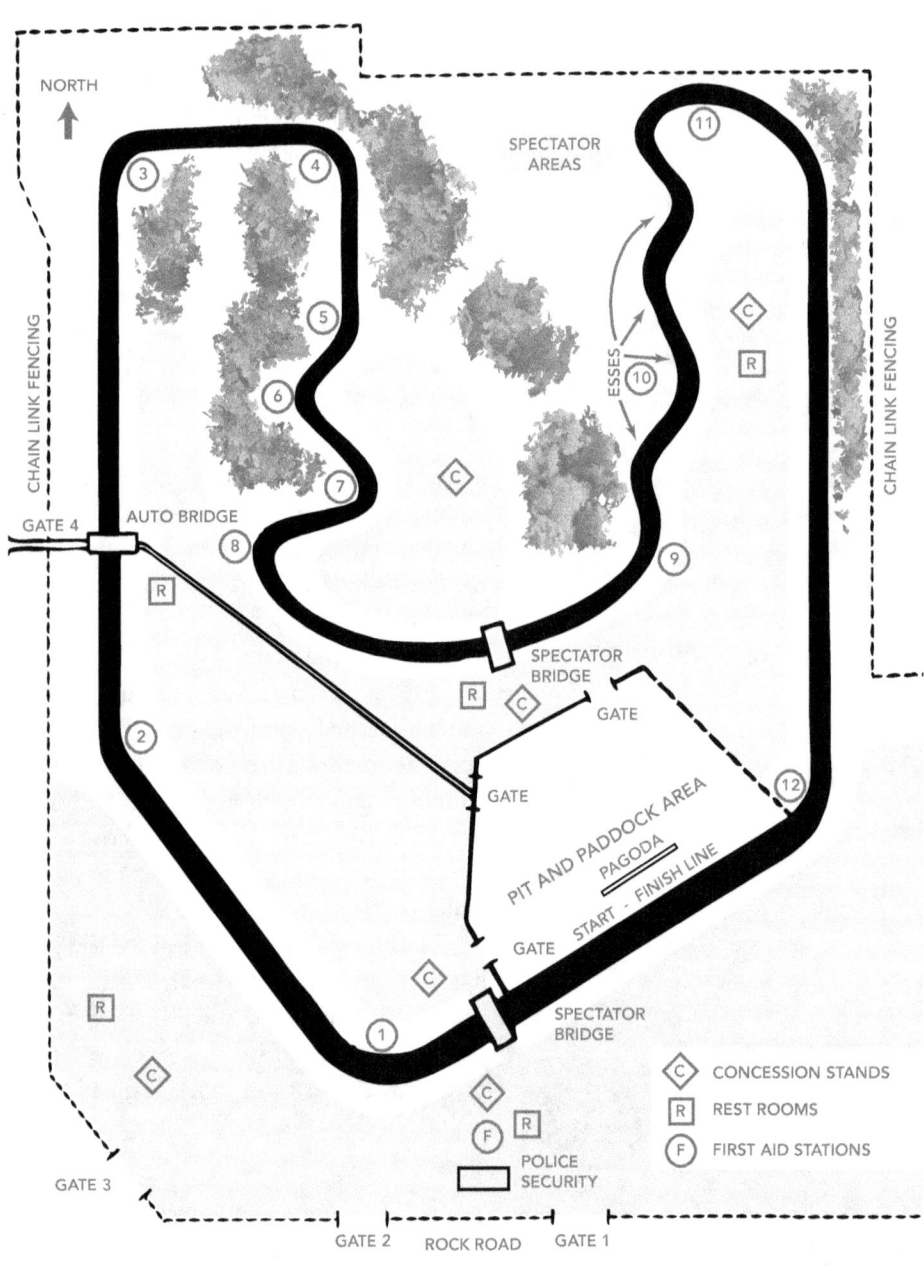

The 3.2-mile, 12-turn Greenwood course has a very steep downhill straight between Turns 2 and 3. (Illustration Courtesy Martin Spetz Program Collection)

Greenwood Roadway was the brainchild of a group of Iowa sports car enthusiasts who were tired of traveling hundreds of miles to race. They were not experienced in fund raising or in building tracks, but they knew what they wanted as drivers from their own personal experiences. Led by members Paul Schwartz and Ray Phillips, among others, they decided to form a corporation, Greenwood Roadway, Inc., sell shares, and simply go for it.

The site chosen for the track was on rolling farmland in rural Iowa. Land in the area was cheap and so was labor, and locals were mostly pleased to have a facility that promised to bring in money from out of the area. The main spectator base was in Des Moines, about a 30-minute drive on two-lane country roads, but several medium to small towns were also not too far away.

The first plans for the racetrack called for it to be fairly basic and built for drivers, but quickly these simple plans were greatly expanded. Soon Greenwood Roadway was to include hotels, restaurants, and recreational facilities. The investors evidently never had the money to realize these dreams and it may be that their plans were actually nothing more than an attempt to drum up enthusiasm for selling shares in the track. On the other hand, they may have been completely sincere but naïve. The end result was the same at any rate.

To help raise capital the group sold stock in Greenwood Roadway, Inc., at $1 per share. You probably can still find

CHAPTER 6

Indianola, Iowa
1963-1966

Facility 3.2 miles
Principal Events SCCA Nationals, USRRC, USAC stocks
Current Status Course is mostly intact but privately owned

Greenwood was a twisty course with some dramatic uphills and downhills and a curving, uphill start/finish line. In 1964, the start/finish line was later moved up the straightaway for the USRRC race. (Frank Manley Photo, Courtesy Martin Rudow Collection)

these stock certificates in garage sales and papered on walls around Iowa, but unfortunately they are worthless now. After an early 1963 kickoff luncheon keynoted by none other than Jim Kimberly, at the time the Midwest's most famous road racer, enough shares were sold to get the project underway. The track was scheduled to open for business in the spring of 1963. Paving would begin after the winter snows melted. But in mid-April the news was leaked that the track would not be ready that year after all, despite substantial work already being completed. In fact, there was speculation that the track would be lucky to open for the 1964 season. Funding had slowed and there was not enough in the coffers to make the course fully ready.

But then Ray Phillips took over as president and general manager of the track. He soon announced that his personal appeal to the SCCA and to investors to ready the track and have it inspected for a race as soon as the weekend of June 8 and 9 had worked and the track would open that weekend.

On June 1 an invited group of racers came to the track and gave it a final shakedown and approval, although the paddock in particular was not what they would have liked. The June 8 and 9 opening event was already being promoted as much as management could afford.

Local SCCA official Pete Winburg described the final 3.2-mile 14-turn course as "extremely challenging and demanding. It sports several high-speed turns, fast downhill straights, and blind corners." About $300,000 had been spent constructing the track. Pie-in-the-sky plans still called for the quick addition of a swimming area, covered pits, restaurants, and a concrete timers' building. All would have been welcomed, especially the swimming pool and the timers' building, if it had been air-conditioned. The weather was hot during racing season in that part of Iowa.

1964: Debut

With the schedule confusion and with other area race events already scheduled that same weekend at Meadowdale and Indianapolis Raceway Park, Greenwood management was looking at a very disappointing entry field with just a week to go. Personal phone calls and frantic appeals to every driver within a couple hundred miles resulted in a respectable but not great final field of 80 cars. Many drivers reported coming (some pulled out of the Indianapolis event upon being cajoled to come to Greenwood) because they were excited about having a purpose-built racetrack in their area and wanted to help make its first racing weekend respectable.

The first race day on Saturday June 8 saw 3,100 paid spectators, a reasonable turnout considering everything. The schedule for the inaugural weekend included a car show, skydiving, and even a falconry demonstration. The Des Moines paper was positive in its reporting but knew it was writing for

Midwestracer Frank Manley had a great day in his Deutsch-Bonnet at this 1965 Greenwood SCCA event. (Photo Courtesy Frank Manley via Martin Rudow Collection)

Formula Vee driver Dick Abney strikes a heroic pose before jumping into his formula car for a Formula Vee USRRC prelim. (Photo Courtesy Doug Dyar)

fans used to seeing oval track racing: "Like all Grand Prix [sic] races, it wasn't possible to watch all the proceedings from one vantage point. The finish line and the hairpin curves on the course drew the bulk of watchers.

"If they came to see someone hurt they were disappointed, for there was only one mishap. One driver, Dave Spensley of Cedar Falls, went off the track on a twisting turn and failed to get back into the race." A breakdown in telephone communications caused an hour's delay in the start of Saturday's preliminary races because officials were not able to stage practice laps during the morning. But this seemed just a minor hiccup, something you could expect for any course's inaugural event.

Art Bunker, a 35-year-old Kansas City foreign car dealer, won the 60-mile feature on Sunday after early leaders faltered in the late stages. Bunker took the lead on the 14th lap and wheeled his Class F modified Porsche 1600 across the finish line almost 30 seconds ahead of the rest of the field. An estimated 10,000 fans were in attendance for Sunday's events. Out-of-state racers were not pleased to discover that a post-race beer was difficult to come by; Iowa was "dry" on Sundays.

Drivers were, however, generally pleased with the track and it certainly was in a beautiful setting: rolling green hills and, as summer wore on, fields of corn and grain as far as one could see. Veteran racer Ed Leslie said, "The track can best be described as 'not level.' The start/finish line can only be seen coming uphill from the last, very fast right-hand turn. Standing starts require several very tall flagmen, or a helicopter (and a good parking brake); and this is the level part of the course! The surrounding area in the back part of the course is lush-green swampland that fortunately has been cleared of alligators, leeches, and the like, and incorporates a serpentine downhill, which sets a stray driver or two off, cutting corn or dropping into a ravine where the search and rescue people carry machetes."

The second event that first year was held on September 23 and did see a few cars go off the track edges and roll down slopes into ravines, fortunately without injury or alligator bites. The 21,000 fans saw Monroe, Wisconsin's, Dr. Curt Gonstead win the feature in a Lotus 23.

One notable driver was future top national-level racer John Morton, just getting started and not even yet possessing a national SCCA license. Morton came from Illinois with his Lotus Super Seven and beat a fast big-bore production field that included a Cobra among other bigger-engined cars. The track received some great reviews in reports of this race, one writer calling it "a 3-mile beauty that promises to be one of the nation's best."

In the 1964 USRRC preliminary production race, Tom Payne (Shelby Cobra) leads Dan Gerber (another Shelby Cobra) as well Robert Crane (Lotus Super Seven). (Photo Courtesy of Mick Enabit and Doug Dyar)

Despite this kind of praise, as early as the first year of operation the track struggled and its future began to unravel. Greenwood Roadway's management fell behind on its bills and it only became worse in the months that followed. Soon everything had to be done on a cash basis. Employees weren't paid regularly and began leaving. Greenwood might have been an artistic success, but it was not producing enough greenbacks!

Facing these cash shortages, the group's management decided to go for broke and see once and for all if it was even possible for them to muster enough spectators to make the track pay its way. Despite the apparent odds, they received the sanction to hold a USRRC race during the 1964 season. The series was just in its second year but was attracting the biggest names and most exciting cars in the road-racing world.

The USRRC Comes to Iowa

Before the USRRC weekend, the track's first races of the year were held in May. "After our two weekend events last year, the reputation of Greenwood Roadway spread like wildfire among drivers," said Harold E. McKinney, chairman of the Greenwood board. "We've been receiving inquiries all winter from drivers who want to try our roadway. Sports car racing really gives the spectator something to do besides sit in a grandstand. At Greenwood Roadway, spectators are encouraged to move from point to point, seeing how drivers perform under the varying challenges offered by the roadway. Unlike oval racing, roadway [sic] racing requires drivers to shift gears almost constantly as they slow down for turns, go up or down hills, or strain for top speed on the straightaways."

Since last year, McKinney said, many improvements had been made to increase spectator comfort, including expanded refreshment facilities and sound systems. It was about time, but the course still always suffered from hot and dusty conditions, and portions of it were simply not accessible to spectators. Also, Iowans were used to sitting in stands and having their racing brought to them on oval tracks, not having to walk for the privilege of watching what they had paid for.

On the USRRC grid, Ed Leslie is in the King Cobra (#96), along with eventual 2nd-place finisher Bill Wuesthoff's Elva-Porsche (#77), Joe Buzetta's Elva-Porsche (#7), and Ralph Salyer's Cheetah (#25). (Photo Courtesy Doug Dyar)

This May 30–31 weekend was the chance for all those drivers apparently frothing at the mouth to go back to Greenwood. Just over 100 showed up for what turned into an unusual and wet weekend. A 1956 Jaguar XK-140 driver, Ron McConkey, stole the show as the old beast showed its teeth to a field of TR4s, Healeys, Porsches, and Alfas to win the first race of Sunday. A Morgan SS in the hands of George Schauer also surprised, winning the big-bore production race over Stingrays, Corvettes, and Cobras. But the biggest upset came in the all-formula race that saw four Formula Vees beating the ex–Roy Salvadori Cooper-Maserati. Rain made the F1 car almost impossible to handle for driver John Rulon. That rain, heavy at times, slowed the proceedings all day long and the final race was shortened due to increasing rains and premature early-evening dark conditions.

Now for the USRRC race. Greenwood was able to generate more local publicity than had previously been thought possible for an event of this type in the area. TV stations and newspapers carried feature stories and frequent updates as the race date drew nearer.

The front row of the 1964 USRRC race is shown prior to the start. Jim Hall's Chaparral (#65) is on the pole, with Charlie Hayes' Elva-Porsche (#77) on the outside of the front row. Hall recorded the fastest laps in the race, too, but oil heating problems dropped him to 3rd overall. (Photo Courtesy Doug Dyar)

Chapter 6: Greenwood Roadway 63

The USRRC starting field also included Ken Miles' Cobra (#98), Bob Markley's Elva-Porsche (#75), Tom Payne's Cobra (#14), Bob Johnson's Cobra (#99), Chuck Parson's Cobra (#10), Don Wild's Elva (#11), Mike Hall's Elva-Ford (#69), and Hal Keck's Cobra (#88). (Photo Courtesy Doug Dyar)

Ken Miles' Cobra is on the USRRC starting line as the crowd shows how it's coping with the heat. The heat was tough on Miles, too, but he still came in 4th. (Photo Courtesy Doug Dyar)

In one of the largest starting fields yet for Formula Vee, 33 of the little guys are just about to crest the hill and race down the main straight to the new start/finish line. (Photo Courtesy Doug Dyar)

The Des Moines Holiday Inn was race headquarters and there were even live newscasts from the parking lot as the big rigs pulled in with their teams . . . Hall, Shelby, and the rest.

It all paid off, apparently, as 18,500 paid spectators (or so it was claimed) came out in 85-degree heat to watch the show. And quite a show they saw, too. The USRRC drivers got the hang of the challenging course quickly and soon were turning laps under 2 minutes, compared to a previous lap record of 2:05. Top speeds on the not-so-long straightaway exceeded 144 mph. Jim Hall and his Chaparral set the record in qualifying: 1:57.8. He led the race when the flag fell, too, for several laps until Ed Leslie, driving the late Dave MacDonald's King Cobra, took over. But Hall was too quick and once again had a good lead when he pitted with oil temperature problems. He was never able to get the Chaparral back up to speed again, eventually finishing 3rd behind Leslie and Bill Wuesthoff (Elva-Porsche), who also won the under-2-liter title.

Reporters noted that by attrition alone, it was one of the toughest races yet on the USRRC circuit. Only 20 cars finished, and some just barely, from a starting field of 30. Driver changes were frequent, too, as the sun blazed down. The fastest GT car was Bob Johnson in a Shelby team Cobra, but he went off course and sustained too much damage to continue. Ken Miles in another team Cobra took over and finished 4th. Miles' car showed the effects of the tough course by finishing with almost no brakes left. The Ford Cortina contingent delighted the crowd by continually lifting their front wheels off the ground around turns, and there were plenty of those to keep everyone happy.

An accompanying 17-lap Formula Vee race with a purse of $1,000 went to Lynn Blanchard. It's interesting to compare that group's lap record set that weekend with the one set by Hall: 2:27 to 1:57. Spectators appeared to enjoy watching the Formula Vee cars, when they could see them. The very low profile of the Vees tended to make them invisible from viewing areas for much of the course.

Everyone was pleased with a twist particularly important to the Iowa location: The concessionaires provided free beer after the day's races concluded. Ed Leslie wrote after the USRRC that Greenwood was perhaps more suited to production cars, and there were plenty of them when the next race, an SCCA division bash on September 27, rolled around. But as

Jim Hall's Chaparral is about to lap Jack Ryan's Porsche 904 and Bill Allen's Elva-BMW. Hall was in the lead here but soon suffered from oil heating problems that caused him to drop back to 3rd. (Photo Courtesy Doug Dyar)

Frank Manley takes a victory lap with his wife Joan. (Photo Courtesy Frank Manley via Martin Rudow Collection)

usual it was the feature that produced the most excitement as Ralph Salyer in a Cro-Sal Chevy won the 30-lap main event.

The crowd of 7,000 went wild watching the race for 2nd as Don Skogmo in a big Genie-Ford barely beat out the little 850-pound Elva of Mike Hall after a duel of several laps. Almost every class saw a new track lap record set, so drivers were getting used to the course. Greenwood was producing its share of great racing, but the crowds were still not what had been hoped for. Karts and motorcycle racing did not help much and the track proved to be really tough on bikes.

Now the results of budget cuts that had repeatedly forced compromises in building the track began catching up with Greenwood Roadway. The track's pavement, applied too thin to begin with, was having problems. Two tough Iowa winters and two seasons of racing, albeit with a fairly skimpy schedule, had proven to be too much. The surface was becoming rutty and irregular. Erosion ditches lined the track, even cutting under it in places.

Research into the track's original plans and their execution revealed that while the surface was planned to be 2 inches thick throughout, the contractor had instead laid down what he thought would be enough to do the job by tonnage, but when it fell short, simply left the surface as little as 1-inch thick in places. It would take another $30,000 to resurface it according to estimates, money that neither track management nor the many $1-a-pop original shareholders would or could come up with.

1965: Ambitious Season

An ambitious seven-race schedule was announced for the 1965 season. Highlights were to be a USAC stocker in June and the second USRRC race in July. Pro motorcycle and kart races, as well as regional SCCA events, would fill out the schedule.

The first big race was the USAC stock car races on June 12 and 13. Dubbed the Greenwood 200, it offered a purse of $12,000, with $2,000 going to the race winner. Greenwood organizers had caught a break in the quality of the field. Many

Spectators enjoy the sun-drenched action through the esses as a Lotus 23 chases an Alfa Spider in a 1965 regional SCCA race. (Photo Courtesy Frank Manley, Martin Rudow Collection)

of Mopar's NASCAR regulars switched to USAC for the 1965 season in an organized boycott of NASCAR's rules that banned the Hemi engine from NASCAR competition.

Two star drivers who came to compete had their first look at the race course on Thursday, June 3: Paul Goldsmith of Munster, Indiana, former USAC champion (1961 and 1962), and Bobby Isaac of Catawba, North Carolina, who drove the previous year in NASCAR competition. Goldsmith was terse in his reaction to the course after driving it in a stock 1965 Plymouth: "It's dangerous."

Jim Hurtubise, USAC's 1965 Comeback Driver of the Year, and who had earlier competed in his sixth Indianapolis 500, had this to say: "Road racing is hard. You have to know what you're doing all the time. It's a lot more difficult than the steady 'left-hand turn' driving you find on the half-mile and mile tracks. And on top of this you are up-shifting and down-shifting all the time. It's challenging, but it's also fun. I'm looking forward to Greenwood."

But not enough other drivers were. Race weekend brought grim faces from both USAC and track officials. Only 14 cars were on track for Saturday's qualifying sessions, after entries from 25 had been received. Qualifiers tore out several corners and a paving crew went into action when the day's competition ended. Lap speeds ranged from 77 to 85 mph. David Pearson, among the Chrysler Corporation's refugees from NASCAR, clocked his lap in 2 minutes 6.65 seconds to lead the qualifiers. Only minor spins were reported during the daylong qualifying activity as the drivers dealt cautiously with the turns.

Finally, on race day, a few more cars arrived and 19 finally took the green flag. When it was all over a 25-year veteran of stock car racing, Norm Nelson, took home the 1st-place money. The 44-year-old driver from Racine, Wisconsin, passed early leader Paul Goldsmith while Goldsmith was in the pits on the 63rd mile of the race. Attempting to make up for lost ground, David Pearson was clocked at 150 mph on the straight, the fastest speed ever recorded at Greenwood. The most serious incident ended up humorous rather than tragic when Jim Hurtubise went off the road at Turn 1 and ended up almost submerged in a pond, but there were no disasters. Only a dozen cars were running at the end.

In the last event at the track, an SCCA regional was held over the 1966 Fourth of July weekend at Greenwood. A program of seven races, divided as usual according to classes, started at 1 o'clock each afternoon. Upwards of 150 cars were expected. Far fewer showed up, but racing provided drama nonetheless. After 15-lap production races on Saturday, the feature on Sunday had a lot of excitement. Jerry Hansen, 28, a Minneapolis stock broker, and Ralph Salyer, of Hammond, Indiana, drove one of the hottest duels ever at Greenwood. Hansen, wheeling a 370 Chevrolet-powered Wolverine, nosed out his veteran rival (McKee-Olds) by slightly less than a car length at the end of a thrilling 45-mile battle.

The (claimed) paid crowd of 7,108 was the largest attendance since the USRRC event of the previous year. Spectators spent most of the two days huddled under any shade they could find, as temperatures were almost 100 degrees F at the track. No surface problems were reported, but it certainly was little better than it had been for the USAC race a month earlier, despite some patching.

Financial Backing Runs Out

In the August 14, 1965, issue of *Competition Press* it was reported that the track had officially announced bankruptcy. Just two weeks before the USRRC date of July 17–18, Norman Ackerman, now president of Greenwood Roadway, Inc., had stated that the track could not afford to risk the $25,000 in expenses they would incur from staging the USRRC event, and canceled it. Even if it were true, Ackerman did not endear himself to local racers as he blamed the Des Moines and Iowa Valley SCCA associations for many of his problems, citing a vague "lack of cooperation and understanding." He admitted that from a financial viewpoint, the track was a "complete disaster."

Meanwhile the local SCCA associations pointed out that their members had purchased thousands of dollars in shares to start the whole thing, built the entire sound system, and supplied the volunteer labor that the track had called for to help in putting on races. Ackerman was accused of exaggerating or shaving spectator counts depending upon guarantees that sanctioning bodies had made. National SCCA officials

Greenwood as it appears today. This shows Turn 1 and the long straight that ended downhill at Turn 3. The early spring Iowa backdrop is breathtaking. (Photo Courtesy Judy Rudow)

still expressed hope for the track, stating that its basic layout, grading, and cyclone fencing were all good and still in place. Effort was put forth to keep racing going at the track, but the needed financial support could just not be found. Greenwood closed its doors before the end of its fourth year in existence.

Because it was far from any major towns, and the area was more important for farming than building homes, the Greenwood track has not suffered the inroads of development since its closing. The course remains virtually intact, and even though erosion and weathering had made the surface unraceable, it is possible to drive around it in a family sedan. Although the same challenges of dust, heat, and limited spectator viewing options remain, there has been talk of reopening the facility. It's probably best that the track remains a testament to racers' dreams and that one memorable USRRC race in 1964.

Time has taken its toll. This is the view today of the straight toward Turn 3. Greenwood had two long straights, and this one was the longer and steeper. (Photo Courtesy Judy Rudow)

At this part of the track, you're looking at the start of Turn 8, the long sweeper that connected the two halves of the course. (Photo Courtesy Judy Rudow)

HILLTOP RACEWAY

STILL STANDING AFTER ALL THESE YEARS

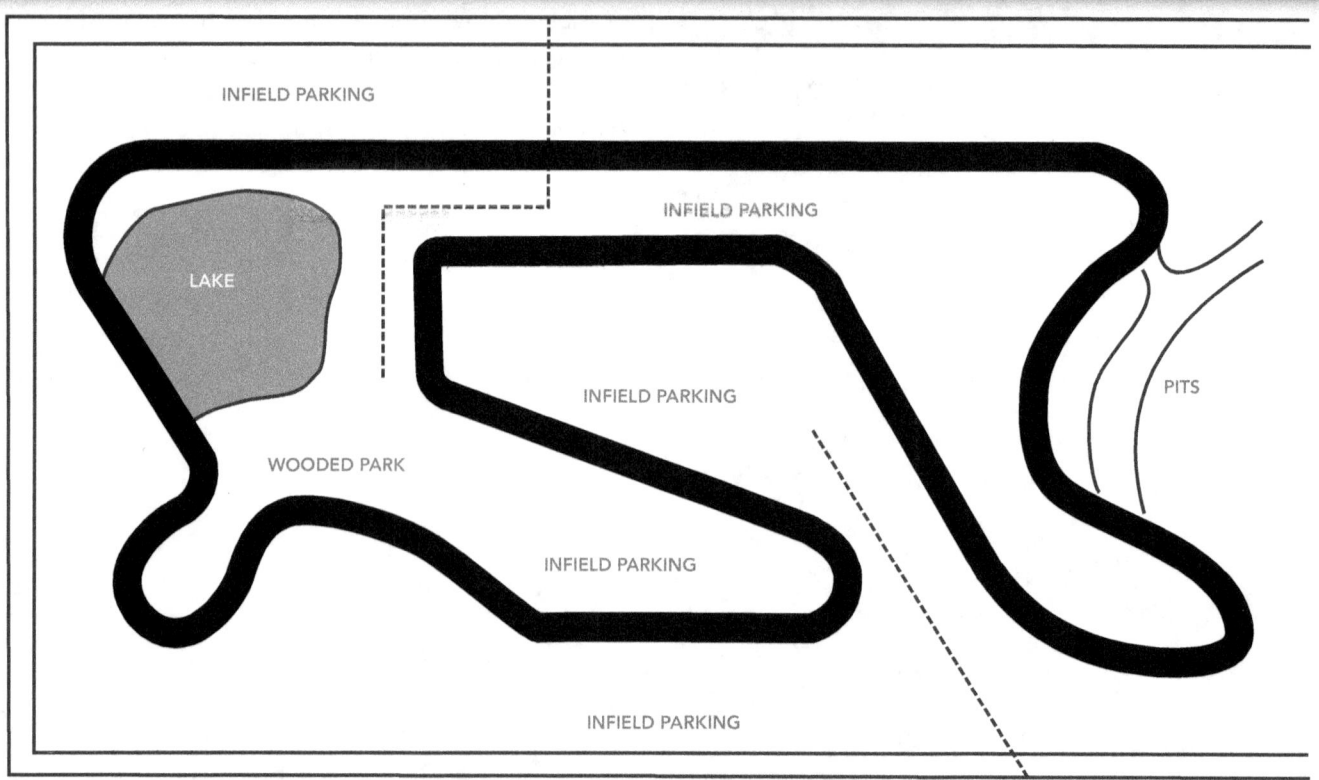

The only course map available of Hilltop is pretty basic. The start/finish line and pits were on the short straight right below the long straight. (Illustration Courtesy Martin Spetz Program Collection)

One glorious race day made the money, sweat, and tears that went into Louisiana's Hilltop Raceway all worthwhile. For that one day in 1962, many of the country's top cars and drivers converged on the out-of-the-way racetrack to stage a memorable event. In an interesting twist of historical irony, the least used and seemingly the best preserved of the tracks in this book is Hilltop Raceway. You can drive almost all of the course today, and along the way you'll find at least one of the track's old buildings still standing.

In 1960 two road courses became available in the South: Louisiana Hilltop Raceway near Bossier City and Roebling Road near Savannah, Georgia. Hilltop was purpose-built and beat Roebling Road by a week in hosting its inaugural event.

Louisiana Hilltop Raceway (also known as Top o' the Hill) was the brainchild of air-conditioning engineer Steve Robinson of Bossier City, an accomplished Alfa Romeo club racer. He found land located around Top of the Hill, a heavily wooded area 12 miles east of Shreveport. Few hills are in that part of Louisiana and Top of the Hill was one of the highest. Previously a popular resort area, the property had been abandoned when Robinson bought it in December 1959. Robinson founded Louisiana Hilltop Enterprises, Inc., and inspired by the recently completed Continental Divide Raceway in Colorado, started construction work right away, using some of the old resort roads as a starting point.

Word spread in local circles that a new circuit was on its way. Places to race in the area were in short supply after a couple of well-known airport courses were declared off limits for racing. The result of Robinson's construction efforts was a twisty up-and-down course of 2 miles and 12 turns, with only

CHAPTER 7

Bossier City, Louisiana
1960–1964

Facility 2 miles, 12 turns
Principal Events SCCA, USAC
Current Status RV park; course is mostly intact

A large field of typical small-bore cars of the day (Porsches, Elvas, MGAs, Abarths, Sprites, and some specials) roars off for the September 1960 race. This was at the older, top-of-the-hill starting line. (Photo Courtesy Willem Oosthoek Collection)

one straight of around 1/2 mile. A few turns were slightly banked. Even the starting line was on a curve. The course partially circled a small lake. Drivers would have little margin of error because there were virtually no run-off areas.

In addition, Robinson took advantage of former resort buildings on the site by quickly converting them and being able to offer permanent buildings right away. Timing stands, shower facilities, an air-conditioned motel with garages, and a swimming pool were all part of the facility. A beach on the lake and several barbecue-pitted picnic grounds made Hilltop a family-friendly destination. Overall, a reported $100,000 was spent ($800,000 in today's money) preparing Hilltop for racing. Robinson estimated that another $150,000 would be needed to fully realize his dreams for the facility.

1960: Hot Opening

The track opened on a blistering hot and sunny weekend, June 4–5, 1960. More than 100 entries showed up for the inaugural weekend, an SCCA event sponsored by the Southwest Louisiana region. Saturday offered six races, followed by five on Sunday. Among the hot shots in the feature race were Louisiana lumberman Bill Fuller with his Jaguar D-type and Delmo Johnson with a Jaguar XK-SS. Both had substituted Chevy power for Jaguar. Bill Janowski was on hand with his *Monsterati*, an appropriately named special also featuring Chevy power on a 1939 Ford chassis. Five Formula Juniors were also part of the field, including a Volpini driven by Robinson himself.

Chapter 7: Hilltop Raceway 69

This view from the start/finish line and pit area shows the great spectating opportunities offered at Hilltop during its short existence. This view, taken during the 1962 Pipeline 200, is overgrown today with tall trees and the old track is completely obscured. (Photo Courtesy the Henry Ford)

In Saturday's 7-lap warm-up for the top contenders Janowski led the field until he spun on lap 4, diving down an embankment. To the crowd's delight he managed to get back onto the track, but by then Fuller was firmly in control of the race, keeping Johnson and Norm Scott (Porsche 550RS) behind him.

On Sunday it was Fuller all the way again in the 20-lap feature, averaging 63.5 mph. Johnson and Kansas City's Tom Newcomer (Lotus 11) followed him home. Janowski's gear lever snapped off in his hand, and as a result, he finished farther back, stuck in third gear. Robinson was able to win the Formula Junior title, a reward perhaps for personal risk he had taken in financing the course.

The big-bore drivers turned in the best races of the weekend. A novice, Bill Cantrell, barely prevailed over Gil Steele's AC Bristol in a Corvette. The race for 1st was so hard fought that the turn workers applauded the top three finishers on the cool-down lap. Most drivers who took part in the race weekend had never been on a course like this, airports being the norm in the area. Hilltop was a dramatic change in what was demanded of them and their cars. Hard braking and tight turns were new to them. As a result, spinouts were common and at least a dozen cars were damaged in collisions and off-course excursions.

The SCCA's Red River region of Shreveport hosted Hilltop's second event, the Heat Wave Races on July 30–31 of the same year. Two races on Saturday, six on Sunday. Perhaps learning from his own racing experiences a couple of months earlier, Robinson had made a few adjustments to the course. Most notably the start/finish was off the turn and back on the straightaway, a more traditional location. The paddock area was now on the infield. Welcome changes, but only 52 cars showed up to take advantage of them.

Among the people to watch were Janowski's *Monsterati*, now with a 5.7-liter Chevy engine, and local VW dealer Harry Washburn, who showed up with two cars: a Porsche Carrera and a Chevy-engined Ferrari Monza. The Monza had seen a lot of use by then and was a bit tired, but installing the new powerplant made the car competitive again. Washburn and Fuller shared the Prancing Horse car over the weekend, with Fuller getting the berth for Sunday's feature.

Janowski's *Monsterati* set a new course record on Saturday with a 1:50.4 while easily winning a 10-lap feature race. Washburn's Monza/Chevy finished 2nd. Robinson again was in his Volpini and finished an impressive 3rd overall. Janowski was the heavy favorite for Sunday's 20-lap feature, especially since the aging Ferrari, now driven by Fuller, was having brake and transmission problems. *Monsterati*, though, threw a rod on lap 18, giving Fuller the lead. His final average for the race was just 60.2 mph. The Porsche Carreras of Washburn and Harry Martin finished 2nd and 3rd.

It was a busy summer at the new racetrack. The Red River Region hosted a third regional at Hilltop on September 3–4, the Dedication Races, with two races on Saturday and six on Sunday. This Labor Day event attracted 69 entries, headed by some familiar names: Janowski's *Monsterati*; Fuller, now back in his D-type/Chevy; and Washburn, who brought the

One of the stalwarts of the early days at Hilltop, Bill Janowski in his fearsome Monsterati, a Chevy-powered, home-built special. He was often the fastest on track but rarely finished. (Photo Courtesy Willem Oosthoek Collection)

This first weekend Hilltop race is being run clockwise; contrast the view to the first photo. The Jag XK-150 of H. E. Fraser chases a Ferrari 250 in the hands of Woody Boyles. (Photo Courtesy Willem Oosthoek Collection)

This is a good view of the start/finish line and pit area for early races. Two Formula Juniors wait for the call to action. (Photo Courtesy Willem Oosthoek Collection)

Carrera for himself and the Monza/Chevy, which he offered to Bob Schroeder for Sunday's feature. The only other entry with an off-hand chance of winning the feature was Memphis dentist Don Horn in a Porsche RS-60, a car that had finished 2nd overall at Sebring that year.

In Saturday's 10-lap warm-up Fuller beat Janowski and Horn. Fuller was the favorite to win the 20-lap feature on Sunday. After a hectic race that saw spinouts and drop outs, Fuller won again.

The weekend saw a lot of good racing but paid attendance was down again. From an initial strong turnout of 8,000 for the first race, only 1,500 paid to watch the Labor Day festivities. Racers liked the course, but perhaps it was too far from population centers. Despite this praise from veteran official Paul Shattuck, who called Hilltop "a honey . . . one of the best courses for spectators in the country, even better than Lime Rock," not enough of those spectators were showing up. Maybe something bigger than an SCCA regional race was needed to stir things up. The USAC's professional Road Racing Championship series provided such an opportunity.

USAC driver Lloyd Ruby tested the course late in 1960 and waxed enthusiastic about it. After driving the course in Robinson's Volpini and Alfa, Ruby stated: "This is the finest spectator course I have ever observed. It is the second best racing layout. My ratings would put Road America first, with Hilltop second." After such an endorsement, it seemed only natural that the USAC or the SCCA would hold a major race at Hilltop, but for some reason nothing happened in 1961.

1962: The Pipeline 200

Track owner Robinson reorganized his company late in 1961, renaming it Louisiana Racing, Inc. Then, early in 1962, he announced a major new event for the track: the Pipeline 200. To be held March 31–April 1, it was the season opener for the five-event USAC Road Racing Championship, scheduled as a two-heat event of 100 miles (50 laps) each. The event was open to formula cars, sports racers and production cars, in other words, Formula Libre.

This was a first for the USAC, and they hoped to attract American Indy-type cars as well as the "usual" foreign contingent. None showed up, but it was still a diverse and exciting group of cars and drivers. Eight open-wheeled formula cars were on hand, including an old 250F Maserati and Dan Gurney in a brand-new 2.5-liter Lotus 18. Sports racers and fast production cars made up the rest of the 26-car field, from Bob Donner's Porsche RS-61 to a Ferrari 3.0 TR. The race was run counterclockwise.

Practice was especially interesting as Gurney could be seen tooling around in a dead-stock Corvair. His Lotus was hastily being put together in the background from parts that had arrived at owner Frank Aricero's Los Angeles warehouse just in time for the long tow to Bossier City.

The fastest 24 qualifiers were allowed to take the start in each heat. The purse was $8,000, with additional lap prizes of $100 offered by local sponsors for the leading driver on the 1st, 10th, 20th, 30th, and 40th lap of each heat. Among other starters were Lloyd Ruby (Lotus 18), Jim Hall (Lotus 18/21),

In this wild production-car race action at a June 1960 Hilltop race, the #56 car is in a big slide. Truett Helms in the Corvette won this one over Bill Steele (AC/Bristol), Harry Washburn (Carrera), and the others. (Photo Courtesy Willem Oosthoek Collection)

If you weren't careful at Hilltop, you could end up in the trackside lake. Four cars went into the lake over the years; none of the drivers were hurt, but they did get wet. (Photo Courtesy Willem Oosthoek Collection)

Chapter 7: Hilltop Raceway   71

Spectators check out Alan Connell's Cooper-Climax at the start/finish line and pit area for the 1962 Pipeline event. (Photo Courtesy Willem Oosthoek Collection)

The starting grid for the 1962 Pipeline 200 event. From front to back, #96 Dan Gurney (Lotus 18), #6 Roger Penske (2.5-liter Cooper), #77 Bob Schroeder (deTomaso Iris), #45 Bob Donner (Porsche RS-61), #16 Chuck Cassell (Porsche RS-60), #47 Harry Washburn (Porsche 550), and #36 Bob Hurt (Ferrari TR). (Photo Courtesy Willem Oosthoek Collection)

Shortly after the start of the first heat of the Pipeline 200; Dan Gurney is already pulling away from Roger Penske. (Photo Courtesy the Henry Ford)

and two T53 Coopers in the hands of Roger Penske and Alan Connell. All equipped with 2.5-liter Climax engines, along with Gurney they were the most likely candidates for overall victory. Two Formula 1 cars did not make the start. One was the ex-Nürburgring Fangio 1957 Maserati 250F so famously driven by The Master to victory that year, the other a new Tec-Mec. Even though neither started the final two heats they added some luster just by being on hand.

Among the sports racers the favorites appeared to be Donner (RS-61) and Bob Hurt, with the only Ferrari present, the 1959 Sebring-winning 250TR. Hilltop regulars Bill Fuller and Delmo Johnson were on the entry list with their Chevy-powered Jaguars but did not show, while Bill Janowski practiced but withdrew. Too bad, especially because these three had considerable experience with the tricky course while the other top contenders were neophytes there.

Friday and Saturday saw disappointing weather that ranged from gloomy to downpours. The fastest qualifying time was turned in by Ruby: 1:39.91. At the last minute Sunday morning, Gurney's car finally got going and Dan wasted no time in turning in the fastest qualifying time of all: 1:39.127. Formula cars were proving to be much faster at Hilltop than sports racers; the fastest qualifier of that group was Chuck Cassel's Porsche RSK at 1:48.84.

Race Day Dawns

Sunday dawned with great sunny weather, and an estimated 18,000 spectators showed up at $3 each. Seventeen cars finally started the first of the two heats. Heat 1 ended with Gurney taking an easy win with an average speed of 70.01 mph.

At 3 pm, Heat 2 started with a grid based on the first heat's finishing positions. Penske led Gurney after the opening lap and then Gurney pitted with severe vibration caused by a faulty tire. When he was moving again he was dead last, five laps behind Penske. After a very rapid rise through the ranks, he was gaining on Penske when Roger had to pit with a broken gearshift lever. That was all Gurney needed and he won before an approving crowd. The final top three were Gurney, Donner, and Penske. Gurney's winning average speed was 66.97 mph.

Sold and Closed

Robinson was extremely pleased with the day's turnout for both entries and spectators, and figured that his racetrack

At the far end of the course, Bob Donner's Porsche RS-61 leads a pack around a tight hairpin. Note the dangerously placed telephone pole, one of several similarly placed around Hilltop. (Photo Courtesy the Henry Ford)

had turned the corner. He promised that the Pipeline 200 event would become an annual event. But it was not to be. Despite generally good reviews, spectator turnout even for the USAC race had not financially supported racing at the track. Robinson tried to sell the whole facility for $125,000, and *Competition Press* commented that it was an excellent investment. They rated the track and its accompanying facilities top-notch. The poor spectator attendance that had doomed the track under Robinson, they felt, was due to poor advertising and publicity. A buyer was found: the Ark-La-Tex Amusement Corporation (the final purchase price was not announced). Reportedly well capitalized, they announced plans to revitalize and upgrade the track in many respects and lure big-time events back.

Big time maybe not, but a sports car race was held at the slightly improved road course on September 27 of that year. The event was a regional SCCA event and it was marred by the death of a local racer. Dangerous culverts were in evidence alongside the course and were at least a factor in the fatality. Heavy rain showers further made the day miserable, and few spectators were in attendance. It seems that all concerned then simply slunk off into the mist and the once-promising road circuit at Hilltop was never used again.

In 1965, Hilltop was converted into an RV park, sort of akin to its former resort status. Today the park shows some wear around the edges, but still holds a mostly permanent population of RVs in various states of repair. The course remains almost intact but the infield has grown so much that it is almost impossible to see more than a small portion of the track from any one spot.

This is the view from the timing tower in the Pipeline 200 as Gurney hastily pits to consult with his crew. The consultation must have been productive because Gurney tore through the field to win by a good margin. (Photo Courtesy the Henry Ford)

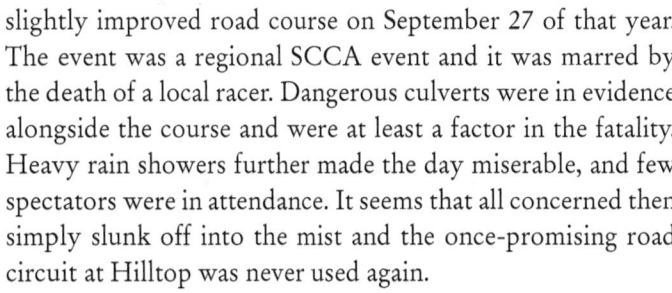

Dan Gurney (#96) laps Bob Shroeder in the deTomaso Iris (#77) and the rest of the field at the Pipeline 200 on his way to the win. (Photo Courtesy Willem Oosthoek Collection)

The woods have reclaimed most of the track. Trees replace the spot that was occupied by that precariously placed telephone pole shown earlier. (Photo Courtesy Judy Rudow)

A portion of the old course still circles the lake that had a few drivers swimming during the track's short life. (Photo Courtesy Judy Rudow)

It appears that the last of the Deadheads have taken refuge in the RV park that is still circled by remnants of the old track. (Photo Courtesy Judy Rudow)

You can clearly see the course-side mud holes that made the course messy at times. (Photo Courtesy Judy Rudow)

Chapter 7: Hilltop Raceway   73

MARLBORO MOTOR RACEWAY

THE GRAND LADY OF THE EAST

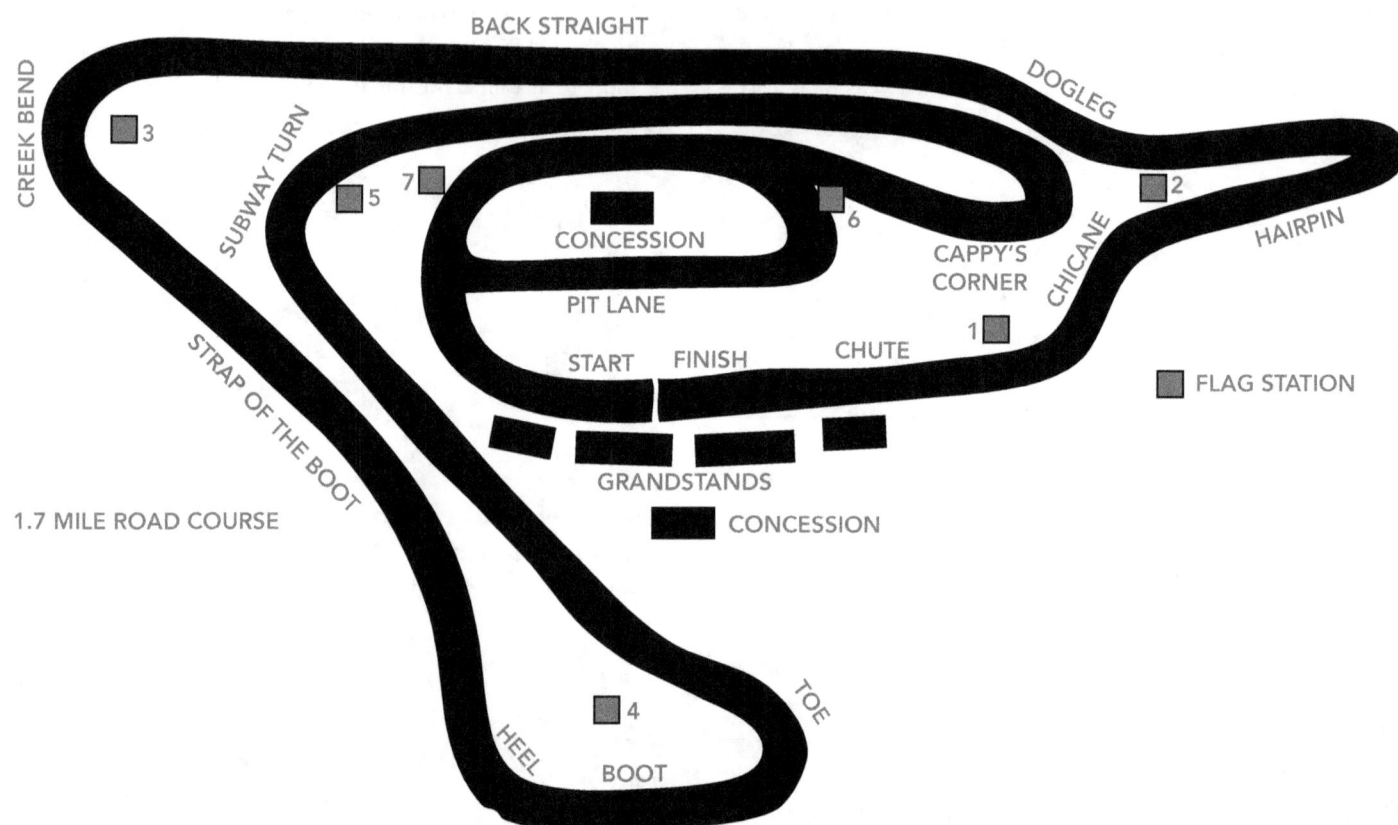

It looks like a Mad Mouse Maze, but this is the tight and twisty circuit that was Marlboro. The Start/Finish line and the grandstands indicate the oval portion. (Illustration Courtesy Martin Spetz Program Collection)

Similar to many of the tracks profiled in this book, Marlboro started life as a dirt oval track. Its upgrade began when a rudimentary road course was added in 1954 and the 1/3-mile oval was paved at the same time. It ended up being used strictly as a road course circuit; it had a proud and prolific record of racing that included many of the decade's top names. And, because of its location near fragrant tobacco-drying warehouses, the circuit was often referred to as "tobaccoland."

Owner Eugene Chaney took longer than anticipated to grade and pave the new road circuit, which was puzzling because he owned a large concrete company. You would think he'd have known what he was getting into. Or maybe he did. According to many reporters as well as participants, the road course that he built was a low-budget short course, more like a go-kart track in layout and tightness. Of course the same complaint was lodged against many of the purpose-built road courses of the time, a complaint almost certainly fueled by racing experiences on the World War II airport circuits that had dominated racing. Such courses were built as runways for big planes and therefore featured long straights and hairpin turns for the main, as well as flat surfaces and ample runoff areas.

Tight purpose-built courses, such as Marlboro, were less comfortable and more challenging. It was indeed a tight

74   Lost Road Courses

CHAPTER 8

Upper Marlboro, Maryland
1955–1968

Facility 1.7-mile road circuit; 1/3-mile oval (dirt and paved)
Sanctioning Bodies SCCA, NASCAR
Principal Events Trans-Am, President's Cup, Refrigerator Bowl, 6- and 12-hour endurance races
Current Status Undeveloped private property; course is mostly intact

In a photo that shows the diversity of feature race fields at Marlboro, the 1963 version of the annual Refrigerator Bowl gets underway. Yes, that is a Ford Galaxie out there. (Bill Dobbins photo, Courtesy the Washington D.C. Region, SCCA)

course. When it opened in 1955, Marlboro was just a 0.7-miler and half of that was the oval. But then, the entire plot for the track and its infrastructure was only 28 acres total. Even if the management had wanted it, a potentially moneymaking 1/4-mile dragstrip could not be accommodated.

1955: The Lavender Hill Mob

Founded after their brand of driving for trophies was called "egregious pot-hunting" by SCCA official M. R. J. Wyllie, some Washington, D.C.–based SCCA drivers started calling themselves the Lavender Hill Mob Racing Association (LHMRA). The odd name came from a contemporary Ealing Studios movie with the same title about a miscast gang of bumbling English crooks who despite themselves made off with millions in gold melted into little Eiffel Tower statues (okay, you'll have to see the movie to understand).

It might have been the main part of a too-short road course, but the oval track had grandstands erected along it that could accommodate a large crowd in covered comfort, at least by 1955 standards. Also, from the stands, spectators could see almost all of the entire road course. Although some sports car racing had taken place on the oval under the auspices of the local MG club, the first official race on the new road course for the Mob and the rest of the Washington, D.C. SCCA region racers was held on May 22, 1955.

Dick Thompson

Heralding things to come, a young racing dentist and LHMRA founding member named Dick Thompson was the big winner that day. Thompson, however, won his events in his own Jaguar XK-140MC and a borrowed Mercedes-Benz 300SL, instead of the Corvettes with which he became well known. Jaguars were so popular and dominating in production circles that year that a special race was held just for them. Ten races in all were run on a day that saw enough rain to flood the backstretch before giving way to a weak sun by day's end.

Racers were glad to have anywhere to race because airports were increasingly being ruled off-limits to them, but the sinuous 0.7-mile course was going to limit any serious racing. So the Mob managed to have it expanded to 1.7 miles, partially by coming up with most of the money for the construction. Track owner Chaney was delighted with the support and pledged to work mainly with Mob members from then on.

The oval was still a big part of the track; drivers exited and entered it at opposite ends. Later, bigger-engined cars often became airborne at the transition from oval to road, and then again a few moments later, from road to oval.

In the first road race at Marlboro in 1955, Jaguars tangle with one another. Dick Thompson, the race winner, is in one of them. (Photo Courtesy Birmingham Automobile Racing Club)

Added to it was a twisting and turning road course with two of its straightaways separated by just a few yards of grass and wood barriers. It was not a setup that would fly today. At some point in the 1959 season, the track's grandstands, guardrails, control tower, corner stations, and other buildings were painted lavender, startling drivers passing by on nearby Route 301.

A 1957 *Sports Illustrated* article celebrated the opening of the bigger track and noted that the day was crammed with events; no fewer than 11 races were offered. The Mob managed to win most of the first-place trophies, too, led by Dr. Thompson, who was now in a Corvette.

The mid-July day was, as expected, hot and humid, but 6,000 spectators showed up and enjoyed the views from the grandstand seating. *Sports Illustrated* opined that spectators would really enjoy the intimate track with its excellent viewing opportunities (although perilously close to the track), while drivers might be less than thrilled. Carroll Shelby, for example, was quoted as saying that the frequent shifting and braking demanded by the course was tiring on the drivers; it was "like beating each other with short sticks." Denise McCluggage later called Marlboro a "squirrel-cage-like twisty, curling, [but] sporting circuit."

Walt Hansgen

In addition to Thompson, Walt Hansgen was a frequent Marlboro competitor and winner on the circuit in the early years. The genial East Coaster went to most races in that part of the country, and always drove big, fast machinery, and drove it well. He almost won an early-1959 SCCA National race there in a Lister-Jaguar despite a qualifying race tangle that earned him a starting position at the back of the pack for the feature. He was beaten by a Porsche RSK whose tight wheelbase made it a natural for Marlboro.

That same race weekend, April 18 and 19, was also notable for the first non-Sebring appearance of the Corvette body style that became famously known as the Sting Ray. Other big (or soon to be big) names included Bob Sesslar, Bob Holbert, Augie Pabst, "Pup" Pupulidy, Charlie Kolb, and Roger Penske.

Winning at Marlboro was prestigious. The central location of the circuit, its proximity to Washington, D.C., an eager team of race reporters who made sure each race received national coverage, and the aggressiveness of the Mob's Washington SCCA region officials saw that the track received its share (and more) of races, both large and small. The instantly famous Old Brick Inn, a nearby watering hole with a lot of character, also made the track a popular destination.

Dick Thompson, driving a borrowed 300SL, stays ahead of Bill Kincheloe in the Healy in a July 1955 race. This was one of two races Thompson won that day. (Photo Courtesy Lou Schroeder from the Mike Eaton Archives)

Dick Thompson created quite a stir on this 1960 starting line for the President's Cup with his new Stingray. Despite the novelty of the car, he did not place in this edition of the race. (Photo Courtesy Birmingham Automobile Racing Club)

76   Lost Road Courses

1957: SCCA National

The Mob hosted the track's first SCCA National in the summer of 1957. The event met with enthusiastic praise despite some complaints about the tight course and the way the heat and humidity hung in the infield. Walt Hansgen continued to show the most speed, this time in a locally owned D-Jaguar, and won the main event after the Maseratis of Carroll Shelby and John Fitch retired. The cars that finished 2-3-4 behind Hansgen are worth a note: a Jaguar XK-SS, a Mercedes-Benz 300SL roadster, and one of the first Ferrari Testa Rossas seen in those parts.

The Mob hosted no less than three cocktail parties over the weekend and provided great trophies. Shelby, sidelined for the day, opined that the challenge of driving both tight courses, such as Marlboro, and the elaborate longer courses, such as Road America in Elkhart Lake, Wisconsin, would soon produce American drivers the equal of any in the world.

1958 and 1959: The President's Cup

At the time, the President's Cup was one of the most prestigious races on the East Coast. In the early days, the president of the United States actually presented the cup to the winner. The Cup race was held at Marlboro for the first time in 1958; it was a natural location, given its proximity to Washington, D.C. Hansgen won again, this time in a Lister-Jaguar, on a day that changed from sweltering heat to a violent thunderstorm. The day's races were reportedly lackluster, but one of the highlights was General Curtis LeMay awarding the cup. The general was the man most responsible for the growth of sports car racing in the early 1950s when he made military airports available for racing.

The 1959 President's Cup races made up for the unexciting 1958 races. Held again in mid-April, 225 drivers entered, led by Hansgen, who was winning races all over the East Coast. This time, however, he started last because of a qualifying accident, and then could not hold off eventual winner Don Sesslar's Porsche RSK, which had taken 4th at Sebring a month earlier in the rain.

Reporter and racer Toni Cappiello spun out so many times on the turn leading from the road to the oval that it was named after him: Cappy's Corner. He noted that the course, already considered the toughest in the country by many, was even more difficult when it rained.

The day attracted 8,000 spectators, and entrants filled the pits. Even when rain fell and flooded the course and the pits, it didn't dampen the enthusiasm of the spectators or the drivers. The rain contributed to a popular win when a Jaguar XK-150, in the hands of Lou Hatcher, won the big-bore production race over a bevy of slippery Corvettes. (Dick Thompson was not racing that day or he might have won.)

The course officials made a lot of friends when they had each class winner join the outright race winner on the victory lap, each holding aloft his own checkered flag. As with most Marlboro races of the day, the event was reported extensively in *Road & Track* magazine. Someone at that magazine obviously liked Marlboro because the track received more than its fair share of coverage in *R&T*'s popular "Race Results" section. Dave Roethel, SCCA regional exec during much of Marlboro's history, was publicist for the facility, and can probably be given much of the credit for this coverage.

Bob Holbert gets his Porsche RSK ready for the 1960 President's Cup race. He came in 2nd to Roger Penske, who was in another RSK. This was one of the races that gave Marlboro its reputation as a "Porsche track." (Photo Courtesy Birmingham Automobile Racing Club)

No less than two Ferrari Berlinettas grace the starting line at the 1962 SCCA Nationals; they are driven by Bob Grossman (mostly hidden at the left, #6) and Charlie Hayes (right, #7). Grossman won the big-bore production race as Hayes' Ferrari blew an engine while fighting for the lead. Dick Thompson, in the Corvette, raced them hard but was a DNF. (Photo Courtesy Birmingham Automobile Racing Club)

Even before the days of the "unfair advantage," Roger Penske was a prolifically winning driver, as here at the 1962 SCCA Nationals in a Cooper Monaco. (Photo Courtesy Birmingham Automobile Racing Club)

The 1959 6-hour was typical of the way things went in this type of event. A D-Jaguar driven by Graham Shaw and Dick Robinson (not Hansgen) was fastest but flighty; it eventually crashed and was out of the race. A 2-liter Maserati was also quick but broke down after two hours. Finally, an Elva Mk IV, driven by Bob Davis and Art Tweedale, won over, of all things, a Triumph TR3.

1960: Bizarre Accidents

The President's Cup continued to kick off the year at Marlboro. In 1960, Roger Penske showed his ability at a young age. He was just 23 and two years out of driver's school, which he had attended at Marlboro. He drove an older Porsche RSK to the Cup win. Smaller cars often dominated at Marlboro because the tight course did not allow the big-engine cars to rev up and use their horsepower. In fact, three Porsches led the first larger car, a Birdcage Maserati, at the end. A total of 204 cars were on hand for the event. One of them, a Ferrari California, would be worth well over $15 million today. However, the car was far from being just a beauty queen. That day, in the hands of successful Ferrari driver Bob Grossman, it beat all of the Corvettes in Big-Bore Production.

An early June 6-hour race that year was bizarre and saw terrible accidents and fires both on the track and in the grandstands. In the end, no one was hurt, but an Elva and two Corvettes were burned to a crisp. One of the accidents saw Collier Miller and his Deustch-Bonnet take a 45-foot dive into the creek. The car went all the way under and he had to swim for his life. This time a Ferrari 250 California (VA) specially brought in for this event was competitive but did not win. Art Tweedale and Ed Costley won in an Elva.

1961: Mark Donohue Begins His Rise to Prominence

Marlboro began its 1961 season with the appropriately named Refrigerator Bowl event. The first one was held on January 8 and accompanied by snow flurries and freezing temperatures. The SCCA agreed to this date after some negotiation to open the SCCA's new competition year. Not many spectators were expected to brave these conditions, but more than 1,000 came. Most notable was the appearance of two youngsters, Mark Donohue and Jay Signore, who went on to fruitful careers in motorsports. Donohue's life was tragically ended 14 years later, but Signore was involved with stock car racing for many more years.

At the time, both were just young kids with a lot of enthusiasm and raw talent. Good friends, they often traveled to races together and diced for class and race wins. On this day, they were both in Elva Couriers and had a memorable race. Signore was ahead, with Donohue's front bumper right at his rear wheel when the checkered fell. Bruce Jennings, the top Porsche driver in the area at the time, won the Refrigerator Bowl. He described the trophy as "big enough to hold a dozen coconuts."

Marlboro's reputation as a "Porsche track" was reinforced when Bob Holbert won that year's SCCA National (the Governor's Cup) in a Porsche RS-61. To date, it was the most dominating victory at the track in a major event; Holbert lapped the entire 22-car field. Donohue was there again and made another big impression, as did another youngster just getting started, Peter Revson. He was driving a Morgan and, according to *Competition Press*, made "one of the

Bob Grossman was the top East Coast "production" Ferrari drivers in the early 1960s. Here he wins Marlboro's 1962 SCCA National in a Berlinetta. (Photo Courtesy Birmingham Automobile Racing Club)

hairiest showings ever" at the track, sliding furiously around the course but staying in contention until his hood blew off. Almost continuous rain that weekend caused a lot of sliding.

The President's Cup was held at another track that year, so Marlboro held one of its infamous 6-hour enduros on the early-summer date that might have seen the more prestigious race. An RS-60 driven by Pete DeCosta and Bill Mayberry outlasted a large field to win the 6-hour go.

After a couple of regional races, the season ended with a long bang when a 12-hour sedan enduro was held on October 22. Drivers agreed that the demands of a 12-hour race on the tight circuit provided one of the toughest tests of gearboxes, brakes, clutches, and suspensions, not to mention drivers. Despite the presence of famed mechanics Smokey Yunick and Ray Nichels, two Swedish Volvos easily beat a team of Yunick and Nichels–aided Pontiac Tempests as well as other cars. To make a final statement, both Volvos were driven to their homes at the conclusion of the race; one was 400 miles away.

The race drew so much attention despite its challenges to man and machine that it was immediately scheduled again for the following year at an earlier and warmer date. Sensing that sedan endurance racing would become highly marketable, the Washington D.C. region's SCCA exec applied for and was granted a full FIA international sanction for all 12-hour sedan races at Marlboro.

1962: Mixed Field of Drivers

The Refrigerator Bowl was back in January 1962. The promoters added some spice to the day by attracting stock cars, midgets, and even a go-kart to run together. Dick Thompson in a new Corvette beat Elmo Langley in a 390-ci Ford stocker in the main event. Langley, though, surprised the crowd by wrestling his big beast around the tight little course in surprisingly fast and smooth fashion. He turned in lap times in the 1:45 range, something only Thompson could match in production ranks. The two had a rematch on the oval later in the day, with Langley smacking Thompson when Thompson spun in front of him.

It was obvious that the Ford, set up for right-turn superspeedway racing, could be a match for anyone if set up for road racing. To further annoy purists, a match race held later between a go-kart and a Morgan ended with the kart prevailing, as it was able to take many of the course's turns flat out.

The biggest crowd in the track's history, 12,000 people, attended the SCCA National in April. Braving freezing temperatures, they witnessed an epic Corvette versus Ferrari duel in the A-B-C production race. Dick Thompson held off three Ferrari Berlinettas until his engine quit. Lap times of the leaders in the race dipped under 1:40. Bob Grossman finally prevailed in his Berlinetta.

Roger Penske in his Cooper-Monaco was the winner of the main event. Both he and the Formula Junior Cooper of Tim Mayer turned laps in the 1:35 range. Reports from the race indicate that of the 250 cars raced over the weekend, all appeared to have crumpled fenders.

Volvos prevailed again at 1962's 12-hour enduro race, this time they were the new PV-544 fastbacks. Harry Brack and Brad Howes drove their car to the win over a Saab driven by Hal Mayforth and Louie Braun. The real excitement of the day, though, was provided by a little Austin-Cooper in the hands of no less than Dick Thompson and Roger Penske, who must have had a ball as they hurled the diminutive car into a 4th-place finish. The speed of Renault 1093s and Corvairs also surprised onlookers. The 2nd-place Saab actually did a complete somersault in the second hour. It was driven to the pits, inspected, and went back out.

1963: The Mob's Swan Song

Many of the same contestants that had made the 1962 Refrigerator Bowl so enjoyable entered the 1963 Bowl. Again the go-kart raced against a Morgan (and just barely lost this time) and Elmo Langley showed up in another Ford Galaxie stocker (still in the final stages of preparation for Daytona). Despite plenty of snow on the ground and cold temperatures, the stands were reportedly half full. The locals evidently liked the novelty of this event. Langley was 5th this time when Thompson and other Corvettes led him in. More match races were held between three Formula Juniors and a V-8-60 midget followed. The oval-track car beat them in an oval track race but could not handle the road course.

It was Penske again in the 1963 SCCA Nationals, the first of the season anywhere. Penske drove the Zerex

At least one national magazine thought that Marlboro's annual Refrigerator Bowl races were worth a cover. (Photo Courtesy Martin Rudow Collection)

Roger Penske won several Marlboro races. Here, he sits in the controversial Zerex Special (a Formula 1 car with fenders) waiting the call to grid at the 1963 Nationals. (Bill Dobbins Photo, Courtesy the Washington D.C. Region, SCCA)

Cooper Special. The mid-April weekend also marked the first local appearance of the new lightweight Sting Ray, which was not yet accepted into production ranks. In the capable hands of Dick Thompson, it turned some fast laps but did not do particularly well in the open race. During the race, spectators had dangerously congregated in the branches of trees bordering the course, so track workers used fire hoses to dislodge them. Eventually, the owner charged a fee for using the leafy perches to watch the race.

Overall, 10,000 spectators showed up, which was a great showing. The track had hired a new publicity firm and its work appeared to be paying off.

The 6-hour race continued to be popular with spectators. About 5,000 came to that year's race, even though it was extremely hot. The high temperatures almost sucked the life out of several drivers. One who made it the whole way single-handedly was Art Tweedale, a frequent competitor at the track who also won the Index of Performance in a GM Lotus. A Bob Mouat/Paul Hyatt–driven Cooper-Monaco won overall.

That year's 12-hour enduro, again held in high mid-August temperatures, saw some big names participate. Included in that group were Walt Hansgen, Curtis Turner, Charlie Hayes, Bruce Jennings, and Dick Thompson, all driving small-bore sedans. Ford Cortinas and Falcon Sprints were the fastest and most durable that day, with a team of Jack Seas and Bob Olthoff winning in one of the Cortinas. These FIA events for sedans were starting to attract attention for how popular and competitive they were, although, at the time, true sports car fans couldn't quite digest sedan racing at this time.

This event is also notable for a meeting that day between Alan Mann and Ford's John Holman, which resulted in Mann becoming Ford's European race shop.

1964: New Management

The 1964 Refrigerator Bowl saw nice weather for the fifth year in a row, confounding locals who had experienced five weeks of cold and snowy weather leading up to the weekend. A new management team greeted them as well. Mark Baden, a local attorney operating as Baden, Inc., took over after he bought out the ownership of the Mob and Eugene Chaney. The new SCCA classes were used for the first time anywhere with promising results, but overall racing was reported as being "rather dull." The most notable incident was Mark Donohue showing up in a Cobra and winning his production race, albeit not without a mid-race spin. Still just a kid, Donohue was continuing to make his mark on the racing world.

The President's Cup was back at Marlboro in 1964 as part of the SCCA National weekend. The field was lacking star power that year but made up for it with some exceedingly good racing through the entire eight-race day. Ed Lowther in a Genie-Ford won the cup and a handshake from General LeMay.

Who should win the 12-hour enduro this summer but a young Scottish driver named Jackie Stewart. At that time, he was still a relative unknown in this country. He co-drove with Mike Beckwith in a Cortina. Colin Chapman himself was on hand, as the Cortina team was one of his pet projects, and his cars took the first two places.

Regional races rounded out the year, and it should be noted that Porsche driver Bruce Jennings won many of them in a Porsche Carrera and a Porsche Super. Jennings has to be acknowledged as the "Little King" of the circuit (at the very least), because he never raced big-engined cars there.

The Marlboro track had been around for almost ten years as the 1965 season shaped up. It had never been able to pull in the really big crowds as had other tracks built around the same time: Watkins Glen, Riverside, and Elkhart Lake. The short, tight circuit was just too small to warrant the kind of

Don Yenko, one of the top East Coast Corvette drivers of the day and a frequent Marlboro competitor, gets the checkered flag after winning Class B in a 1965 SCCA National Classes A-B production event. (Photo Courtesy Birmingham Automobile Racing Club)

races that attracted those crowds. And smaller crowds meant a smaller cash flow.

1965: End of an Era

After the conclusion of the 1964 season, oval-track racing ended at Marlboro. A couple of late-1960s attempts to revive it did not work out.

Small crowds indeed were on hand for the sixth annual Refrigerator Bowl. No real headliners were present either so it was a local's race, with the ever-present Bruce Jennings and Bob Tullius staging the best race of the day. Tullius' TR4 and Jennings' Porsche brought the freezing crowd out from under their blankets as they staged an exciting finish with Tullius getting the nod that day. Only 100 or so spectators showed up and the day was halted a bit early, to no one's real sorrow.

The year's early-season National was little better. However, an exciting car in the hands of Harold Keck created a jolt of adrenaline. Keck was in a brand-spanking-new 427 Cobra and won the production race easily. Ed Lowther duplicated his main-event win from the year before in his Genie-Ford. A cold rain fell throughout the weekend and the April 25 event drew few spectators.

As the 1965 season moved along with a few regional races, word came that Les Netherton had purchased the track. Netherton ran a Valiant with an automatic transmission in sedan races and was known for his winning ways. He promised to keep the race schedule pretty much as it was, but he wanted to enlarge and improve racer and spectator facilities. He also called out the 12-hour race, citing it as an example where a bigger purse and better publicity could bring major teams and transform the event. Aware of the limitations of the total land available, he also spoke of acquiring adjacent property so the course itself could be expanded.

An expanded $3,000 purse was offered for the 12-hour enduro that year, and the event drew the factory team from Lotus and factory backing for two Plymouth Barracudas. But a lone Alfa TI beat them all. Jackie Stewart led everyone in qualifying and for the first hour of the race, but his Cortina soon broke. So did the fast Barracudas and other Cortinas. The Alfa of Pete Van der Vate and Monty Winkler took the victory.

The biggest race of the season in terms of number of cars was the Nationals in late September. Stirling Moss was even on hand as 220 cars filled the pits. The feature race was chaotic because of the high attrition rate. At one point every turn station had a broken-down or wrecked car to deal with. A big car won, too; the Chevy-powered Carliss-Schall Special beat Gerry Crawford's Lotus 30 over the line. Plenty of good racing went on all day, especially in the Formula Vee and EP races.

The last race weekend of the year saw a repeat win by the Alfa of Pete Van der Vate. Track officials staged the event as a preview of the upcoming SCCA sedan category, hoping to receive sanction from the national organization to hold one of the series' races. They were rewarded on this weekend by a 25-car turnout for the sedan event.

1966: Big Time Arrives?

The 1966 season's Refrigerator Bowl started off with a new "unofficial" lap record of 1:26.1 by Charlie Hayes, veteran of the track, who was driving a hot Elva-Olds on a demonstration lap. Mark Donohue also set a record for production cars with a 1:35.2 in a new Mustang. Also notable was the first U.S. appearance of an Alfa GTA, which won both small sedan races.

Sedan racing continued to steal the show as the season began at the April 3 Governor's Cup. Despite an overall feature win by Hal Keck in a 427 Cobra, a duel between Monty Winkler's Alfa GTA and Bob Tullius' Dodge Dart really had the crowd on its feet. The Alfa eventually beat the Dart by a nose.

Drivers signal their readiness for a Le Mans start at a typical Marlboro sedan 12-hour enduro race, the roots of Trans-Am. The three-car Cortina team that included Jackie Stewart is at the far right. (Bill Dobbins Photo, Courtesy the Washington D.C. Region, SCCA)

The Marlboro road course went straight ahead to the left, so cars such as the Ferrari in the foreground are actually on pit row. In the background, Hal Keck's 427 Cobra is getting the checkered flag from a very energetic S/F flagman in this 1966 SCCA National. (B. D. Dobbins Photo, Courtesy Mike Eaton Archives)

The Washington region and the Marlboro track were finally ready for the big stage, at least they hoped they were. A Trans-Am race was scheduled for the track's annual 12-hour. Trans-Am was in its first year as a series and it was still developing into the headliner it later became; nonetheless, it was the biggest thing that the track and the region had seen and they pulled out all stops. They were rewarded by a memorable event that local *Sports Car* correspondent called "by far Washington's Greatest Day of Racing."

In the end, Bob Tullius and a young Tony Adamowicz pulled off the win in a Dodge Dart as Chrysler products took the first four places, followed by an Alfa GTA. The winning duo completed 405 laps of the 1.7-mile course in the 12-hour period. The pre-race favorite Mustangs suffered mechanical ills of one sort and another. They were fast but often in the pits. In all, 36 cars had started the event and 27 cars were still running at the end. Big-time racing had come to Marlboro and it had worked. At least this time.

1967: Legal Issues Loom

But reality set in again when the 1967 season started with the inevitable Refrigerator Bowl. It drew a small entry and attendance lists on a dreary wet and cold day. And then the roof didn't actually cave in, but it sagged dangerously.

The original track president, Mark Baden, was in legal trouble and owed more money than he had. Baden's creditors soon were suing to auction off the track to pay his debts. Netherton, innocent of any wrongdoing as far as could be determined, fought to keep the track open and off the auction block. As a result of this turmoil, the 1967 season was under threat, and that included the now-precious 12-hour Trans-Am race. After some negotiations, the season-opening Governor's Cup on April 8–9 was given the green light because it appeared unlikely that the track would be padlocked right away. The season could continue on a race-by-race basis.

Strapped for cash because of the court costs, Netherton attempted to negotiate racing fees with the SCCA that were more favorable to him. But he also threatened to pull the plug on the season himself. The traditional 6-hour enduro in early May was abruptly postponed until June 25.

A non-spectator event was held in June, with high temperatures and a high entry fee of $35. Drivers grumbled about the fee but 150 of them paid it anyway with the understanding that Netherton had to charge higher rent fees and the SCCA's insurance was going up. Regardless, the strong turnout showed that possibilities still remained for the track. Bruce Jennings was there, of course, and won his E Production race. Local Ferrari dealer Gordon Tatum was there, too, with a 330 *and* a GTO, both race ready. He chose the 330 and won the feature handily.

The word finally came that the traditional 12-hour race would *not* be held. Instead, two 300-mile points-scoring races for Trans-Am cars were scheduled on the same date. It is doubtful that many drivers mourned the loss of the 12-hour race on the demanding Marlboro circuit.

Saturday saw the Little 300, the under-2-liter division, with Bert Everett and Jerry Titus winning in a Porsche 911 after some spirited racing. Good old Bruce Jennings co-drove a Porsche into 2nd. The Alfas had their troubles and did not have a finisher.

In Sunday's feature, Mark Donohue and teammate Craig Fisher drove the well-prepared Camaro to an easy win. Mustangs took the next three spots in front of the only Mopar finisher, Tullius and Jennings in a Dodge Dart. Only 14 cars started the race; 8 finished. But the 10,000 spectators seemed happy. Marlboro and Netherton had kept the faith.

The season wrapped up with the 6-hour enduro, now known as the Les Six Heures de Marlboro, which had originally been postponed from May to June. Porsches again stormed to the finish as they had in the Little 300 earlier in August. Porsches took the first four places and the duo of Gene Hobbs and Rick Mandelson in a Speedster were 1st overall. Both Hobbs and Mandelson were winners of previous 6-hour races at Marlboro, although in far different cars. Hobbs was an overall winner and Mandelson won for Index of Performance.

The troubled 1967 season was not over yet and the legal situation dragged along in the background. A Turkey Bowl was held on November 18 with a field of 193 cars. Old course pros Bob Mouat and Bruce Jennings raced for the win in the feature, with Mouat's Sting Ray finally beating Jennings' familiar Porsche.

1968: Ray of Hope

Interest in racing at Marlboro remained high, but the 1968 Refrigerator Bowl had to be called off on race day when snowstorms threatened to overwhelm the region. Still, 80 cars had shown up to race. Despite continued shows of support, no Trans-Am race was scheduled for the track nor was one held there again. It was sad for the track; its initial dedication to sedan endurance races had probably paved the way for the entire Trans-Am circuit.

Storms also continued to blow over the future of the track, but there was a ray of hope. On February 6 Netherton received the okay to continue his season under strict conditions that included limits on racing hours and sports-cars-only use of the track. Other troubles included vital safety measures that were promised but had not been completed and unpaid insurance premiums. But, surprisingly, 1968 was a very good year at the track.

Formula cars were moving in, and on March 10, Mike Hiss set a new lap record of 1:29 flat during a regional. Otherwise it was a locals-only affair with Hiss winning the feature in an FB Brabham. New safety railings had been installed just a few days before the race date.

A *Competition Press'* race report called Marlboro tired and old, but people kept coming out to race on it. The place was livened up even more on April 7 by the Governor's Cup nationals. The 165 entrants set 10 new class lap records as well as the overall course record: 1:27.8 by George Alderman in a Group 7 McLaren. He also won the featured Governor's Cup race in the same car. Great racing all day long, as well as the fast laps, showed Marlboro's popularity once again.

Dick Thompson returned to the track for a 300-mile endurance race on June 16 in a turbine-powered Howmet. He showed both the car's speed and his ability when he cut half an hour off Mark Donohue's 300-mile race record, which was set the year before. Thompson and his co-driver, Ray Heppenstall, lapped the field every half hour in an awesome display of dominance.

Good fields and close racing continued as the 1968 season ended with non-spectator regional races and one national. In the national, Bob Welch, in an FB Brabham, set a new lap record of 1:27 flat. He also won the feature. Jerry Crawford won that year's Marlboro Cup in an Mk2 McLaren. Bruce Jennings' Porsche continued to win or show the most speed in his production class.

Good showings, but all was still not well with the track. Netherton had to come up with $35,000 to keep the track from the auction block as part of the Chaney estate. The original owner still held title to the 42 acres on which the track was located. It was a narrow escape for racing in the region as Netherton showed up with the money the night before the auction was scheduled to begin. As it was, a full schedule of racing for the 1969 season was promised, with more spectator events, too.

1969: Not Much Glamour

The Refrigerator Bowl was left out of the 1969 schedule, so the season began with a regional race, March Madness, on March 16. Local racers entered in good numbers, and novelty races were held, including a Formula Vee handicap. Gene

More than 200 race cars, plus support vehicles, sometimes crowded the pit area at Marlboro. The surrounding oval limited pit space so it was often close quarters for all. (Photo Courtesy Steve Lloyd)

Chapter 8: Marlboro Motor Raceway   83

Bruce Jennings (#77) ruled the Porsche roost during the 1960s, but he and competitors including Gene Dobbs (#76) were friends, too. Here they all pitch in to keep Jennings' Porsche going. (Bill Dobbins Photo, Courtesy the Washington D.C. Region, SCCA)

Fisher in a 427 Cobra won the feature; interestingly, the big-engine car beat the 289s over the line on this tight circuit. Big cars continued to dominate at the annual Governor's Cup, which Jerry Crawford won in a McLaren. Crawford had been chasing the cup for years and finally won it in what turned out to be the last time the Cup race was held on the Marlboro track.

Land developers purchased the whole complex in early May 1969. They cited the proximity to rapidly growing metropolitan complexes in the area, but evidently failed to research the stability of the land on which Marlboro was built. Ponds and loose gravel did not make an acceptable base for any serious construction. Netherton, staying on as track manager, promised that racing at the track would continue for the foreseeable future.

Sure enough, a full season was held at Marlboro. However, it held none of the glamour races (such as Can-Am and Trans-Am) that other circuits were featuring, but did host plenty of good regional racing. Rick Mandelson reigned supreme in Formula Vee ranks in his Zink. As always, Bruce Jennings was on top in the Porsche ranks. Pete Sherman was a frequent feature winner in an Elva. The Marlboro Cup winner that year was Jerry Crawford in a McLaren Mk2; his 327-cc Chevy was not too much for the course to handle. Crawford beat out several Cobras with that car and finished the race with only second gear; it was a good gear to have for the Marlboro circuit.

The Final Race

You could say that Marlboro went out with a bang: The largest field ever for a regional race there came for the last race

Pit work finished, Jennings leads Dobbs at the start of a late-1960s Marlboro race. Jennings won, as usual, thanks in part to Dobbs' sportsmanship. (Photo Courtesy Steve Lloyd)

This historic racing facility is a shell of its former self. In 2015, piles of scrap wood are where bleacher seats and the shell of the covered grandstands were located. The ruins of a once-great track are sad reminders of the glory days past. (Photo Courtesy Judy Rudow)

at the track, the 1969 Turkey Bowl. The 189 cars made for a lot of great racing throughout each class. Two Lotus 23s, a car that was perfect for this track, led the feature, which was won by Ken Butler, a longtime competitor at Marlboro, in a Lotus 23. Fittingly, Bruce Jennings was among the class winners.

The day was marred by the death of Dick Lord, an original Lavender Hill Mob member, who suffered a heart attack behind the wheel of his H production car on the cool-down lap. He had raced every year at Marlboro since 1955.

And then the curtain fell on Marlboro. Unceremoniously, the track was padlocked after that Turkey Bowl. Local racing shifted to the new Summit Point track in West Virginia. Although it was not much longer (2 miles), the track was safer and more accommodating to a wider variety of cars. The SCCA was simply no longer willing to put its members at risk at Marlboro, and the track ownership could not or would not make any further modifications to the track for the sake of safety.

Surprisingly, the track was never plowed under and the site was never developed for alternative use. As of the summer of 2015, the road course still exists, but the grandstand and other support buildings are pretty much reduced to rubble. Reunions have been held at the track, and some even included members of the old Lavender Hill Mob. The entire facility is fenced off, though, behind a padlocked gate. It was recently offered for sale for $3.5 million as a racetrack. A new track could probably be built over the old surface if floodplain-zoning problems are overcome. Whether or not such a project would be profitable is certainly debatable. Eventually, the circuit will likely be totally lost to a developer's bulldozer.

The far side of the track's oval still remains. You could drive a car around the old course very slowly today, but the surface has deteriorated alarmingly. (Photo Courtesy Judy Rudow)

Today, the hairpin turn is lost in the spooky woods that have grown up around the track. (Photo Courtesy Judy Rudow)

Chapter 8: Marlboro Motor Raceway

Meadowdale International Raceway

THE MIDWEST MONSTER

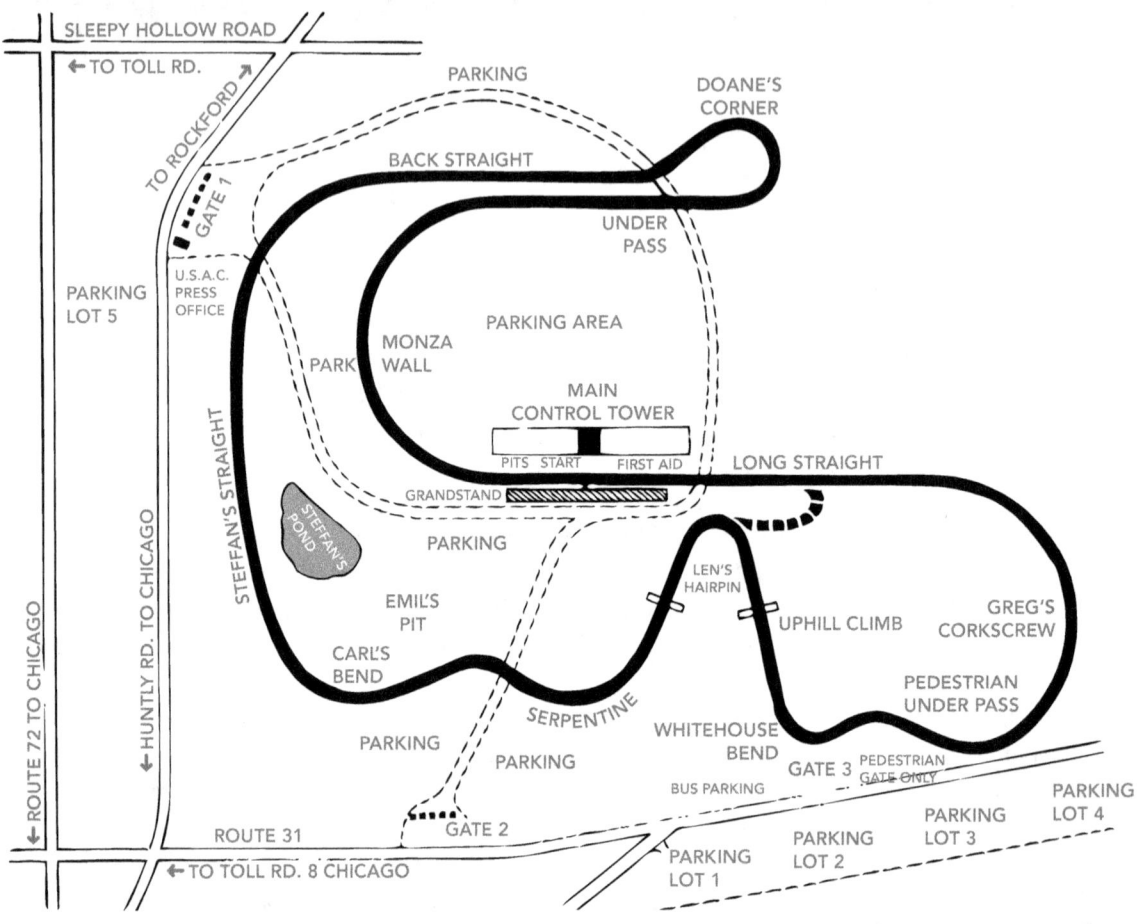

This is one of the better course maps from the day. The dotted line shows the shorter, 2.2-mile course turn-off. (Illustration Courtesy Martin Spetz Program Collection)

Meadowdale Raceways became known as the Midwest Monster because the excessively banked and unconventional track produced thrilling races and terrified drivers. Of all the racetracks in this book, none came anywhere near to generating the level of controversy as Meadowdale, yet none has a more dedicated following and is better preserved today.

In design alone, the Meadowdale racetrack was a bold move forward for road racing in this country. American amateur racers were not used to track features such as Meadowdales's high Monza-wall-style corners, scant run-off areas, and steep ups and downs. The airport courses on which they had learned to race had flat turns and wide run-off areas that helped the less skilled. And it also had many other features that generated its share of controversy.

The Meadowdale course was the result of the dreams of Leonard Besinger, a pioneer builder in the area just southwest of Chicago. His success as a developer building low-cost modern postwar housing did not dull an appetite for farming. He bought an old farm near the little town of Carpentersville in

CHAPTER 9

Carpentersville, Illinois
1958–1969

Facility 3.27 miles, 2.2 miles
Principal Events USAC sports cars, SCCA Nationals, Trans-Am, USRRC
Current Status County park; much of course remains

It was an awesome starting field for Meadowdale's 1964 USRRC race. From left to right, it's Ed Leslie (King Cobra), Bobby Unser (Lotus 19), Bob Makely (Elva Porsche) on Row 1; Al Unser (Lotus 23) and Jim Hall (Chaparral II) on Row 2; Charlie Hayes (Elva-Porsche) and George Winterseen (Cooper-Chev) on Row 3. (Photo Courtesy John McCollister)

a mostly empty stretch of land near Illinois Highway 31. He named the farm Meadowdale and planned to use it to raise specialty horses and have a place for his grandchildren to play. Unfortunately, these plans did not work out and a fire razed the farm. He left the few remnants alone, including a large concrete silo that was a landmark in the community, and turned his energy into building another housing development near the farm property.

1958: Debut

The Chicago region of the SCCA conducted the track's inaugural event on September 13 and 14, 1958. Although it was just a regional race, it drew a big crowd of drivers and spectators eager to see what all the fuss was about. Banked turns, fully equipped pit areas, big grandstands? Wow, bring it on! To say that the actual reaction to Meadowdale during and after the weekend was mixed is a vast understatement.

Perhaps the massive pre-race hype could have warned some of the more thoughtful. Fangio himself was rumored to be showing up and his voice (or that of someone who sounded like him) was used in some of the many commercials that flooded the airwaves. A special color supplement appeared in local newspapers. The advertising exaggerated slightly when it claimed the track to have "the longest straightaway in the world" at 6,000 feet. The Monza Wall sounded thrilling, if not actually terrifying. It was trumpeted that cars would have to be at absolutely top speed going around it, and if they were not, they might actually tumble off the high banks. Attracted by all this publicity and the promise of big crowds of voters, Illinois Governor William Stratton himself came out to cut the ribbon for the first weekend's races.

The Monster

Writing about the weekend in *Sports Cars Illustrated*, in an article titled "Midwest Monster," reporter Dic Van der Feen (later to become the SCCA's PR director) stated that Meadowdale is "one of the most dramatic circuits yet built; and one of the most disgraceful." His report, which is summarized in the next few paragraphs, paints a picture of a venue and event that bordered on the ludicrous, and events that would have been downright funny if first the potential and then the reality of tragedy had not been present.

According to Van der Feen's no-holds-barred report, the most stunning feature of the track, the Monza Wall, proved to be the most troublesome. The 45-degree wall's cup-and-saucer shape was paved with the help of a conventional flat-pavement roller winched up and down each section. The end

Building a Menacing Beast

In 1957, spurred on by the interest of his sons, Besinger decided to build a racetrack near the silo on 232 acres of his abandoned farm. As much as anyone, through his developments he was aware of the enormous growth coming in the Chicago area. He was sure that a properly built and promoted racetrack would draw big crowds. Then, as a benefit, it would draw attention to his nearby housing development. For proof, anyone just had to look at the big crowds drawn to Elkhart Lake, not too far away in Wisconsin, but not nearly as close to a large population center. Evidently not one to do things halfway, Besinger and his fellow enthusiast investors toured the leading U.S. and European road tracks, including Le Mans, Reims, and perhaps not the best choice, Monza. His worthy plan was to incorporate the best features of each for drivers, spectators, and officials.

Besinger and his sons, who were also deeply involved in the project, designed the track themselves with help from Dick Doane, a local Corvette dealer and experienced race driver. Track construction commenced in June 1958. Accustomed to building housing developments in as short a time as possible, Besinger's crew rented some road-building equipment and managed to get the track up and ready for use in just 90 days. And it was much more than just a road snaking through the woods. The whole layout appeared to be first class, offering (on paper) far more for everyone than any other American circuit.

When originally opened, a lap of the asphalt-topped track was 3.27 miles. Its most immediately notable features were two steeply banked turns, quite a novelty in this country. These turns were at each end of a 4,000-foot straightaway. The steeply banked, 180-degree curve leading onto the straight was dubbed the Monza Wall, obviously inspired by Besinger's visit to that track. Drivers would supposedly come off the Monza Wall already at very high speed, rocketing them on to the straight and down to the second banked turn. Originally called "Greg's Corkscrew" (Besinger named several turns after his children), the second banked curve became known as "Little Monza." It was also a 180-degree turn, tighter and even steeper than the first, with the added challenge of being steeply downhill. It ended near the old farm silo (left next to the course for paid advertising). The course had serpentine turns, fast turns, and dramatic elevation changes. It was dramatic for its features off the course as well, with bridges, underpasses giving access to the infield, permanent pits, and space for more than 100,000 spectators.

The parking lot was crowded for the track's opener. If stories can be believed, more than 150,000 people paid to watch the races that day. (Photo Courtesy Don Devine)

88   Lost Road Courses

Jim Jeffords drove the famous *Nickey Nouse Special*, a Scarab, in the summer of 1959 to two USAC victories at Meadowdale. (Photo Courtesy Ron Shaw)

In a 1959 USAC race, a Corvette-powered Maserati in the hands of Sonny McDaniel stays ahead of a T-Bird Special driven by Jim Moseley. Although colorful, the T-Bird eventually crashed and McDaniel's car did not place. (Photo Courtesy Ron Shaw)

The leaders are about to lap slower cars as they come out of Doane's Corner heading for the Wall in a 1959 race. Note the trash blowing toward the track from the spectator's area. Jim Jeffords won the race in *Nickey Nouse Special*. (Photo Courtesy Ron Shaw)

result looked good to the untrained eye, but drivers immediately found it to be washboard-bumpy, and each of the many sections ended with an up and down transition to the next. Several cars bottomed out on the wall, and it was far from the ultra-high-speed corner that was planned.

Tom Stephani, eight years old at the time and part of his dad's Nickey Chevrolet team, was at the event. He confirms that the wall beat up cars badly, and it often forced early retirements because shocks could not take the pounding.

Zooming down the long straight past the pit area, the drivers encountered an unsettling sign painted right on the surface of the track: "PRAY." Pray indeed, drivers; Little Monza was coming up. It was previewed by a sharp bump upon entering, which further unsettled drivers. Moreover, it had a concrete wall behind it and no escape road. According to Van der Feen, Little Monza soon became the "most cautiously respected racing circuit bend in the entire country." This was not written as a compliment. But Van der Feen's most scathing criticism was reserved for the circuit's final turn, Doane's Corner, located right before entering the short straight prior to Monza. He described it as "the most deceptive and treacherous curve combination of the course . . . a left-handed 'dog leg' develops immediately into a perfectly flat right-hand hairpin built on a 210-foot radius." It was a difficult and dangerous corner and drivers were required to slide while under power to come out with any momentum. Most amateur American drivers were not accustomed to powersliding a car in competition, so it produced some interesting racing.

Coming Up Short

The outcome of the first race feature proved that, far from what had

August Pabst wins the 1960 National at Meadowdale in his Meister Brauser Scarab. After an early race scrap with Dick Thompson's Sting Ray was stopped by Thompson's retirement, the Scarab had an easy victory. (Photo Courtesy Ron Shaw)

been planned, the course was not particularly fast. Chuck Daigh won in a Scarab with an average speed of 85.5 mph; his fastest lap was just 87.5. Reading Van der Feen's fevered description of the course it seems amazing that anyone survived. Run-off spots were almost non-existent, and sliding cars faced dirt embankments that could flip cars over or they could crash into concrete walls. The much-hyped Monza Wall proved almost a joke. It had been claimed that cars would have to average "120 mph" to keep from actually falling off of it. But a parade of Model Ts went around at putt-putt speed and had no problem whatsoever.

Beyond the previously stated concerns, Van der Feen was critical of Besinger's very quick construction work and the landscaping, or rather, the lack thereof. As most contractors would do, he first had scraped the area clear of everything, right down to the smallest blade of grass. He had no time to replant, if that had even been part of the plan. The result was windblown loose dirt that was stirred up by 25-mph winds during the first race weekend that cloaked the whole facility in thick clouds of dust that lasted all day. Van der Feen did not spare his words. "Drivers proceeded half-blinded through storms of grit, cardboard cups, plates, and papers in a mad cartoonist's world of racing in a nightmare. Spectators were plastered black by the filth, literally caked with dirt." The wire mesh fencing

Harry Heuer in the Scarab leads eventual winner Roger Penske in the Maserati Tipo 61 Birdcage down the long straight hill in the 1961 SCCA National. The hill was really not as steep as it looks in this photo. (Photo Courtesy Ron Nelson/classicvintagemotorsports.com)

The pits, looking down the track toward the drop-off of the long straight. You can just barely see the controversial Paddock Club to the left. (Photo Courtesy Ron Nelson/classicvintagemotorsports.com)

Jerry Hansen keeps his Scarab ahead of the famous M. R. J. Wyllie, here in a Lola-Climax, at the 1962 Meadowdale SCCA National. Hansen was a DNF; Wyllie took 5th in the race won by Harry Heuer's Chaparral. (Photo Courtesy Nelson/classicvintagemotorsports.com)

used instead of standard snow fencing did not help. The wide mesh allowed the dust and garbage to blow right through while snow fencing would have caught at least some of it.

But the failure of the fencing's material was nothing compared to the worst failure of the fencing: its placement. Spectators gathered behind the fencing were much too close to the track. Van der Feen stated that one errant car could "positively mow down dozens of people in split seconds." Hyperbole, perhaps, but two spectators were actually hit by flying debris from crashing cars. Spectators got even, though; they pelted the cars with beer cans, cigarettes, rocks, and spittle from overpasses and the fenced-off areas that were also too close to the track. And drunken spectators beat up a policeman who attempted to stop them from throwing rocks at the passing race cars.

Another dangerous spot was the paddock club, which was built over the pits; well-heeled spectators paid top dollar to watch the race from this area. Evidently no one had warned them about fire safety, or they just did not care, and throughout the weekend they dropped cigarette butts into the pits below with abandon. Luckily, a fuel fire never broke out. Some of those who would have been most in danger if such a fire had broken out were "friends of Mr. Besinger." These individuals wandered through the pits with aplomb, smoking and banging on cars, and in general making dangerous pests of themselves. They usually refused to leave when asked to do so by pit marshals because of their "friend" status. And those pits. Billed as having full service including fuel, they were actually rickety wooden stalls with few comforts and no fuel.

The long walks from the parking areas and poor viewing at different locations around the track probably irritated spectators despite the fact that the track was built more with spectator access in mind than drivers' safety. Areas that offered really good sweeping views were limited; spectators could likely catch only a (too close) glimpse of the cars as they sped by. Van der Feen summed up his story by speculating that the sport had been sullied beyond repair, but that the promoters, whom he portrayed as nothing more than cold-hearted villains of the first order (or at the very least dim-witted fools), would be free to continue their evil ways.

Van der Feen's article is so over the top that you have to wonder if a competing track commissioned him to write it. However, his account is pretty much backed up by a 2010 story in *Vintage Motorsports* magazine. Bert Levy, who is a respected motorsports writer today, attended the race as a teenager, attracted by the enormous pre-race publicity and advertising. He confirms what Van der Feen wrote and adds that he also remembers the blaring, screechy, relentless PA; ads for local stores; and terrible sanitary facilities for spectators.

Both Bert Levy and Tom Stephani remember another thing from when they were youngsters, though: They found the event as exciting as could be. And, because of it, they were hooked on road racing for life!

As hilarious as the various stories around this first weekend are, there is no joking about the death of a reportedly dust-blinded race car driver at Doane's Corner, Ferrari pilot Robert Walker from Kansas. Surprisingly, he was the only fatality during the track's 11-year run. That terrible incident, along with the facility's wide-ranging problems, produced numerous bad reports of the race. As a result, the track earned a negative reputation from which it never really recovered. In addition to Walker's death, there were 10 flips that first day. Lost in all the turmoil was the win by Chuck Daigh. He and his boss, Lance Reventlow, piloted their Scarabs around to a relatively no-contest 1st and 2nd place in the feature.

The Scarabs were in the early stages of their brief but convincing place in the top echelon of American sports car racing and they had a loyal following. But how many spectators were really there to see the Scarabs or other cars is open to debate.

Obviously, the promoters wanted to claim the biggest crowd possible. The monumental traffic jams before and after the races may have given the impression that 150,000 paid spectators was an accurate count. However, that many spectators were almost certainly not present. And that's just as well, because the access roads and only highway were woefully inadequate for those who did attend.

Tom Stephani says that, as the crow flies, the course was very close to large population centers. And that made it difficult to get there without suffering through terrible traffic jams. He feels that this is the main reason that the facility ultimately failed. But I'm getting ahead of myself.

Not everyone was as completely negative as Van der Feen. An article in *Modern Man* magazine acknowledged many of the circuit's shortcomings but made them seem more challenging than suicidal. Daigh himself acknowledged that the banking on the Monza Wall was rough, but, in his opinion, the course was the second best in the country (after Riverside). It must be acknowledged that Daigh was an experienced professional race car driver, and up to the course's challenges. Many other drivers simply were not.

The local Chicago SCCA was upset about the whole weekend, from the dangers of the course to the rowdiness of the crowds. It was also offended by the hype surrounding the event and the type of spectators it attracted. In fact, Van der Feen wondered, in an editorial he wrote for *Competition Press*, if the unhappiness of the SCCA wasn't one of the main problems. Many prominent members of the Chicago club wondered if this was the direction they wanted their family sport to go. It began a long series of negotiations with track management about necessary improvements. Besinger was evidently open to these improvements. He was reported as being "devastated" and "near tears" over the death at his first weekend of racing. And that was *before* he read Van der Feen's first article!

1959: Sports Cars and Stock Cars on the Monster

Bills needed to be paid, so another race was held as scheduled, local SCCA blessing or no. This was a 222-mile stock car race sanctioned by the MARC (Midwest Association for Race Cars). It was held on the full road course. These drivers and their cars were used to ovals so this road race was a rarity for them. They may have felt more at ease with the banking, which was, after all, more similar to the ovals. During the race, an errant tire struck and injured some people in the crowd, but thankfully, there were no fatalities. Daigh and Reventlow were back, but veteran stocker Fred Lorenzen won the race in a Ford with Daigh 3rd. A crowd of 88,000 was reported, which was very likely an accurate count.

That first race in September proved how popular sports car racing was. The SCCA would not sanction a race at Meadowdale, so Besinger and his cohorts sought (and received)

At a 1962 Nationals, Dick Thompson leads the field in a Corvette, followed closely by Bob Grossman's Ferrari Berlinetta. The Besinger farm is in the background. (Photo Courtesy Ron Nelson/classicvintagemotorsports.com)

By the 1962 SCCA Nationals at Meadowdale, Ferrari TRs were already being left behind. These two are in the hands of Robert Hunt (#36) and Wayne Burnette (#94). Burnett did win Class DM honors. (Photo Courtesy Ron Shaw)

Shown is the pace lap in the 1961 SCCA National. By rows, one is Don Devine, Scarab, with Harry Heuer in a Chaparral. Two, Dick Thompson and Dick Doane in Grand Sport Corvettes. Eventual winner is #5 Maserati Tipo 61, Roger Penske. (Photo Courtesy Ron Nelson, classicvintagemotorsports.com.)

By 1964, even Chevrolet-powered D-Jaguars were being outclassed. Jerry Dunbar, driving this D-Type, suffered a DNF at the USRRC that year. (Photo Courtesy John McCollister)

sanctioning from the United States Auto Club (USAC) and pulled together a respectable field for the May 30, 1959, Meadowdale Grand Prix. At the time, the USAC was a professional circuit and was basically at war with the SCCA over this professionalism. It certainly did not have lower standards for driver safety, but did hold three races at Meadowdale that year.

The starting field of the first USAC 313-mile feature included such luminaries as Jim Jeffords, Harry Heuer, Lloyd Ruby, and Augie Pabst. The headliners were the Rodríguez brothers, young hotshots from Mexico City who were flashy and fast. However, their Porsche did not finish. It rolled and caught fire in the feature while running 2nd. The USAC also sanctioned the next road race, the Meadowdale 444, held on the Fourth of July weekend. Almost 40,000 spectators attended, although race photos show mostly empty grandstands. Jim Jeffords won every heat in both of these USAC events, driving an ex–team Scarab sponsored by Nickey Chevrolet. It was famously known as the *Nickey Nouse Special*.

The third and probably biggest of the three USAC events was a Formula Libre race held on Labor Day weekend. It attracted a top field, including Rodger Ward's Offy midget, which had stunned the sports car world by winning the main event at Lime Rock a few weeks earlier. Ward set a new lap record in qualifying with 92.7 mph, but even the tough oval-track midget could not stand up to this course. Augie Pabst, in a Meister

Ernie Erickson in a Porsche RS-60 braces himself for the high-banking Monza Wall that was the talk of the racing world when it was built. Domestic drivers simply were not ready for it, but this challenging portion of Meadowdale actually produced no serious incidents over the years. However, its pounding took a toll on cars. (Photo Courtesy Ron Nelson/classicvintagemotorsports.com)

Ford Cortinas were a hit everywhere they raced because of the way drivers such as Dave Clarke threw them around turns. Here, Clarke leads the Alfa GTZ of Chuck Stoddard. (Photo Courtesy John McCollister)

Brauser team Scarab, proved to be the class of the field and won the race. However, two serious accidents and several rollovers and flips overshadowed the race weekend.

1961: SCCA Beginning

The USAC events had attracted big crowds and fine fields, but it did not return to the track. In addition, the Chicago SCCA region would not relax its boycott of Meadowdale. Therefore, management found other SCCA associations more willing to sanction races at Meadowdale, and the National SCCA races were run there beginning in 1961. The track gained some traction with local drivers when track manager Bob Hallet let anyone come and use the facility for testing, for free. The Chicago region SCCA even held a drivers' school at Meadowdale in early 1961 and brought in Stirling Moss to run it! The 1961 National was held under the auspices of the Milwaukee SCCA. The weekend produced an especially notable result. Well-known motorsports journalist and race car driver Denise McCluggage won the production main in a Ferrari 250 over a field that included most of the top production drivers of the day. McCluggage remained faithful to the track until the end, declaring it as one of her favorites. Roger Penske, in a Maserati Tipo 61, won the feature that day.

1962 and 1963

The Milwaukee SCCA was evidently happy enough with the track and the event because repeat Nationals were scheduled in 1962 and 1963. The track saw at least one great race at the 1962 Nationals when Roger Penske, in a Tipo 61, cannily held off young Peter Ryan's Sadler. This event was also notable for several suspended SCCA drivers being allowed to race. It was an attempt to lure spectators to help save the track financially. Track improvements continued, but they were often more promise than actual progress. The SCCA events were not drawing the kind of crowds that the track management needed, although the 1962 Nationals supposedly drew a "record crowd" of 18,000. If this number was accurate, it was not a "record." Even so, it was not enough and the attendance recorded in 1963 was not enough either. Track management kept going mainly by leasing the track to private clubs for non-spectator races and allowing the police department to hold high-speed driver training there.

In 1964, a new management group took over at the track. Headed by a Chicago public relations man, Ralph Banghart, the group pulled a rabbit out of its hat. It received sanctioning for the SCCA's biggest attraction: the United States Road Racing Championships (USRRC). The SCCA had finally relented and welcomed professional drivers into its events and created an entirely new series for them.

1964: A National USRRC Race

By 1964, the USRRC was in its second year and attracting top drivers, the best cars, and the biggest crowds. Meadowdale hosted the eighth USRRC race for 1964 on August 8. The Chicago region came back into the fold and conducted the race. This time there was no argument over the importance of pre-race publicity. The promotion for the event was exceptional, and it managed to garner major attention from the Chicago press. The result was a spectator turnout of 20,000, which *Competition Press* stated was the largest crowd ever at Meadowdale . . . they should have checked their own back issues! But it *was* a good turnout considering that it was a busy sports weekend for the Chicago area.

According to USRRC results, the Cobras continued their winning ways in the Manufacturers' Race, with Ken Miles and Bob Johnston taking 1-2 for the Shelby team. In the feature Drivers' Race, Jim Hall won in his Chaparral, after Ed Leslie in a King Cobra had set a new lap record of 1:58.4 in qualifying to sit on the pole for Sunday's race. Hall won by a considerable margin and in so doing clinched the Drivers' Championship for that USRRC season. The Monza Wall claimed another car when the experienced oval-guy Bobby Unser ran into the guardrail. Because this was Meadowdale, all accidents were under a magnifying glass.

Track management was making the effort to properly promote events and make the facility profitable. In addition to non-spectator races, it held go-kart events, auto thrill shows, late-model stock car races, motorcycle races, and a couple of local SCCA events. The SCCA events were run on a shortened 2.2-mile course, easier on drivers and cars but still tough. A good chunk of the main straight was eliminated in this shortened course, making it more competitive for smaller-engined cars. The Little Monza wall section was also eliminated in this

These are three shots of cars in action on the Monza Wall at the 1964 USRRC race. Here, Bob Markley was a DNF in an Elva-Porsche that competed in several USSRC events that year, with a best of 7th overall at Greenwood. (Photo Courtesy John McCollister)

Here, oval ace and future IndyCar champion Al Unser was still early in his career but should have felt right at home on the Wall in his Lotus 23. He eventually DNF'ed here as well as in his other two USRRC starts with the Lotus 23. (Photo Courtesy John McCollister)

Scott Beckett crammed a big Ford block into his Maserati Tipo 61 for the USRRC race. Here he leads Charlie Hayes in an Elva-Porsche. Beckett and Hayes were both DNFs. Hayes and the Elva-Porsche did well enough in other USRRC events to place 3rd overall in the series that year. Beckett raced the hybrid Maserati locally a few more times in the Midwest without particular distinction. (Photo Courtesy John McCollister)

shortened course. But still, it was not working financially, and the track continued to suffer from dust, uncontrolled weeds in spectator areas, and a shabby feel in general.

The Monza Wall was not getting any better, either. It was noted at the USRRC event that several cars had top-of-the-fender damage after the race resulting from the pounding the shocks took from that part of the course. It seemed that every race, no matter how long or short or held on what course, produced more than its share of damage to cars. But it must be noted again that there were no fatalities at Meadowdale after that very first race.

1965 Through 1969

Even a turnout as great as 20,000 was not enough, and the track closed for racing after a shortened 1964 season. No racing took place at the track in 1965 and 1966, and only a small regional race was run in 1967. Police training and non-spectator events went on and a new management group, Meadowdale International Raceways, took over in late 1966. After all, here was an established track all ready to go. Maybe it had a few problems, but it also had a lot going for it. The new group was enthusiastic and promised many improvements, including dealing with the troublesome Monza Wall. It removed the Monza Wall and replaced it with a sharp turn on top of a large new asphalt patch. It also proposed building two oval tracks to make the facility "the most versatile in the world."

Bolstered with these promises, it managed to land a Trans-Am race for the 1968 season. Trans-Am was by then the country's second most prestigious road racing series after the Can-Am.

A claimed attendance of 25,000 people showed up for the event. This number is entirely believable given the series' popularity that year. That number may or may not be accurate, but the people who did attend had to brave heavy rains that turned the usually dusty dirt spectator areas into quagmires, sucking off shoes and generally spoiling everything. The rain did stop for the race, just before the green flag was scheduled to fall, and there were apparently few effects from the wet track as the race went on. Mark Donohue won that day (as he did so often in his Penske Camaro) even though he started last on the grid because he didn't qualify on Saturday. Several local drivers filled the 19-car grid; many of them were not in the same league as Donohue, Jerry Titus, and company. Despite the last-minute revision to the turn that had replaced Monza, as well as some paving work that occurred throughout the Saturday practice sessions, no serious course problems were reported.

That was the last hurrah for Meadowdale. Despite everything, the track simply could not generate enough money to keep going. It limped through an aborted 1969 season and that was it. Speculation arose that pressure from developers had forced the track management's hand. That might have been the case, but no development went up on the deserted

The wall at Little Monza bears some scars as four USRRC cars head in. Front to rear, it's Joe Buzzetta, Special (finishing 6th overall); Bud Gates, Genie-Chev (DNF); Tom Terrell, Lotus 23B (13th); and Don Skogmo, Genie-Ford (11th). (Photo Courtesy Ron Nelson/classicvintagemotorsports.com)

Maybe stock cars were used to high walls, but not so much coming out of them onto a road course. Workers scatter, some more nimbly than others, as two cars collide in a mid-1960s stocker race. (Photo Courtesy John McCollister)

The pavement curves to where the famed Monza Wall started. It was torn down in 1967 when the new track management did not want the upkeep it required. Not a trace of it remains today. (Photo Courtesy Judy Rudow)

remnant of the course. Rather, it was allowed to gradually sink back into the woods.

Meadowdale's Second Life

Was Meadowdale indeed a "monster" or really just a big pussycat? Despite the fact that other tracks of the day had worse records, the remaining feeling is that it was closer to monster. It became so feared and respected that everyone approached it with a certain amount of caution. In the end, that proved to be a good thing.

The track site, now known as Raceway Woods, is a forest and nature preserve. The Dundee, Illinois, Township Park District and the Forest Preserve District of Kane County maintain the recreational area. However, the site is recognized for its racing history, and much of the original track is in place in the form of a hiking trail. The surface is paved over in some areas; in others, the original surface remains. Mothers now push their children in strollers and people walk for fitness where Miles, Pabst, and Hall once reigned. Except for the silo, almost all of the original structures are gone or covered with brush. The overpass for cars into the infield viewing areas is still in place, although many parts of it have rotted or rusted away so even crossing by foot would be hazardous. The silo, still a landmark, is preserved and serves as a highly visible reminder of where the track once stood. Reunions have been held in recent years; people gather with their cars and remember this valiant but flawed attempt to bring big-time road racing to the Chicago area.

About a third of the famed downhill main straight that ended with the "PRAY" sign and Little Monza is grown over with a walking trail put over the remnant. (Photo Courtesy Judy Rudow)

The silo landmark that was present before and all through the track's history was preserved in its original location between Turns 3 and 4. Today, it is at the entrance to Raceway Woods Park, the county park that includes all of the old racetrack facility. (Photo Courtesy Judy Rudow)

Bahamas Speed Weeks

PARTY CENTRAL FOR THE RACING SET

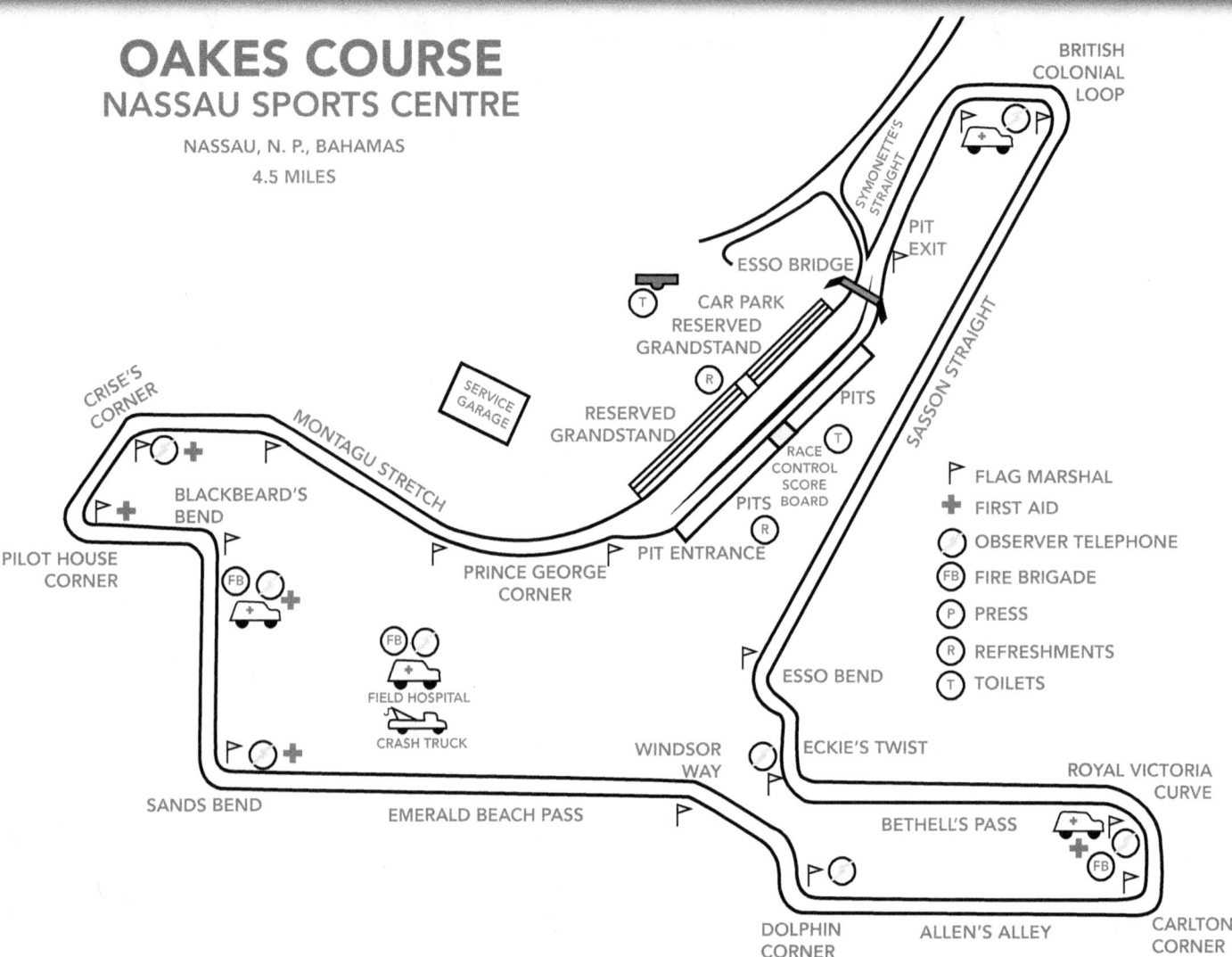

The 4.5-mile, 17-turn Oakes Field Course at Nassau was used from 1957 on. Nearly $100,000 was spent on making it suitable for racing. Note the colorfully named corners. (Illustration Courtesy Martin Spetz Program Collection)

Parties and racing don't mix, right? For the most part, that is a rule that has always been followed by the racing fraternity, until after the weekend's racing is over at least. But when it came to racing at Nassau in what became the Bahamas Speed Weeks, all rules went by the boards.

Nassau was an end-of-the-season blow out, a mid-December time when everyone let their hair down, but it also produced spectacular racing. The racers and crews took advantage of Nassau's unparalleled hospitality. Drivers took full advantage of the sun, women, beverages, and general party atmosphere that the event fostered. But between partying and good times, some of each year's best and most exciting racing took place. It is not an exaggeration to say that for a short time, the Speed Weeks were

CHAPTER 10

Nassau, New Providence Island, Bahamas
1954–1966

Facility Windsor Field, 3.5 miles; Oakes Field, 4 and 4.5 miles
Principal Events Nassau Speedweeks
Current Status Both fields are still in operation; Windsor Field is now known as Lynden Prindling International Airport

This is the last Le Mans start at Nassau. Eventual 4th place finisher Hap Sharp in the Chaparral is nearest the camera, winner Mark Donohue is hidden at this point. (Photo Courtesy Bill Sadler)

next to Le Mans as the most important event on the motor racing calendar.

Nassau is the capital city of the island of New Providence in the Bahamas, about 160 miles off the coast of Florida. But no one referred to the race site as New Providence Island, nor did the general tourist brochures. "Nassau" is how everyone referred to it, whether as a venue for racing or as a tourist destination. It became a tropical getaway for Americans who wanted to escape the cold and wet winter months. One of these visitors, Sherman "Red" Crise, was the initial driving force behind the establishment of what became Bahamas Speed Weeks.

Crise had the idea in 1953 when, on a sailing trip through the Bahamas, he found a large amount of open, unused, runway space at Nassau's Windsor Airport. At that time races were held with great success at similar airport locations all around North America. This seemed to be the perfect time and place to introduce the sport to the Bahamas.

Crise had the credentials to pull off such an event. In prewar years he had been a successful oval track midget car race organizer and promoter. Crise contacted local Nassau businessmen and received enthusiastic interest from such luminaries as Sir Sydney Oakes and Robert Symonette, both members of the Nassau Development Board. The three formed an organization, the Bahamas Automobile Club, to get the whole operation going.

Nassau was still a British colony at the time, so approval for any such plans was needed from the Royal Automobile Club as well as cooperation from local government officials to hold the race at the airport. Cooperation to allow their drivers to race was also needed from the SCCA, which was already holding on to its amateurs-only rules for dear life. They were convinced to let their members race with professionals and for money, two SCCA no-nos, on the basis that the event was being held on British soil.

1954: Windsor Field

The first edition of the race, called the Nassau Trophy Race (later known as Bahamas Speed Weeks) was scheduled for December 6–12, 1954. Using an airport course should have made things relatively easy, no land to grade or trees to cut down. The biggest challenge was the runways themselves, which were composed of crushed coral rock and asphalt; it was tough on tires. The first race was announced kind of late in the American racing season, so not that many entrants came in, and race organizers buttressed the field by encouraging local entries. After all, they reasoned, local entries would build local interest. Enough local entries came in (14) that a special residents-only race was organized and became a permanent part of the schedule. That first year only three races were held, including the one for residents, the Bahamas Automobile Club Cup, and the featured Nassau Trophy Race.

The international draw of the race was evident immediately in that Alfonso De Portago won the Cup race and Masten Gregory the Trophy. Both were internationally known race car drivers who drove Ferraris for this event. Jaguars were the most prominent marque that first year. Several officials flew in from Miami to help with the race, experienced race officials being scarce in Nassau in those early days. The majority of cars were shipped from the United States to Nassau aboard the SS *Queen of Nassau*. The event was well received by drivers and the spectator count was good. Tourism officials were pleased, which was the whole idea as far as local government and business people were concerned

1955: Trophy Races

Buoyed by the success of their first foray into racing, the Bahamas Automobile Club enthusiastically promoted their 1955 race, again called the Nassau Trophy Road Races. The more than 200 entrants was more than they could handle. The organizers were in the enviable position of being able to pick and choose who they wanted to race with them. Not surprisingly, they went with cars that tended to be the most popular with spectators. That primarily meant Ferrari, of course.

De Portago took the Governor's Trophy Race, which had permanently replaced the Bahamas Automobile Cup, and Phil Hill won the Nassau Trophy Race in cars bearing the prancing horse symbol. Among others, Stirling Moss showed up that year, probably attracted as much by the promise of Nassau-inspired bikinis as by racing opportunities. A trend was started that year in which race organizers arranged all kinds of special races, which might or might not be repeated in following years. That year there were special races for the little Formula 3 bombs, Jaguars, Ferraris, and Porsches.

These were simpler days and cars were shipped by boat. Actually, their arrival in port was part of the magic of the week, as they first unloaded and then drove through city streets to their hotels. Adulation along the way was the norm as well-wishers and race fans lined the route.

The event now had a permanent place on both the international race calendar and the tourism plans for Nassau.

Nassau Week impresario Sherman "Red" Crise in 1965. (Photo Courtesy Bahamas Speed Weeks Photo Archive)

The first Nassau course: Windsor Airfield. Red Crise was delighted to find this large facility available, but the surface was partially composed of crushed coral that proved to be tough on tires. (Photo Courtesy Bahamas Speed Weeks Photo Archive)

In those simpler days, David Ash simply put on a helmet and raced in the 1954 Bahamas Cup in his MG TF. History only records that the car was totally outclassed. (Photo Courtesy Bahamas Speed Weeks Photo Archive)

Tourism had jumped significantly during race week, and that was enough to spur everyone's enthusiasm. For drivers the parties were becoming legendary, as each hotel and bar on the island tried to outdo the others with parties that rotated among them every night. Although many other races were held in years to follow, and the exact makeup of their fields may have varied, the Governor's Cup and the Nassau Trophy Race remained the feature events. Although the week produced great racing, it also produced some confusion for fans. In addition to the two permanent feature races, the organizers also staged the Governor's *Tourist* Trophy, and the Nassau *Tourist* Trophy. Oh well, as long as you call me in time for the parties.

1956: Windsor's Final

The last year at Windsor Field proved to be trickier than the first two as the track surface continued to deteriorate and sand was blowing over it as well. And this was on a track that had to accommodate more and more top-name drivers and their cars, and even the first factory team of three Corvettes. This welcome factory involvement saw the cars equipped with ram fuel injector systems and slightly modified bodywork that included a small headrest and fin.

This year the entire event became known as the Bahamas Speed Weeks as it stretched on for more than seven days with the addition of a regatta. The regatta did not return, but the name was appropriate even with car racing only, as in later years the event indeed took more than a week to complete.

Carroll Shelby won the over-2-liter Governor's Cup, Howard Hively the under-, both in Ferraris. It was all Italian cars as Stirling Moss in a Maserati 300S won the Nassau Trophy Race. The Marquis De Portago made his last appearance at the track in this one. He was tragically killed at the following year's Mille Miglia in an accident that effectively ended open-road point-to-point racing worldwide (except, oddly, for Sicily's Targa Florio). The good-time Marquis was a symbol of the charms of the Nassau week in its infancy.

A bevy of Corvettes leads eventual winner Marquis De Portage's Ferrari Monza (#13) and Lou Brero's zebra-striped D-Jag in the 1956 Nassau Trophy Race. The Marquis earned 3rd place; Brero was farther back. (Photo Courtesy Mike Martin)

That was the last year for the Windsor course, but certainly not the last for racing at Nassau. The race was so popular and such a boon to the island's economy that almost anything would have been done to keep it going. Despite the challenges Windsor presented, racing might have stayed there except for increasing pressure to use the facility for passenger planes. A new course was found at another island airport, Oakes Field.

1957: The Oakes Field Course

If Windsor Field had been barely acceptable, at first glance the new course for 1957 at Oakes was even worse, but not impossible. A rather long course was laid out, consisting of 17 turns over a 4-mile loop. Some enhancements to the facility really improved it. They included a footbridge over the track, a press box, and 104 covered pit areas. The coverings were welcome in this sunny climate, but they did little to cut the heat and humidity. And that was all those covered pits offered: a cover. No outlets, not even a bench. The event continued to be highly popular, whatever the course changes, and again more entries were received than could be accommodated. One subtle reason might be that all the car magazines, which reported colorfully and lavishly upon the race each year, were not available until January, when most readers were deep in the cold and chill of winter. The seeds for a sunny Bahamas trip the following year were planted.

Despite a few close calls between cars because the pit area proved to be too close to the track, there were no major incidents that year on the new course. Drivers included Phil Hill, Carroll Shelby, and Stirling Moss, adding prestige to the event. The week began with the Nassau Tourist Trophy (run on a shortened 3-mile course), and Masten Gregory in a Maserati 450S took victory.

It was four days until the next race, and no doubt everyone took advantage of the interval to explore the island's many delights. Ed Crawford won the under-2-liter race in a Porsche 550 and Phil Hill repeated as winner in a 4.1 Ferrari in the second section of the Governor's Trophy. He famously crossed the line on a flat tire, having made the last half lap in this condition but still taking the checkered first.

Stock car racing legend Curtis Turner, not known for his road-racing prowess, won a new-that-year GT race in a Corvette SR2. In the big race of the week, the Nassau Trophy, the future Sir Stirling earned the win in a hastily reconfigured 3.5 Ferrari that had arrived with a center-mounted throttle. Moss showed his mastery even with this unfamiliar car as he won by more than a minute. In addition, everyone was amazed at the precocious ability of 14-year-old Mexican Ricardo Rodríguez, who could race his Porsche wheel-to-wheel with anyone.

Local police and other officials gave the racers a warm and welcome reception. In this photo from 1957, Brian Naylor gives a local gendarme an introduction to his *Sadler Special*. (Photo Courtesy Bill Sadler)

Brian Naylor (left) drove Bill Sadler's *Sadler Special* to a 1st in Class B in the 1957 Tourist Trophy. (Photo Courtesy Bill Sadler)

1958: Course and Purse Changes

The first years of the Bahamas Speed Weeks had seen a lot of Italian dominance, Ferrari and Maserati. But Lance Reventlow, a young American driver, had been there, too, since 1957, albeit starting out in a Maserati. He soon built his American cars, the famous Scarabs, to challenge the world. In 1958 Reventlow drove his Scarab to dominating victories, winning both the Governor's Trophy Race (no U-2 division that year) and the Nassau Trophy Race, co-driving the latter with Chuck Daigh.

If you did not know the length of the course you might think that these races were all sprints, but a mere five-lap race at Nassau was, after all, 20 or 25 miles. That's right, the course had been changed again and in 1958 a lap was now 4.5 miles long. The tourism board tried to keep the conditions of the 1958 races under wraps. The area had a week of tropical rainstorms that forced postponement and rescheduling of some races, and the track was often flooded or at least very wet. Those covered pits leaked, too.

A conflict arose between professional and amateur racing, and it had deeply affected the 1958 edition of the week. But this conflict illustrated a difference in philosophy between the Bahamas Automobile Club and the SCCA. The SCCA was trying hard to run against the tide and keep the sport on an amateur basis. But all over the world and even in the United States professional racing for money was more prevalent.

The amount of prize money being so bitterly contested by the SCCA for "professional" races seems laughable by today's standards, but in 1958 even $100 went a long way toward keeping a race car running. The Bahamas Automobile Club had to offer prize money to keep the quality of the field up to the established standards. The SCCA, however, did not even allow their members to receive expense money, and the trip to Nassau was not cheap.

The SCCA stated that it would suspend any of their drivers racing in the same race as professionals. The SCCA's edict finally forced Crise to forego offering appearance money, and that led to several top drivers staying home, most notably Stirling Moss. Evidently the lure of all those well-stuffed bikinis and endless parties was not strong enough to overcome this lack of cash incentives. But the following year saw a big change in the appearance money controversy.

1959: Big Prize Money

Crise and his fellow club members went all out in 1959 to secure the appearance of the world's top drivers. The staggering total of $96,000 was offered for prize, appearance, and expense money. This made the Bahamas Speed Weeks the richest event in the sports car racing world. Cannily, Crise also offered free accommodations to members of the press who continued to give his event a lot of love.

Events had been added to Speed Weeks all along, and in 1959 there was a residents' race; a ladies' race; an Austin Healy race; the President's Cup; the Nassau Memorial Race; a Governor's Trophy Race, which was for both over- and under-2-liter cars; and the featured Nassau Trophy Race. Kart racing was even added that year as Crise sniffed another opportunity.

Speed Weeks went on from November 27 through December 7. Johnny Cuevas opened this sixth Speed Weeks with a win in his 356a Porsche Carrera for the Nassau Tourist Trophy. All three big races were held on the final day of the

Lance Reventlow's winning Scarab (#37) and Carroll Shelby's DNF Maserati 450S (#98) in close company at this point in the 1958 Nassau Trophy Race. (Photo Courtesy Bahamas Speed Weeks Photo Archive)

At the Le Mans start of the 1960 Nassau Trophy race, a Chev-powered Healy driven by Forrest Dana jumps into a short-lived lead. Eventual winner Pedro Rodríguez' Ferrari (#57) is still in line. (Photo Courtesy Bill Sadler)

week. Stirling Moss won the over-2-liter Governor's Cup in an Aston-Martin DB2, while Bob Holbert took the under- in a Porsche RSK. George Constantine took the Nassau Trophy Race in another DB2, a race that was shortened slightly by approaching dusk. The most motley collection was in the residents' race, which saw a surprising 18 starters.

At some point someone had to ask, "Who is paying for all of this?" and the answer of course was the island of Nassau through the public-funded Bahamas Development Board. The event brought a lot of tourists and international publicity as a tourist destination. However, the benefits really flowed to the wealthy on the island, and the less wealthy (as in poor, of which there were many) island residents did not enjoy an increase in their standard of living. But they did notice the lavish event and party atmosphere enjoyed by Speed Weeks participants. Opposition to the whole thing began to be heard.

1960: Big Ups, a Final Big Down

As the new decade dawned, Bahamas Speed Weeks continued to expand, especially in the open-wheel ranks. Two days of kart racing were featured, including a race billed as the world championship for the little guys, and the First International Caribbean Classic for Formula Juniors. Both karts and Juniors were exploding in popularity and were still a crowd-pleasing novelty as well.

To accommodate the extra racing the event dates were extended to November 21 through December 5. Although all events were popular, the most excitement continued to be for the 252-mile Nassau Trophy and the Governor's Trophy. The Le Mans start that year saw the sudden departure of Stirling Moss because his Lotus 19 suffered a mechanical failure in the first turn of the first lap and he had to call it a day.

Even Moss may have been tired by the parties that still went on nightly. Moss did manage to win the Nassau Tourist Trophy in a Ferrari 250SWB and a Ricardo Rodríguez–driven Ferrari 250TR took the Governor's Trophy Race, which was back to only one division: open. However, even with Moss out, a Lotus 19 won the Nassau Trophy race in the hands of Dan Gurney. Moss . . . the Rodríguez Brothers . . . Gurney. The week was still drawing the top talent.

1961: A Short Week

Gurney was indeed a "top talent" and he really showed it in the 1961 week when he again won the most prestigious race in the somewhat shortened Speed Weeks schedule, December 3–11 this year. The week was preceded by a full week of karting events, which, incidentally, was the last for the karts. After a fast start, they just did not prove to be popular enough.

The schedule that year had the 112-mile Nassau Tourist Trophy for GT cars slated for December 3. Despite a year of efforts by the organizing committee, the course surface was still rough and bumpy enough to draw complaints. As the cars were becoming faster, conditions that might have been tolerated just a couple of years earlier were no longer acceptable.

Gurney noted that you had to specially prepare your machinery for it. In Gurney's case that meant down to disassembling the car and Magnafluxing it to be sure it was up to the challenge. Of course many, if not most, of the cars entering the week did not have the luxury of such a regime.

Stirling Moss was in the twilight of his racing career at that point, although no one knew it, and the Nassau fan favorite won the Nassau Tourist Trophy. Gurney took the Nassau Trophy in another Lotus 19 after Moss' car broke. Pedro Rodríguez, who, along with his ill-fated brother Ricardo, had been a regular at Nassau, won the Governor's Cup in another Ferrari 250TR. The Formula Junior Pan-Am team attracted another great field, including Team Rosebud out of Texas, who shipped over a whole truckload of cars; one of their drivers, Pete Lovely, won the Juniors race that year.

In addition to his teammate Pat Pigott, who took 2nd, Lovely also bested Mark Donohue and Roger Penske. Races were also

Pete Lovely and Team Rosebud teammate Pat Piggot motor to the start/finish line for their Formula Junior race at the 1961 Nassau. Lovely won, Piggot was 2nd. (Photo Courtesy Pete Lovely Collection)

The start of the 1961 Formula Juniors race. For a while, the Juniors looked to be the next big thing in racing. Eventual winner Pete Lovely is on the right in #65. (Photo Courtesy Pete Lovely Collection)

Not a lot of Nassau racing glamour here in 1961 as Bob Holbert's mechanics set to work on his Porsche 718 RS-61. He was eventually a DNF in the Governor's Cup. (Photo Courtesy Bahamas Speed Weeks Photo Archive)

held for midgets and quarter-midgets but these did not prove to be overly popular. Karts and midgets used a special half-mile, 19-turn circuit designed out of the airport grounds just for them.

1962: Back to Racing

These were the years before Lotus 19s began to carry American V-8 engines, but the original configuration was enough in those days for them to post wins for the third straight year.

Innes Ireland drove one to victory this time in the Nassau Trophy affair.

The Nassau Tourist Trophy, on the other hand, was now split into two divisions, one under-2-liter, one over-. Ferrari GTOs swept the over-2-liter division, taking the first four places. Roger Penske led them all in.

In the Governor's Trophy event, Hap Sharp took first in a Cooper Monaco.

Juniors began losing their luster, but they again had their own race and Jack Nethercutt led from start to finish. Team Rosebud was not back after one of their star drivers, Pat Piggott, was killed at Riverside the year before and his friend Pete Lovely cut back on racing.

1963: Low Excitement

The event really became Bahamas Speed *week* for 1963 as the dates expanded to December 1–8. Karts and Juniors were gone. VW Beetles and Formula Vees had taken their place. Although these classes were less exotic than the Juniors, these cars had fallen so rapidly out of popularity that it would have been extremely difficult to assemble a good field. Both VW beetles and the Vees had their own races. Unlike the Juniors in their heyday, though, they did not attract top drivers.

The week also offered a more exciting new dynamic as only one Ferrari 250 GTO was entered and it seemed that Modena had given the GT honors to whomever proved superior between Cobra and Corvette. The two American makes had been duking it out all year and both were determined to end the year proving their superiority.

Shelby brought his "A" team (had he any other?) with Ken Miles, Dan Gurney, Dave MacDonald, and Bob Holbert leading the charge. Corvette ran its cars through the Mecom team and had Roger Penske, Jim Hall, Augie Pabst, and Dick Thompson behind its wheels.

The much-anticipated GT race, however, was not as exciting as was forecast. A Lola MKVI GT was allowed to race with them and won easily in the hands of Augie Pabst. In 2nd place was that lone Ferrari GTO entry, which was driven by Mike Gammino, a privateer who had raced the car all around the United States that year.

Festive Atmosphere

For the 1961 race week, *Competition Press*' Art Peck had a special report that caught the atmosphere of the week during those halcyon years. His party report went something like this: Sunday, all on hand were annoyed that the kart folks had taken over the traditional Sunday night hangouts, Dirty Dick's and Blackbeard's Tavern. But substitute locations were found, not to worry.

Monday night was the Junkaroo Tavern with dancing. Peck reported that Mr. Moss was quite the dancer.

Tuesday was the Pilothouse, which featured a traditional all-in-the-pool-with-clothes-on event.

Wednesday saw all hands on the second deck of the Windsor Hotel BaMa Lounge.

Thursday was "Fort Montague" night at which a few drivers and crewmembers traditionally joined the band for impromptu jam sessions.

Friday was the Nassau Beach Party night, after which at the British Colonial, Long Island's Lou Comito threw his annual party on the terrace off his room. Dancing a-plenty went on at both locations, with the twist and the limbo proving to be the favorites.

Saturday was at another terrace location, this one at the Emerald Beach. A Mercedes-Benz party nearby that year was a little more genteel, but since the big race of the weekend was to be held the next day, all that night's parties were a bit more restrained.

Sunday saw plenty of post-race team parties no doubt, but nothing was scheduled for all hands.

On Monday, however, there was one last big bash, the annual Fort Montague Hotel Motor Ball.

A Ford Galaxie with veteran driver Darel Dieringer joins the fun at the 1962 Nassau Trophy Race. He did well, too, taking 7th overall. (Photo Courtesy Speed Weeks Photo Archive)

Eventual winner A. J. Foyt in his Scarab Mk IV is about to pass Jim Hall's Chaparral on the way to a win in the 1963 Nassau Trophy Race. Hall was a DNF. (Jack Brady Photo, Dave Freidman Collection, Courtesy the Henry Ford)

The best showing by the Grand Sport Corvette team was in the Governor's Trophy Race, in which they came in 3rd, 4th, and 6th but well behind winner A. J. Foyt. Chevy power was the big winner, though, that weekend as Foyt was driving a Chevy-powered Scarab when he won the Nassau Trophy Race.

1964: Serious Tone

For 1964 there seemed to be a certain note of desperation seeping into Red Crise's announcement: "We have a fabulous field of entries, far better than in any other year. These races are going to be the greatest in the world." He was no doubt being encouraged into justifying the expense that the week was forcing from local groups. At least Crise did not have to work extra hard to entice John Mecom to bring his team back to Nassau. The Texas oilman entered five cars, including two Grand Sports.

The appearance of the new Ford GT-40s created the most buzz. They had been shipped from England especially for these races and were equipped with 289 engines. In the end, though, Roger Penske won the Nassau Tourist Trophy GT race in a Grand Sport, and then came back to win the other two feature races as well. With Hap Sharp he won the Nassau

1961 Governor's Trophy winner Pedro Rodríguez is about to lap fellow Ferrari TR driver Bob Major. (Jack Brady Photo, Dave Freidman Collection, Courtesy the Henry Ford)

The Shelby Team is offloaded for the 1964 week. The team's best results were Ken Miles, who earned a 2nd in the GT race; Bob Johnson, a 4th in the Nassau Tourist Trophy Race; and Tom Payne, a 9th in the Governor's Trophy. (Jack Brady Photo, Dave Freidman Collection, Courtesy the Henry Ford)

Trophy Race in Sharp's Chaparral, and driving alone he won the Governor's Trophy Race in another Chaparral. It was the first time that one driver had won all three features.

Phil Hill and Bruce McLaren arrived with their Ford GT-40s, but these cars were not prepared for competition. After a dismal showing in the Nassau Tourist Trophy race, they were abruptly pulled out of the week and shipped back to England. Whether the drivers stayed on for the week's parties is not recorded.

And about those parties. The bars and restaurants were crowded, but things were more serious and the drivers were less likely to be seen taking in parties and complimentary drinks at bars. Spectators, media people, and assorted hangers-on, yes; people who had to drive very fast cars on a challenging course the next day, no. At least for the most part.

1965: Turn and Face the Change

Winds of change swept over the island, and as a result, the 1965 race week saw a major decline in the number of entrants and top-shelf race machinery. American cars were being made ready for the next domestic racing year, and even Team Mecom did not show up this year, nor did they again.

Crise, ever resourceful, declared 1965 the Year of the Rookie, but no one was fooled. Among those not fooled were the members of the new political party in power on the island. The United Bahamian Party was under pressure to spend money on such mundane things as schools and sewer systems, not to mention better sports opportunities for the island's residents. The party ruled that no more public money would be targeted toward Speed Weeks. The track would be converted into a sports complex.

Some exotic cars and top drivers made the journey, but there were fewer of them, and the glamour was fading. Bruce McLaren won the Governor's Trophy Race in one of his early McLarens, an M1-B. The Formula Vee field had grown substantially, and the little guys loved the special attention they received at this event; 33 showed up to race. Chris Amon, an international driver, competed and won.

The ladies' race that year was peopled entirely by borrowed Vees, and there were plenty to choose between. A few fast cars showed up that were being prepared for the following Can-Am season. The Nassau Tourist Trophy Race was won by Charlie Kolb in a Ferrari 275 GTB/C. Hap Sharp won again, this time in the Nassau Trophy Race in a Chaparral. His teammate Jim Hall had a nasty off-course excursion in his own Chaparral during

Ford GT-40s made a big splash when they arrived but they did not do much in the 1964 Nassau Tourist Trophy races. Here, Phil Hill chases eventual winner Roger Penske and Jack Saunders, both in Grand Sports. (Photo Courtesy Don Markle)

Surprisingly, there were all-VW races in 1964 at Nassau. They were beautifully prepared, too, but the drivers' names have been lost. (Photo Courtesy Dan Markle)

The mid-pack lineup for the 1964 Nassau Trophy Race shows the fully developed structures for the pits and the timing tower. (Photo Courtesy Don Markle)

the race and hit a car that had gone off earlier. No one was hurt but the result was a lot of bent metal and shredded fiberglass.

1966: Last Bahamas Speed Weeks

The writing was on the wall, and the 1966 event, the 13th edition of the Bahamas Speed Weeks, was the last. The event's decline was speeded along by the death of Sir Sydney Oakes, one of the event's originators and strongest supporters over the years. A strong and respected voice for continuing the event had been lost. If it was not too late anyway.

The Nassau Tourist Trophy and the Governor's Trophy were combined this year. Hap Sharp won again, again in a Chaparral, this time lapping the entire field while doing so. Mark Donohue won the Nassau Trophy Race in his familiar Lola T70. His speed average set a new record, one that will never be broken, of 105.7.

Unfortunately, the weekend also saw the only death in the event's history when a Ferrari driven by Rodrigo Borjes Zingg rolled over and burned. The Bahamas Speed Weeks had almost made it through without a fatality.

1967: The Season that Wasn't

When everyone left after the 1966 race they probably assumed that they would be back the next year. But early in 1967 it became final: The development board had shut off its money spigot for good, and Red Crise and his team had to face the inevitable. Without public support the Bahamas Speed Weeks event was done. The last hope went out with the ruling party losing control of the government to an even more restrictive and racing-intolerant group.

Crise reportedly had tried to somehow lure Can-Am racing to the island. When that failed, he went in an entirely different direction and tried moving the whole operation to Grand Bahama Island, and hold races just for Formula Vees. The effort failed and racing at Nassau was gone ... or was it?

Recently a vintage racing festival has been held in downtown Nassau. It's a wonderful idea, but after a couple of years, the event's future is unclear. For a short time at least some of the cars that both thrilled and irritated island residents years ago were there again.

Walt Hansgen in the rear-engined Scarab Chevrolet took a 3rd in the Governor's Trophy race and an 8th in the Nassau Trophy in 1964. The car was, by then, just too old and slow for even the talented Hansgen to challenge for the lead. (Photo Courtesy Bahamas Speed Weeks Photo Archive)

Nassau islander Patsy Kenedy raced with the locals in her Porsche 356B Carrera. (Photo Courtesy Bahamas Speed Weeks Photo Archive)

In the 1966 Nassau Trophy race, Peter Revson took 3rd place in his McLaren-Elva MIB-Ford. This was the last race at Nassau. (Photo Courtesy Bahamas Speed Weeks Photo Archive)

Ontario Motor Speedway

WHERE HOLLYWOOD GLITTER MEETS MOTOR RACING

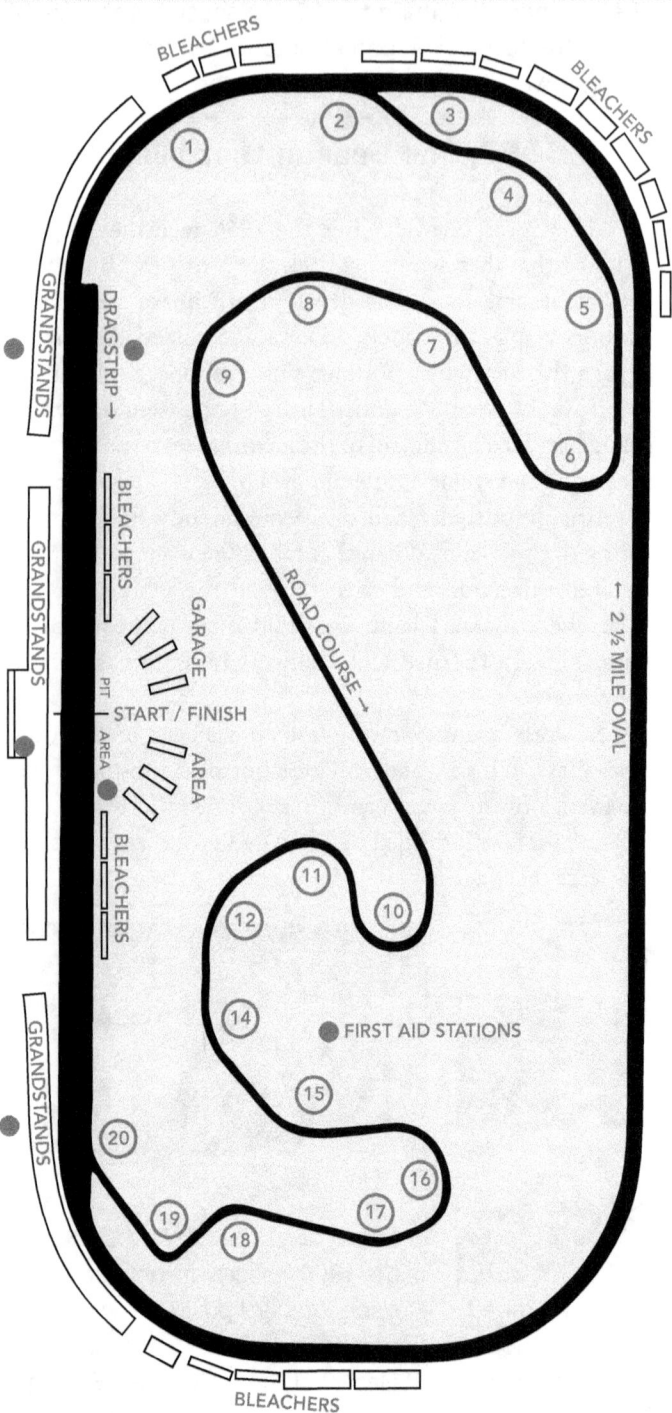

This comprehensive description of the road course and oval is from the 1971 Questor Grand Prix program. The road course ultimately proved to be too far from the grandstands for easy viewing. (Illustration Courtesy Martin Rudow Collection)

Ontario Motor Speedway was a full-throttle attempt to bring big-time racing closer to Los Angeles, just 40 miles away. Ontario was the home of an international airport and was right next to Interstate 10, the area's only major east-west freeway in those days; access was convenient and easy. Ontario was not much developed outside its city limits, especially toward the east where the garish town of San Bernardino beckoned (or not). It was a perfect spot for a racetrack, and at apparently the perfect time.

Ontario planned to attract major races by all of the dominant sanctioning bodies of racing: the Indy Car series and USAC for open-wheel oval car races, NASCAR for oval stock car races, the NHRA for drag races, and the SCCA and FIA for road course races.

During the 1960s, radio ruled the Los Angeles airways. Millions of commuters (me among them) were stuck in long traffic jams twice a day. The postwar generation loved rock and roll on the radio, and those stations were huge. More mainstream stations catering to the tastes of middle-agers stuck in those same traffic jams also drew big audiences. Radio and billboards captured the attention of this often-motionless motoring public. It was a perfect setting for a massive media campaign to launch a new racetrack, and the new racetrack at Ontario took full advantage of all of these promotional opportunities.

1966: The Build Begins

The facility was the result of five years of hard work started in 1966 by Ray Smartis, a Southern California race promoter who initially went out to build a dragstrip and soon had bigger plans. He focused on what seemed an ideal site, the Cucamonga Winery's 800 acres across the freeway from

CHAPTER 11

Ontario, California
1970–1980

Facility 3.2 miles
Principal Events SCCA, SCCA Formula 5000, FIA, NASCAR, USAC, IMSA
Current Status Business park and shopping mall; no trace of the track remains

This artist's rendition shows the vision for the Ontario grandstands and pit area, circa 1969. This was one time that the final product looked as good as the vision. (Photo Courtesy Riverside International Automotive Museum)

the Ontario International Airport. William Loorz, CEO of Stolte Construction, one of California's largest commercial construction companies, was designated contractor for the project. He soon hooked up with David Lockton of Sports Headliners, an Indianapolis, Indiana, company that represented several leading international race car drivers.

When Lockton viewed the proposed site it had been subdivided into fourteen separate parcels owned by 150 individual owners. An important Hollywood connection was established because many of those owners were Hollywood celebrities who had bought the land for tax shelters. Lockton convinced the owners to sell their parcels, arranged an important local tax break for investors, convinced the USAC to sanction a 500-mile race there, and raised investment funds for the new Ontario Motor Speedway.

Walter Tyler designed the facility to be state of the art, based on features of the Indianapolis Motor Speedway. Important enhancements were made to make the oval track faster than Indy: The racing surface was one lane wider and the short straightaways at the ends of the track were banked. Most important, a dragstrip and an infield road course were added. The oval course was 2.5 miles with 9-degree banked turns, and the road course was 3.2 miles with 20 turns and a 3,300-foot main straightaway. The city fathers of Ontario were not completely taken in by the track promoter's dreams, even though their tax-free bond offering for the track gave the city eventual sole ownership of the track in 1998. Belief in the enduring attraction of motor racing was obviously high.

Although road racing figured prominently in the track's plans, the promise of a West Coast Indy race was more incentive

This is the road course that was built in the middle of farm fields. When Ontario Motor Speedway opened in 1970, the facility looked like this. (Photo Courtesy Riverside International Automotive Museum)

1970: Gala Hype for the Grand First Race

for the owners. So, the California 500 was launched in 1970 as the track's first truly major event. The track had been completed in just 22 months; fortunately, there were few time-robbing big trees or rock outcroppings to deal with in the area's flat and featureless landscape. Massive covered grandstands with more than 85,000 permanent and 65,000 portable seats were the facility's most spectacular feature. All of the oval and most of the road track was visible from these seats. Parking was available for 45,000 spectator cars. The infield held two man-made lakes. The cost of the whole thing finally came in at $25.5 million or about $145 million today.

The board of directors featured some big names in and out of the racing industry at the time. How involved they actually were is somewhat open to question, but their names lent a lot of prestige. From Hollywood came Kirk Douglas, James Garner, Paul Newman, and Dick Smothers. Familiar to race fans were names including Briggs Cunningham, J. C. Agajanian, Roger Penske, and Parnelli Jones. One famous driver's name not mentioned for obvious reasons was Jimmy Clark. The popular Scottish driver had reportedly been a key consultant in the early stages of design for the road course but his name brought up many sad memories.

Inevitably, it seems, the whole project raised some eyebrows. None were raised higher, in public at least, than those of the respected writer Brock Yates. In an article in *Car and Driver* magazine, Yates stated that the fund-raising aspects of the whole enterprise reeked of "snake oil salesmen." Some other key figures in the sport expressed concern about Ontario because "it is just too big." But the facility jumped the sport into the mainstream. Even though the 60-mile circle of Los Angeles held half the population and economy of California, the track had to compete with Dodger Stadium, Disneyland, and the Memorial Coliseum for the entertainment dollar. The thinking was "go big or go home" and many in the sport thought that the whole Ontario operation was just too much too soon.

The first race, sort of a "soft launch" celebrity go, was held on August 9, 1970, and all went well with the new facility. The first big race, and it proved to be a monster, was the California 500 for Indy-style open wheel cars. Held September 6, 17,000 people attended the dedication ceremony the week before, and then 60,000 paid $2 each to watch the first day of qualifying on the 22nd.

Race day, September 6, was scheduled during one of the traditionally worst times for smog in Southern California. But the threat of high heat, unbreathable air, and clogged freeways did not deter more than 178,000 people from showing up. And at least the threatened freeway jams did not materialize. The race organizers and the California Highway Patrol had worked magic to ensure smooth off and on from several freeway ramps, and the track management wisely did not charge for parking, making in and out from their big lots a relative breeze.

The aforementioned massive advertising opportunities available to the track were a major factor. The facility was promoted in all media as a family-friendly, clean, and safe place to be. Speed, fun, color, and glamour were all played up while racing danger was downplayed. After all, everyone knew that the danger was there but no one needed to be reminded of it.

The race was almost an afterthought after a somewhat overblown introduction that included a parachutist, stunt planes, a visit from then-governor Ronald Reagan, a 17-band parade, and a fireworks show. Fortunately, when it finally started, the race did not let anyone down. After the first 186 laps, it was a wild dash to the finish that saw Jim McElreath beat out Art Pollard for the win by 0.75 seconds.

In addition to teaching everyone a lesson in how to advertise a race, the weekend also saw a great innovation in having each car fitted with a radio broadcast unit. These units kept a three-sided, 65-foot-high scoreboard tower correct up to the minute showing the race leader and the rest of the top ten. Although luxury seating is commonplace now at the top tracks around the country and world, it was innovation for racetracks during this day and age. And Ontario offered this

The huge stands are absolutely packed for the track's inaugural big race: the 1970 California 500. Spectator safety precautions for the 178,000 who attended are evident. The powerful front row includes (left to right) Johnny Rutherford, Dan Gurney, and Lloyd Ruby. Jim McElreath was the winner. (Photo Courtesy Riverside International Automotive Museum)

seating option. Its premium seats offered corporations and well-heeled fans the chance to have the best view of the races in private, luxuriously appointed suites. Subsequent races, a NASCAR event and an NHRA world championship drag race, also drew high numbers.

All this bode well for the future, a future that included the first major road course event for the track: the Questor Grand Prix, scheduled for March 1971. A national SCCA race was held that fall, another sort of "soft launch" for that part of the circuit. It featured the leading club racers of the region. However, spectators used to being closer to the action let out a faint whiff of disapproval. They felt removed from the track in those massive grandstands.

1971: The Questor Grand Prix

The road circuit at Ontario was, eventually, not as well used as the oval. Nevertheless, the Questor Grand Prix was one of the biggest and most noteworthy road events of the 1970s and deserves to be well remembered. It was a noble experiment. Unfortunately, it also proved to be the undoing of the circuit management's plans to stage a full Formula 1 race at the track.

Typical of the way they did things at Ontario in those early days, the Questor was going to be the most intriguing, unusual, and exciting match-up yet between American and European cars. The Questor Corporation was looking to make a major statement and the event offered a great opportunity to do just that. Questor was a corporate conglomerate with subsidiaries as varied as golf clubs, piston rings, and children's furniture. Auto racing seemed to be the perfect tool to make a statement and the glittering new Ontario Speedway the perfect venue. The FIA refused to sanction a race there, so an already-scheduled Formula 5000 SCCA race welcomed Formula 1 cars, whose engines were under the series' 3-liter limit.

Lack of an FIA sanction proved less of a hindrance when Questor put up $300,000 in prize money for the event. Prize money and the appeal of a glittering new track surrounded by Hollywood personalities attracted an extremely impressive international field of teams and drivers. They included Lotus (Emerson Fittipaldi and Reine Wisell), Scuderia Ferrari (Mario Andretti and Jacky Ickx), Brabham (Graham Hill and

Mark Donohue felt that the F5000 cars could not stay with the F1 cars in the Questor Grand Prix, and he was right. Driving an F5000 car, Donohue gave the F1 drivers the stiffest competition, but eventually the Penske driver retired and Mario Andretti earned the win. (Photo Courtesy Dale von Trebra)

John Cannon was a terrific F5000 driver, but he could not keep up with the European F1s; he finally finished 12th. (Photo Courtesy Dale von Trebra)

Pedro Rodríguez gets ready for a Questor GP practice session in his BRM. He eventually came in 10th and never really challenged for a top spot. (Photo Courtesy Dale von Trebra)

Tim Schenken), BRM (Jo Siffert, Howden Ganley, and Pedro Rodríguez), McLaren (Peter Gethin and Denny Hulme), Matra (Chris Amon), March (Ronnie Peterson), and Tyrrell (Jackie Stewart).

West Coast Formula 1 fans had never had an opportunity to see such cars and drivers close up. Matched against this impressive group were America's F5000 stars, including Mark Donohue, Peter Revson, and George Follmer, and non–F5000 regulars, A. J. Foyt and the Unser brothers.

Even last-minute advice from Parnelli Jones could not help Al Unser much at the Questor. He came in 28th. (Photo Courtesy Dale von Trebra)

Tim Schenken was an international F1 driver not well known to American racing fans. Still, he came in a strong 5th overall in the Questor. (Photo Courtesy Dale von Trebra)

Promoting the race was easy for Los Angeles ad men. The radio airwaves were full of commercials with a snotty-sounding British Formula 1 driver. They claimed that the American drivers were uncultured, loud, and unskilled and their cars could never compete with the European Formula 1 teams. And actually, Jackie Stewart did say a few such things. Billboards and newspaper ads featured the same insulting message. Rock-and-roll radio stations gave away tickets en masse. However, European drivers were blown away by the facility's private luxury suites and lavish trappings; they were less so by the track. The night-before dinner party at Ontario was probably the most glittery thing any of them had yet seen, stocked with great food and wine and beautiful people.

A spectacular 126-page program greeted spectators. Here, though, the faults of track management's expectations started to show. The turnout of 68,000 was good but not up to the financial demands of the track, or of Questor, evidently, because they were not involved in future automotive racing events. The Ontario facility had a huge appetite for cash, and crowds had to be exceptional to ensure its survival. Although a Formula 1 Grand Prix points race, which would have been at least equal to the status of the Questor, was planned for 1972, it never came off.

What about the race itself? The agency-written bravado attributed to the European drivers proved more or less true. The American F5000 drivers were certainly fast enough. However, the tight and twisty corners and deceiving Turn 1 configuration favored F1 more than F5000 cars. Basically, the F5000 cars had a higher center of gravity that made the American chassis less agile. As Mark Donohue had predicted, they were faster in the straights but could not hold that speed through the turns. Mario Andretti was the eventual winner. The victory was a sly tease: it was an American driver in the most famous European Formula 1 car of all, Ferrari. So, in a way, both sides won.

Formula 1 cars were at the front most of the day, with Stewart and Ickx doing the early leading. The race was run in two heats,

The McLaren team's Denis Hulme (3rd overall) and Peter Gethin (8th) run their F1 cars in front of a good-sized group of Questor GP spectators. (Photo Courtesy Dale von Trebra)

As smog clouds the track, Tyrrell's Jackie Stewart stays ahead of McLaren's Denis Hulme and others. Stewart and Hulme raced close most of the day and finished 2-3. (Photo Courtesy Dale von Trebra)

The Questor Grand Prix simply had too many empty seats. Even 68,000 spectators could get lost in the huge grandstands. (Photo Courtesy Dale von Trebra)

probably to give people more time to buy souvenirs and the liquid refreshment they needed on what was a pretty hot day. Andretti managed to win both heats with Stewart 2nd, and that is the way they finished in aggregate. Ron Grable, the first F5000 driver, was way back in 7th. Donohue was the only F5000 driver to give any real competition to the F1 cars until he retired in the second heat.

Sam Posey wrote a detailed description of how to drive the course for *Auto Racing* magazine, based on his experiences qualifying for and racing in the Questor. He stated, "It's a track where you use your mind and your powers of concentration more than your guts and strength... the two apex lefts (off the banked turns) are the trickiest, you have to really concentrate, especially at those two points." Although Posey did not mention it, Jackie Stewart said there was a feeling that the action was too far removed from the grandstands.

Of course, nothing but a full-fledged Formula 1 race ever came near the road racing excitement created by the Questor Grand Prix. And such a race never developed at Ontario. Management was discouraged by the 68,000-spectator turnout, especially considering the massive hype that had gone into the event. Without American drivers, they reasoned, a Formula 1 event would be even less popular. Again, it was "go big or go home."

1974: Financial Woes Threaten the Track

Although the speedway successfully attracted spectators and had the potential for success, the operating company had difficulty meeting its debt service obligations on the municipal bonds. Big crowds were a start, but the track needed to attract *monster* crowds and high-end sponsorship for each event to be profitable. The track tried to stage another big race on the road circuit. The 1974 California Grand Prix was an F5000 race that drew all the big names in that series, including Mario Andretti, Brian Redman, and David Hobbs. Redman (Lola T332) led every lap of the 100-mile race and came out on top of that one with Andretti 2nd.

Also in 1974 a stage of the Camel 4-Hour series was held with Peter Gregg winning easily in a Porsche RSR. The Ontario 100 Miles, another Camel Grand Prix race, was the last recorded road course race; it was held on September 5, 1976. Another RSR won this time in the hands of Jim Busby. How successful these last few races were in

Post-race, Jackie Stewart has strength for interviews while still lugging the big 2nd-place Questor trophy around. He proved his pre-race point about F1 compared to American Formula 5000 cars with his 2nd place finish. (Photo Courtesy Dale von Trebra)

A milestone was set at Ontario in 1972 when Jerry Grant made the first 200-mph lap anywhere in an ex–Dan Gurney–team Eagle. (Photo Courtesy Riverside International Automotive Museum)

drawing spectators is not known, but they were certainly not popular enough to keep road racing on Ontario's schedule.

Oval races and drag events became the mainstay of the track. In fact, starting with the 1973 season, track management decided to hold two 500-mile races each year, one for USAC Indy-type cars and one for NASCAR stockers. This was in the day when 500-mile races were still relatively rare and a novelty.

On September 3, 1972, Ontario witnessed the first 200-plus-mph lap for an Indy car. It was a qualifying day for the Ontario 500. In windy conditions, Jerry Grant held on for dear life as he willed his 1,100-hp Eagle through the four turns in less than 44.7 seconds for an average speed of 201.414. It was a harrowing ride. Grant's straightaway speeds exceeded 240 mph, but his cornering speeds were as low as 160 mph.

Later, the *Los Angeles Times* signed on as title sponsor for the 500-mile NASCAR race, which was held in late fall. The event became one of the staples on the NASCAR circuit and saw repeat winners including Bobby Allison and Benny Parsons. The Unser brothers were the biggest winners of the California 500, as it continued to be known, with Bobby winning in 1974, 1976, and 1979, and Al in 1977 and 1978. The event became a CART oval race in its last two years.

The vast facility was natural for many other non-racing events, too. In 1971 motorcycle daredevil Evel Knievel attempted a record jump over 19 cars. His successful jump attracted a crowd of 50,000 in paid attendance on the day prior to the NASCAR-sanctioned Miller High Life 500-mile stock car race. Two huge rock concerts were also held. The California Jam was held in 1974 and drew a crowd of 300,000–400,000, the largest paid attendance for a rock concert. California Jam II was held on March 18, 1978. The second event drew a crowd of almost 300,000 paid attendees.

Special events and popular oval races were not enough. The track was not able to consistently draw crowds and attract sponsors big enough to keep up its bond payments, and the land on which it was built increased in value exponentially as the population grew outward from Los Angeles. The 800 acres of land originally purchased at an average price of $7,500 per acre had risen to a value of $150,000 per acre! For approximately $10 million, Chevron acquired the land through bond deals, land that had a commercial real estate development value of $120 million. This development took place gradually and today is a thriving and attractive business park.

The only remnants of the vast complex that was once Ontario Raceway are streets of the business park that are named after famous marques: Duesenberg Drive, Ferrari Lane, and Porsche Parkway. An indoor go-kart track provides the only racing that takes place today on the 800 acres north of the I-10 freeway.

This is the only remaining racing-related structure, and there isn't anything about Ontario Speedway inside to inform people of the "real" racing that went on here. (Photo Courtesy Judy Rudow)

As of the summer of 2015, the earth-pile created for banking the oval's Turn 3 is still visible. (Photo Courtesy Judy Rudow)

Shopping malls and office buildings stand where the mighty Ontario grandstands once dominated the skyline. (Photo Courtesy Judy Rudow)

RIVERSIDE INTERNATIONAL RACEWAY

MULTI-FACETED JEWEL IN THE DESERT

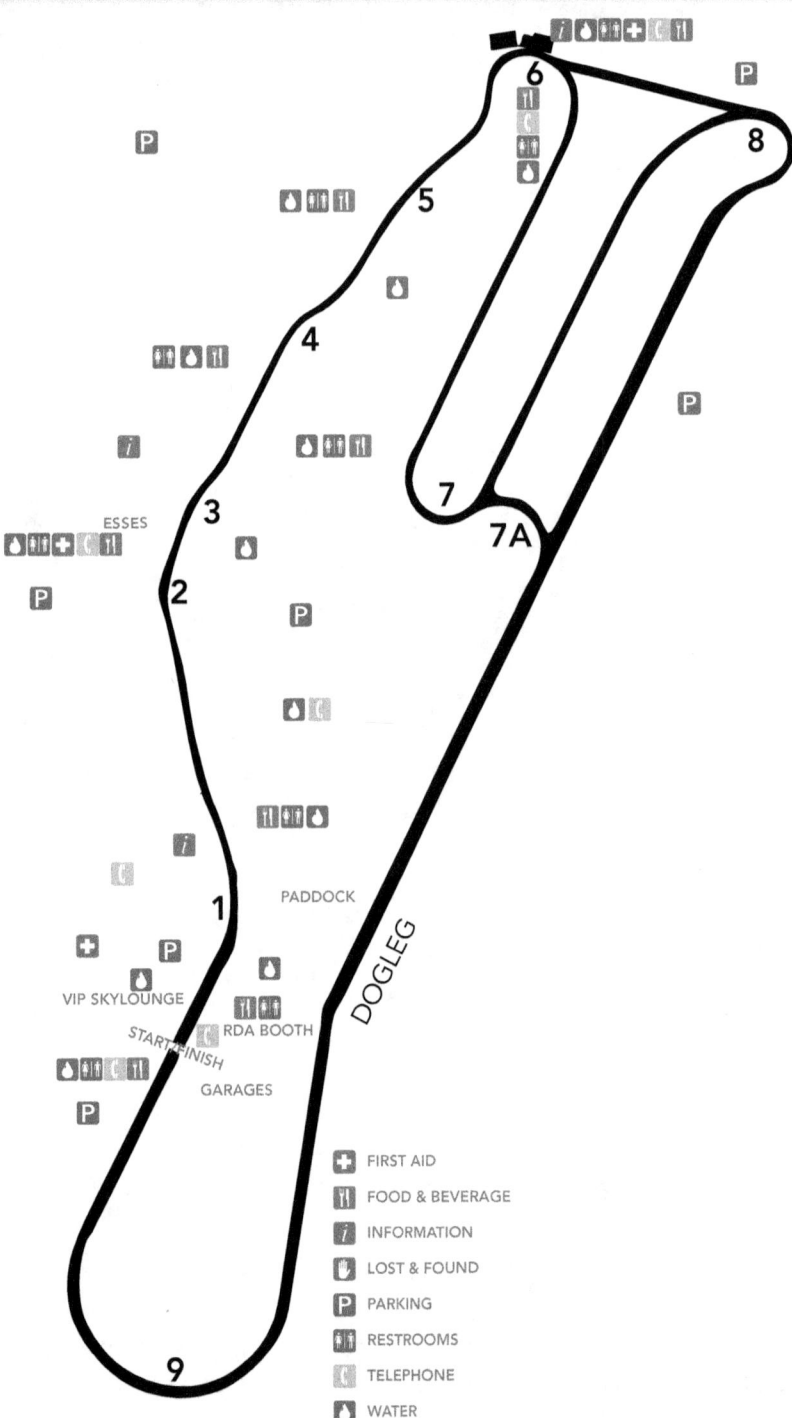

The final courses at Riverside. The first one had no kink at the end of the long straightaway. (Illustration Courtesy Riverside Automobile Museum)

During its 33 years of existence Riverside saw every form of motor racing. Trans-Am, SCCA club and National, Continental, USAC, Can-Am, NASCAR, Formula 1, IROC, NHRA drags, IMSA GT, Indy Car, CART, as well as motorcycles, midgets, and off-road. It saw every car that could be raced in any form and drivers of all abilities, from the most humble to the mightiest.

When Riverside opened for racing business in 1957, it hit the sweet spot of growth for motorsports in this country, especially in Southern California. The entire area was bursting with enthusiasm, money, and vitality. Nowhere else was the car a king as much as it was in Southern California, with its seemingly endless sunny days, freeways, back roads, and long desert highways. This energy was funneled into racing on dragstrips and road courses converted from airports and fairgrounds to become several early-1950s popular racing locales: Palm Springs, Pomona, Santa Barbara, and Torrey Pines, to name only a few. Inevitably these facilities proved inadequate to accommodate the crowds of spectators and faster cars as the sport progressed through the 1950s. Purpose-built race courses were needed, but they had to be built in areas where they would add to the urban congestion and smog that were the downsides of the car-crazy Southern California culture.

An isolated 600-acre turkey ranch 7 miles south of the little town of Riverside seemed

116   Lost Road Courses

CHAPTER 12

Riverside, California
1957–1989

Facility	Long course, 3.27 miles; short course, 2.5 miles; NASCAR course, 2.62 miles
Principal Events	SCCA Nationals and Runoffs, FIA, USAC sports and Indy cars, NASCAR, IMSA, Can-Am, F5000, Trans-Am, IROC
Current Status	Housing development and shopping malls; no trace of the track remains

The start of the 1964 *Los Angeles Times* Grand Prix. The front row is (left to right) Parnelli Jones (King Cobra), Bruce McLaren (McLaren Mk 1), and Dan Gurney (Lotus 19-Ford). Jones won; the other two were DNFs. (Photo Courtesy the Henry Ford)

to fit the bill. The desolate desert landscape, like something out of a Republic Movie Studios B-western, was unsuited for most other uses and land was cheap. The only thing nearby, except for the little backwater town of Riverside, was March Air Force Base, which had already seen road racing on its landing strips. Best of all, a freeway and a four-lane highway connected the racetrack site to downtown Los Angeles. It was on the way to Palm Springs and the interstate went to San Diego. Fans would have a straight shot to the track.

Les Richter's name usually comes first to mind when talking about the development and growth of Riverside Raceway. However, Rudy Cleye of the Blarney Castle restaurant in Los Angeles was initially responsible for the track's development. A visionary, local racer in a Mercedes-Benz Gullwing, and general motorsports fan, Cleye set up an operating company and found and secured the location. He also acquired the necessary zoning and permitting, and contracted a course designer, Jim Peterson, to design the circuit. Peterson was a professional builder who took a tour of European road courses for inspiration and had lots of ideas. Some ideas were perhaps too ambitious, but the basics, a challenging course with elevation changes and a 1.1-mile-long straightaway, were sound. Sound too was the idea of designing the facility so that it could accommodate different types of racing.

The final basic road course was 3.275 miles with nine turns and attractive elevation changes. A shorter 2.53-mile course could be used, too, by eliminating some turns. Plans for an even longer version, to be built later on, were on the drawing boards. John Edgar, a wealthy Southern California race team owner, provided financial backing for Cleye and

An early artist's rendition of how the completed grandstands and surrounding areas would look when they were developed. The vision came true, pretty much. (Photo Courtesy Riverside Automobile Museum)

course construction began early in 1957. A well-publicized mid-June testing date drew many of Southern California's top drivers, and local ace Pete Woods, in a Jaguar D-type, posted a top straightaway speed of 153-plus mph. Press releases made much of this impressive speed and also noted that 100-plus-mph laps could be expected.

1957: Debut Success

The first year of racing at Riverside saw several significant events that bode well for the track's future. About 30,000 fans flocked to the initial race in September. Local hero and future Formula 1 driver Richie Ginther took the victory in a Ferrari. Another good turnout came for the second race that year, an SCCA National that drew racers and press attention from all over the country. This was Dan Gurney's coming-out party. The genial 26-year-old Californian had won a production race in the opening Riverside race weekend. At the SCCA National event, he was in a Ferrari 375 and challenged no less than Car-

Pete Lovely moves his Ferrari inside a hulking "Knobbly" Lister-Chevy driven by Wayne Weller at the 1959 *Los Angeles Times* GP. (Photo Courtesy Allen Kuhn/vintage-sportscar-photos.com)

roll Shelby's Maserati 450S for the feature win. Shelby moved by him in the end, but Gurney had emerged as the course's first homegrown superstar. There would be others.

In late 1957, the USAC sanctioned the first stock car race, which was a 250-mile event. It pulled another good crowd of spectators standing behind the inevitable snow fencing: no grandstands, only a few bleachers had been installed. Jerry of the famous Unser family won in a 1956 Mercury.

1958: Premier *Los Angeles Times* Grand Prix

After some club racing in the interim, including a reverse-track midget race, the USAC and the Cal Club (not yet an SCCA affiliate) co-sanctioned the first premier event at the track, which came off in October 1958. Everything changed, not just for Riverside, but also for the sport in the whole country. Riverside secured the *Los Angeles Times* as a sponsor for its Grand Prix.

The *Los Angeles Times* was the leading newspaper in the area with a huge circulation, and it sponsored the event to support its growing list of car advertising clients. The paper's sponsorship and promotion helped the Grand Prix pull in more than 75,000 people that first year. Spectators were lured to the Grand Prix not only by the paper's great advertising for the event, but also by the presence of many of the world's top drivers and cars. From overseas came Jo Bonnier, Ray Salvadori, and Jean Behra to face off against all the top U.S. drivers.

News from the event was carried in newspapers all over the country, and it received more exposure than almost any other racing event except the Indianapolis 500. Car magazines featured the Grand Prix in major feature stories and on the cover. That first year did not disappoint either. An American

Riverside Superstar Dan Gurney

It was almost uncannily fitting that the first race at Riverside, a Cal Club event, saw the emergence of America's most popular and recognizable superstar driver of the period: Dan Gurney. Just 26 years old, Gurney drove a modified Corvette to 1st in a production race win, then made a great showing in the open feature. Not just his finishes but also his driving skill attracted a lot of attention. Through the years, Dan became the King of Riverside, and in the 1960s he achieved an impressive string of victories, fast laps, and high placings in a variety of cars. As were so many drivers of the era, Dan was seemingly at ease in everything from Indy cars to NASCAR stockers, and he drove all of them especially well at Riverside. He followed up this first race win at Riverside with an even more impressive showing at the season-ending SCCA National on November 17. He was driving an Arciero Brothers Ferrari and dueled wheel-to-wheel with Carroll Shelby before finally losing to the superstar Texan.

Gurney gained more fame outside of sports car circles when he won the first NASCAR event since 1958, the *Motor Trend* 500 in January 1963. He then went on to win three more of the annual Riverside 500-milers in a row, plus another in 1968 and a 400 as well. Years later, Gurney remembers winning those stock car races as his greatest thrill at Riverside.

It was fitting that the last race of Dan Gurney's fantastic career was at Riverside. The 1970 Trans-Am event, the Mission Bell 200, was his retirement event. It would have been wonderful if he had gone out on top, but he did finish a very competitive 5th.

In the 1970s, Gurney built a successful racing team and was a force in the development of drivers and cars. Then, suddenly, in 1980, he stunned the racing world by announcing an end to his decade-long retirement to drive a NASCAR event at Riverside. Despite misgivings from others, Gurney showed that he still had the magic, at Riverside at least. He ran 2nd until his transmission failed. Having shown to all that he still had what it took, Dan retired again, this time for good.

Gurney's prolific career at Riverside is reflected in the number of existing photos of him racing on that fabulous circuit. I wish I could have included more here.

Dan Gurney dominated at Riverside, winning five Grand Nationals and two Rex Mays 300s; he earned the title "King of Riverside." He proved he was a versatile and talented driver year after year and was always very fast in whatever he drove there. (Photo Courtesy Allen Kuhn/vintage-sportscar-photos.com)

---

driver, local boy Chuck Daigh, in an American-built Scarab, won over Phil Hill, Jerry Unser, and, of course, Dan Gurney, as well as the international drivers and cars. Present day Riverside Museum curator Pat Flynn remembers that, as a 15-year-old, he and his parents drove for almost six hours, most of it sitting in long lines on the freeway, to and from Riverside for the event, and did not mind it a bit.

The significance of this 1958 event cannot be overstated. Its popularity forced the SCCA to begin a reassessment of its amateurs-only rules and eventually helped lead to full-fledged professional road racing in the United States. A different kind of significance was the first and only staging of three 500-milers on the same weekend: one for midgets, one for sprint cars, and one for stock cars. The tepid reaction to the weekend gave rise to the feeling that only sports cars could make it at Riverside.

Right after the Grand Prix of that year came the track's first on-screen appearance. *On the Beach*, an apocalyptic major-studio movie, used Riverside for its mayhem-filled car race sequence to spectacular advantage. The track was used in several other movies and TV shows through the years.

Not much new happened at Riverside in 1959, although one USAC club event in mid-July was memorable for its record heat that took out a few drivers. But as Ken Miles said, "This *is* the desert after all." The *Los Angeles Times* (owned by the Times Mirror Company, although the *Mirror* was never in the name of the race) Grand Prix did draw everyone again, including the famous Stirling Moss. In the end, however, Phil Hill, a fan favorite thanks to his Southern California roots, won the day in a beautiful 3-liter Ferrari while Moss, Gurney, and Richie Ginther among others had to retire. Gurney's demise

Carroll Shelby in a Birdcage Maserati (#98) posted his last win as a driver at the 1960 USAC race, beating Jack Brabham (Cooper, #3) and others. (Photo Courtesy Allen Kuhn/vintage-sportscar-photos.com)

Even though it was recorded as just a DNF, Dan Gurney (amazingly) led several laps in the 1960 USAC race in the legendary but sadly outdated *Old Yeller*. (Photo Courtesy Allen Kuhn, vintage-sportscar-photos.com)

Stirling Moss won the 1960 United States Grand Prix (USGP). Everyone was amazed at the skill the famous English driver showed in his Lotus 18, as he won easily and turned the first sub-2:00 lap at Riverside with a 1:55. (Photo Courtesy Allen Kuhn/vintage-sportscar-photos.com)

in the race came in a starting line crunch. The crowd was even bigger than for the previous year's race. The consensus at the time was that the USAC was the future, and the SCCA, trying to cling to its amateurs-only ruling, was strangling itself.

Although the on-track action was remarkable, the amenities at Riverside in 1959 and 1960 left a lot to be desired. Course fencing was substandard. In many places, snow fencing was used to keep spectators from getting too close to the track. Too many places had no fencing at all. Restroom facilities were completely inadequate. Despite the revenue opportunities presented by the heat and dust, relatively few concession stands were available to help people quench their thirst. Still, people came. However, some, including Seattle area racer LeRoy Johnson and his brother, vowed never to return.

1960: Formula 1 Arrives

Despite the drawbacks, huge crowds were still attracted by feature events, but other weekends were slow. By mid-1960 Riverside was suffering from cash flow problems. It would have been unbelievable to people sitting in the huge traffic jams coming to or going home from the *Los Angeles Times* event or waiting in long lines for refreshments at the races but the track was losing money. Cleye was not cash-rich and John Edgar, his principal backer, was losing interest. Local racer Dean Mears was supposedly buying the track and planning questionable changes that included moving the pit area to the inside of Turn 9 and building grandstands on the present pit area. The sales price was said to be $350,000 and two of John Edgar's best racing cars.

With the sale apparently stalled, the season went ahead as planned under the same management. A break came when the other Los Angeles daily newspaper, the *Examiner-Herald Express*, moved its annual spring race from Pomona to Riverside. Nobody knew it yet, but Carroll Shelby was in the last few months of his active driving career. In the race, he drove a Maserati Tipo 61 to the win. The USAC-sanctioned event drew another great field of competitors and a large crowd of again more than 70,000, but the newspaper decided to bow out of racing, citing the expense and the bad publicity when a driver was killed.

The 1960 season was scheduled to finish with a real double-header: the first true Formula 1 U.S. Grand Prix as well as the annual *Los Angeles Times* Grand Prix, this year called the Grand Prix for Sports Cars. First came the *Times* event. *Competition Press* reporter Dennis Shattuck, who had seen a lot of races, called it "unequivocally the best race ever held on the West Coast, (and) it might have been the best ever in the United States." Highly reputed drivers and brilliant machines engaged in field-deep duels. Up front, it was a crowd-pleasing battle between Gurney and Moss for the lead, although both had to retire, letting popular Southern California driver Billy Krause earn the win, famously coasting across the line on an empty gas tank.

Formula 1 was the crown jewel of European motorsport and was becoming the preeminent international racing series. But when the U.S. Grand Prix was held a month after the *Times* event, spectator attendance was astonishingly low. Only 25,000 or so people showed up. It may have been as a result of the small advertising and publicity campaign event promoter Alec Ullman put in, nothing compared to what the *Times* had done for its event. Or it may have been the absence of the Ferrari team. At any rate, the disappointing turnout ensured there would not be another Formula 1 Grand Prix event on the West Coast for some time, and never again at Riverside. Stirling Moss won the race and every true race fan there was awed by the display of superior driving shown by the international Formula 1 drivers. Moss, in his Lotus 18, lowered the absolute lap record to 1:55, the first time anyone had turned a lap under two minutes.

1961: Crashes

Riverside showed its teeth in an early-season Cal Club race when seven bad smash-ups and rollovers occurred. Thankfully no one was badly hurt, but everyone was reminded that it was still a challenging course for both novice and amateur drivers. Riverside management showed that it could be creative by scheduling an early season event that pitted stock cars against sports cars on the short 2.58-mile course. The stockers won, although a Lotus 17 in the hands of Billy Kraus turned

At the 1960 USGP, American privateer Pete Lovely in a Cooper-Ferrari hybrid leads a mid-race pack consisting of, in order behind him, Wolfgang Von Tripps (Cooper-Maserati), Chuck Daigh (Scarab), Ron Flockhart (Cooper-Climax), and Maurice Trintignant (Cooper-Maserati). All finished well behind Moss in his Lotus 18. (Photo Courtesy Riverside Automobile Museum)

in the best lap times. Only 3,500 fans attended; it appeared that West Coast fans were not ready to support stock car road racing. Maybe that was the correct conclusion in 1961, but things were about to change.

In the meantime, fans continued to come out for sports car racing. Even a Cal Club race in early March brought out 8,500 fans. Spectators there saw the latest Riverside hot shot, Dave MacDonald, win in the most recent *Old Yeller*, one of a line of famous local specials that were crowd favorites.

1962: The Grand Prix Marches On

Riverside produced memorable if not historic racing for 1961 and 1962. Low attendance put the track under more financial pressure, but both seasons ended on high notes, and the track had the power of the *Los Angeles Times* behind its Grand Prix. Jack Brabham became the first international driver to win the prestigious event when he drove a Cooper Monaco to victory with Bruce McLaren right behind.

In 1962, Roger Penske won in the controversial *Zerex Special*. Although this car conformed to the rules, it was basically a Formula 1 Cooper with stretched bodywork and a bogus tiny passenger seat so it qualified as a "sports car." The 1962 race was marred by the death of the highly popular Pat Piggott, a Pacific Northwest racer just beginning to make his mark on the national scene. Both events were affected by the weather.

The 1961 race had sweltering 96-degree heat and 30 mph winds. Spectators kept coming out for the yearly Grand Prix (more than 80,000 in 1961) despite such tough conditions. Fans may have noticed that a new type of car was becoming more popular. It was less bulky and noisy, a smaller mid-engined car that could rev high and turn quickly. Fast and interesting maybe, but not as much fun as the bellowing beasts and beautifully-bodied front-engined Italian cars that were crowd favorites from the track's early days.

1963: Les Richter and NASCAR

Les Richter is the name most associated with the track during its years of operation. With a reputation as one of the fiercest and most accomplished pro football linebackers of the 1950s (Los Angeles Rams), Richter brought an imposing presence to all Riverside business and media meetings. When he retired from football in 1962 he was immediately hired to run Riverside as general manager. An odd choice on the surface, but Richter was as smart as he was tough. And, as a youngster in the Los Angeles area he had enjoyed dirt-track racing.

A new ownership group made up of Bob Hope, Fred Levy, Robert Petersen, and Rams football club owner Ed Pauley brought Richter in and told him to make the track profitable,

period. Looking around, he saw that NASCAR had not run at Riverside since 1958 and that other than the *Los Angeles Times* event no other big-time races were on the schedule that could draw the crowds they needed. The spectator potential that was so obvious when the track was built was still there, so Richter went right to work. Under his direction, 1963 was a turn-around year for the track and soon Richter was the face of Riverside.

Dan Gurney (Lotus 19) leads Jack Brabham (Cooper Monaco) and Bill Krause (Birdcage Maserati) and the rest of the field early at the 1961 *Los Angeles Times* Grand Prix. Brabham won, Gurney took 9th, Krause was a DNF. (Photo Courtesy Allen Kuhn/vintage-sportscar-photos.com)

The Talented Dave MacDonald

In researching a book on racetracks of the 1960s, Dave MacDonald's name keeps appearing; he seemingly won races all over the country. To say he was a protégé of Riverside, though, is in large part true. MacDonald sprang onto the racing scene with as much impact as Dan Gurney, and their early careers paralleled each other. Both made their homes and started their racing careers in Southern California. MacDonald started out in drag racing at age 20 with a 1955 Corvette and won more than 100 trophies in four seasons. He burst upon the road-racing scene at Willow Springs in 1960 and was immediately successful in that venue as well.

He first gained national recognition, though, for several outstanding efforts at Riverside where his aggressive sliding style of driving earned him the title "King of Oversteer." His balls-out slides around Turn 6 at Riverside were the stuff of legend. Unlike some drivers whose slides slowed them down, MacDonald had an almost uncanny skill to use slides to his advantage, slowing less going into corners and then accelerating sooner coming out of them. MacDonald's feats at Riverside, as well as his driving style, made him a huge crowd favorite there and he did not often let his fans down. He raced a new Sting Ray wheel-to-wheel with a new Shelby Cobra late in 1962 in a highly anticipated Riverside showdown that saw both cars drop out before the race ended. Impressed with this showing, Shelby hired MacDonald to drive for his Cobra team and he did not let "Ol' Shel" down, winning two races at the team's initial outing at Riverside in February 1963. Shelby introduced a lethal new car, the fabled King Cobra in the fall of 1963;

Dave MacDonald won the 1963 *Los Angeles Times* Grand Prix in masterful style aboard a King Cobra, amazing everyone with well-controlled power slides through the turns. (Photo Courtesy Riverside Automobile Museum)

MacDonald won the *Los Angeles Times* Grand Prix in one. More successes came in 1964 with the Cobra team before MacDonald was killed at age 27 in a fiery crash at Indianapolis that year. Riverside and America had lost one of its most popular drivers and rising young stars.

In his short career he competed in 115 races with 47 victories and 69 top-three finishes. Despite his status at Riverside, there is nothing there to remember him or mark his presence. However, across the country, in the housing development that stands over the site of the old Augusta Raceway, Dave MacDonald Street keeps alive the memory of the two races he drove there, coming in 1st and 2nd. Utterly fearless and immensely talented, MacDonald personified the saying: "There are old racing drivers and there are bold racing drivers, but there are few old, bold racing drivers."

NASCAR saw Riverside's new potential, and with Richter's encouragement it jumped right in. No less than three stock car races were scheduled at the track for its 1963 season: a 500-miler plus a 400- and a 250-mile event. The January Riverside 500-miler was huge, with drivers from all forms of motor racing, ovals to roads, showing up to drive stock cars. The track was off and running again and 50,000 spectators showed up.

After coming close so many times, Dan Gurney won his first feature at Riverside on the short 2.6-mile course. Fans were delighted with the stop again–start again pace of the race, which drew the field close again many times for yellow flags. The race was long, five hours plus in the early years, but that was not a deterrent to fans' enjoyment. The size and color of the cars and their personable but feisty young drivers was appealing, too.

NASCAR had revived the track and brought it new exposure. Considerable doubt existed about the ability of stock car racing to draw fans to Riverside, but the 1963 500 and the other stock car events that year proved that theory wrong. And more good stuff was to come.

Drag racing was added that same year and the track now featured three big events: the 500, the *Los Angeles Times* GP, and the NHRA drags. The 500 was to have more than one name over the years, as new sponsors jumped on. After 1964 it was the *Motor Trend* 500, then in 1971 it became the Winston Western, which ran from 1972 through 1987.

Club races were held, too. Cal Club continued to put on events such as the June 22–23 Pacific Coast Championship race that drew 275 entrants and 8,500 spectators. The numbers were plenty good to keep track management happy and to keep club racing on the Riverside schedule, where it stayed strong until the end.

The *Los Angeles Times* Grand Prix was great again in 1963; 82,000 fans came out to watch one of Dave MacDonald's (and

The immortal Jim Clark in a Lotus 23 at Riverside. He did not have the car to compete against eventual winner Jack Brabham in a Cooper-Monaco, but took 5th overall, 1st in U-2 at the 1963 *Los Angeles Times* GP. (Photo Courtesy Riverside Automobile Museum)

the track's) all-time great performances, wowing the crowd with his sliding, free-for-all style in a King Cobra. The list of people he beat is impressive: Jim Clark, John Surtees, Pedro Rodríguez, A. J. Foyt, Dan Gurney, Jim Hall, and many more. Everyone kept coming to compete in as well as to watch the *Los Angeles Times* Grand Prix!

Soon after the Grand Prix came the second big stock car race of the year, the Golden State 400, where Dave MacDonald once again thrilled the crowd with an out-of-the-box performance, although he brought his ailing car in only 4th. Darel Dieringer won in a new Mercury. The event was tarnished a bit by USAC, which issued a ban forcing its drivers to avoid the event. However, 32,000 fans came out to demonstrate the appeal of stock car racing, even with a reduced field.

The big Riverside grandstands held thousands of fans, and there was hardly an empty seat in the house when stock car races became more popular in the late 1960s. (Photo Courtesy Riverside Automobile Museum)

1964: USRRC Arrives

For 1964, a new professional series came to the desert track: the SCCA's United States Road Racing Championship (USRRC). The country-wide series was gaining a lot of popularity and had missed a stop in the 1963 season at Riverside because of scheduling conflicts. This year they were there in a big way for an early April event that saw Californian Skip Hudson power a Chevy-engined Cooper to the win. Nobody knew, of course, that it would be Dave MacDonald's last appearance at Riverside. He looked good and led for a while but his King Cobra could not hold up.

A new road-racing star was born at that year's *Los Angeles Times* Grand Prix. Although Parnelli Jones had been a top oval driver for a few years, and had actually won that year's Indy 500, his road racing talents were largely unknown. Carroll Shelby gave him a ride in this sports car event in one of his team's King Cobras. He didn't let anyone down as he won the event with apparent ease. Again it was a top-notch field, this time including Jim Clark, who took 3rd in one of those notoriously poor-handling Lotus 30s. Another record crowd was on hand, this time 83,000-plus. Dan Gurney failed to finish, as was so often the case in sports cars here, but he did set a new lap record of 1:29.03.

Even if not that many fans came out, drivers came to Riverside from all over the country in November to compete in the SCCA's first National Runoffs (of sorts), the American Road Race of Champions (ARRC). Competing in regional races all year to qualify for the national championship event, more than 300 drivers showed up for two long days of competitive races in all classes. Everything went well except for some unseasonal weather that saw windstorms and cold temperatures make things very uncomfortable off the track. This was not what drivers from New England had packed their swimsuits and sunscreen for!

Late 1960s: The Golden Era

Stock car racing now started to become much bigger at the track. In fact, everything became bigger at the track and Riverside was able to consistently attract more top talent and bigger crowds than any other racetrack in America.

The annual 500, the first big stock car event of the year, became a showcase for Dan Gurney and this is where he really earned his reputation as the King of Riverside. It was great for local fans to see one of their own beat all the famous Southern NASCAR boys, and they flocked to the track to see it year after year, rarely disappointed in the second half of the 1960s. Both road racers and stock car drivers competed in the 500s, and they also came out for the Can-Am races that followed. It was the headiest mixture anywhere of the top drivers from both disciplines.

By 1967, the attendance for a NASCAR event was almost at *Los Angeles Times* Grand Prix numbers: 76,000. Stock cars were featured at the track twice each year beginning in 1970, with the Winston West 500 taking the place of the *Motor Trend* 500. A succession of beer companies sponsored another 400-miler six months later: Falstaff, Tuborg, and then Budweiser from 1982 through 1988.

In 1967, Parnelli Jones won the 500-mile event, which continued as the most prestigious, but after Gurney's win the following year the good ol' boys did pretty much take over. In 1969, Richard Petty won in a Plymouth and from then on the winner's circle saw names including Bobby Allison, Cale Yarborough, David Pearson, Darrell Waltrip, Terry LaBonte, and Rusty Wallace.

Southern California showed its wet side, too, as the 1972 500 was canceled after 387 miles with Petty in the lead because of heavy fog. Mark Donohue did sneak in there for one last road racing name victory in 1973, but by then it was obvious that stock car drivers could more than handle a road course once they made up their minds to do so. If you were good on ovals, you'd be good on the road.

Riverside Hosts the Premier Series

It was not just stock cars that made Riverside boom. Far from it. The *Los Angeles Times* Grand Prix always drew big crowds, over 80,000 annually, and brought the track press coverage everywhere. The second half of the 1960s saw the emergence of several big series: Trans-Am, Can-Am, the USAC road races, and Formula 5000, all generating a lot of press coverage, and drawing top names and big crowds. Of course, ten years later they had all pretty much fizzled out for a variety of reasons. Let's look at how they played out at Riverside.

Can-Am (the Canadian American Challenge Cup) was the biggest sports car racing event, in terms of publicity and prestige, ever at Riverside. The Johnson Wax–sponsored events offered big prize money, both race-by-race and for the season championship. Can-Am took over from the USRRC series after the SCCA ended the USRRC after the 1968 season, but by then Can-Am was far ahead in popularity with drivers and fans anyway. The USRRC held an event at Riverside right through its last season, seeing winners such as Mark Donohue, Jim Hall, and Buck Fulp. Donohue and others raced both in the USRRC and Can-Am, but their primary focus was Can-Am.

After the 1966 season saw the Can-Am series off to a great start, it really took off in 1967. The *Los Angeles Times* saw which way the wind was blowing and Can-Am became the race series for its Grand Prix from 1966 through 1973.

Mark Donohue winning the 1967 USRRC in his Penske Sunoco Lola T70. (Photo Courtesy Riverside Automobile Museum)

Ken Miles in a Cobra at the 1965 USRRC where he won the Manufacturers' Race but had a mechanical DNF in the Drivers' Race. (Photo Courtesy Riverside Automobile Museum)

International drivers and their imported cars with big-block Chevys took the lion's share of 1st-place trophies in those years. It started with John Surtees in 1966 (Lola). Then Bruce McLaren and Denny Hulme ("the Bruce and Denny show") dominated for a few years in their McLarens, but did it with such independent, seat-of-your-pants flair that no one came to resent them the way they resented Porsche a few years later. Contenders came and went, some were crowd favorites, but in the end it was always an orange McLaren on top. Preparation was the key because other teams had similar resources and could buy their own big-block Chevys, but no one could run at speed lap after lap and race after race the way the McLarens did. The ever-innovative Jim Hall even tried a different kind of ground effect, and the 1970 *Sucker* Chaparral with its snow machine motors sucking the ground made its final appearance at that year's Riverside Can-Am.

Chaparral teammate Hap Sharp won the 1965 *Los Angeles Times* race over the usual strong field that included the great Jim Clark, among others. Hall's best placing in the Grand Prix was 2nd, which he did three times, in 1962, 1966, and 1967. Hall was also 3rd twice, 1961 and 1968. Right after the 1968 event was Hall's famous Stardust crash, which ended his Can-Am racing days.

Jim Hall and the Brilliant Chaparrals

No one was more innovative and persistent than Jim Hall in the 1960s. Storming out of Texas, his Chevy-powered Chaparral team achieved a lot of success, but is perhaps most memorable for pioneering the use of wings, automatic transmissions, and finally the "vacuum cleaner" ground-effects car. Hall raced at Riverside each year of the 1960s, starting with the U.S. Grand Prix, through 1968. He often led or was a top contender and won an overall victory at the 1965 USRRC.

His team put in their best efforts for the USRRC and Can-Am races, and his

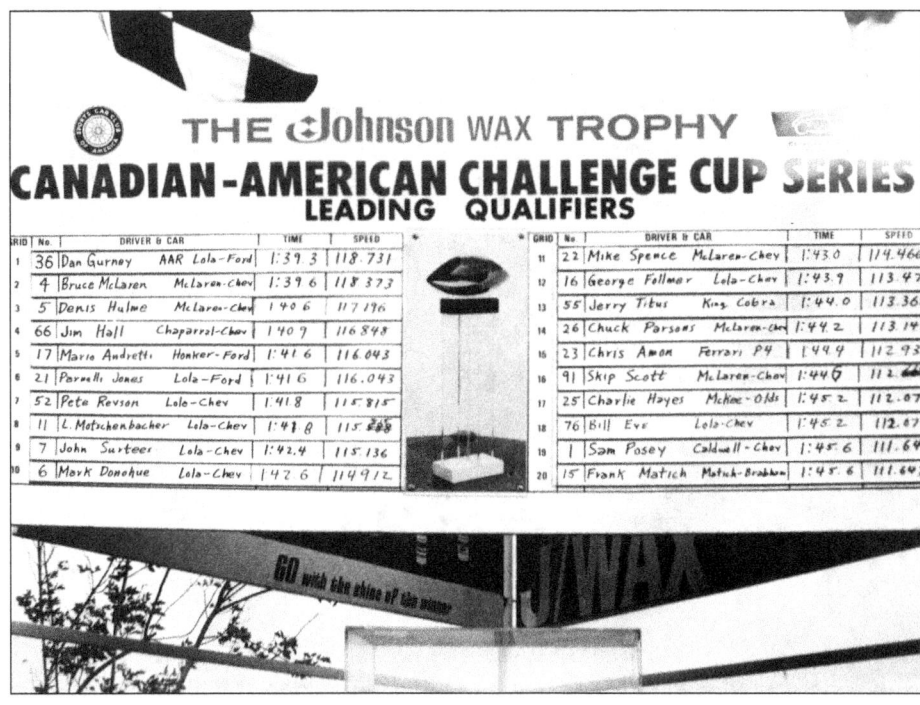

In the days before digital broadcasts . . . The qualifying board for the 1967 Can-Am race shows a terrific field. (John Lacke Photo, Courtesy Riverside Automobile Museum)

A great study of Bruce McLaren winning the 1967 Can-Am at Riverside in one of his fabulously successful cars. (Photo Courtesy Riverside Automobile Museum)

Tommy Smothers was finally convinced to join brother Dick for a Riverside Continental Championship, and it's obvious why. (Photo Courtesy Riverside Automobile Museum)

The spectacularly high-winged and beautiful 1968 Chaparral was fastest at the USRRC race that year, but could not start the final. (Photo Courtesy Riverside Automobile Museum)

He continued to build Can-Am cars, of course, and Hall's ground-effects Chaparral 2J is as interesting and controversial a car as ever raced at Riverside. The ground-sucking Chaparral was amazingly quick and, in fact, set a new Riverside lap record of 1:32.49 in qualifying for the 1970 Can-Am. The car broke down in the race itself, though, when it notably went off track and sucked up yards of desert dirt and sand, spewing it out in a long, dirty, white tail behind. The car was soon banned despite Hall's protestations that this was supposed to be an unlimited racing series, wasn't it? Hall appeared at Riverside again as part of the original Trans-Am series but the cars he designed and built were pretty much over by the early 1970s. Regardless, his white Chaparrals were always beautiful and brutally fast. They are icons of the 1960s racing scene as much as are the curvy Ferraris of the 1950s.

1966–1971: Trans-Am

For a variety of reasons, the SCCA changed Can-Am to reduce its unlimited engine sizes and wild body styles (read: "wings") in the early 1970s. Mark Donohue and George Follmer in factory-prepared and Penske-maintained Porsche 917s came to dominate the series as no one had before in terms of overwhelming victories. The Can-Am fell from popularity so fast that its season was canceled half way through 1984, before the circus even arrived at Riverside. Right through 1983, though, the series' stop at Riverside continued to draw vast crowds as each year's *Los Angeles Times* Grand Prix feature.

Riverside added new attractions to the 1972 *Los Angeles Times* Grand Prix. In addition to the Can-Am racers, Super Vees, 2.5-liter Trans-Ams, and even motorcycles were added to boost attendance, and it worked. But not well enough. The *Los Angeles Times* pulled out after a 1973 Can-Am that drew "only" 65,000 people. Then, to add insult to injury, it switched from roads to an oval and moved the venue for its prestigiously named event to the competing Ontario Motor Speedway.

Trans-Am was not far behind Can-Am in popularity and young Southern California freeway drivers readily identified with the pony cars. The original Trans-Am series ran there from 1966 through 1971. Many of the same names were on top of the standings in Trans-Am: Gurney, Donohue, Jones, Hall . . . but this time in Detroit-prepared cars including Mustang, Camaro, Cougar, Barracuda, Firebird, and then even AMC Javelins.

Starting in 1966, Riverside hosted the final event for the series, and the title was decided right there in 1969. A sensational drive by Jerry Titus cinched the win and the season title for Ford. During its heyday, Riverside's Mission Inn sponsored the annual early-fall Trans-Am event as the Mission Bell 250 (in 1971 it was run as a 200). Dan Gurney was one of

Even on the pace lap for the stockers someone cannot resist dirt tracking. Stock car drivers were notorious for driving straight ahead out of Turn 2 and rejoining the pavement just before Turn 6, saving a few precious yards each lap. (Photo Courtesy Riverside Automobile Museum)

the top contenders in the series, of course, but he never won a Trans-Am at Riverside. Parnelli Jones' 1970 win there was probably the most enjoyable of the series races at Riverside. He simply willed his Ford Mustang around the track, dirt-tracking and frequently cornering on two wheels, and finished 1st with battered bodies: his and the car's.

The 1971 Mission Bell 200 was a far cry in popularity from its 1970 predecessor, and that was the last Trans-Am of the original series at Riverside, something that would have been unthinkable just a year earlier. The climate had changed for auto racing, nowhere more so than in this Detroit-backed form. Ten years later Trans-Am returned with new cars, really shells of current Detroit models with vastly souped-up engines, but they did not attract the kind of following that had been hoped for, nationally or at Riverside. Despite some prestigious sponsors such as Coca-Cola and Meguiar's, the series hosted just four races at Riverside, the last in 1986.

1967: USAC Debuts a New Event

USAC Indy Cars came along in 1967 with a new event: the Rex Mays 300. These events were more prestigious than popular and the series could not wait to jump to the new Ontario track when it opened in 1970. Rex Mays was a popular figure in the area when he was national oval track champ in the 1940s but his name meant little to a new crop of race fans. They did not turn out in vast numbers and so missed some stirring racing. Dan Gurney won the first two editions of the Mays in his own All-American Racers Eagle, with Mario Andretti taking the 1969 version in a Brawner Hawk with Gurney 3rd. The first two races were hard fought and vastly entertaining but played out in front of a small audience. The third Rex Mays event again did not pull well.

1969: Track Upgrades

Although the profitability and popularity of the track was on the rise, Richter invested in infrastructure, trying to make the basically inhospitable locale more inviting to both drivers and spectators. In 1969 Turn 9 was modified with the addition of a dogleg to make it less of an abrupt hairpin and slow down the straightaway speeds a bit. Huge metal grandstands were purchased from the Rose Parade group and installed along the first turns of the course.

Here is the ubiquitous Dan Gurney in a Plymouth AAR 'Cuda at the 1970 Trans-Am race at which he came in 5th. (Photo Courtesy Riverside Automobile Museum)

The Goodyear Tower was purchased (for $1.00!) from the Los Angeles International Airport and installed first at the start/finish line and then moved farther up the track. The Tower featured three levels, one for operations, one for the press, and one as a luxurious lounge for sponsors, VIPs, and others (at the discretion of Riverside management). Grandstands were also installed at Turn 6, one of the most popular viewing spots on the course.

American Raceways, Inc., became virtual owner of the track in 1969, with Richter now a vice president of the new company.

Dan Gurney was usually the master of Indy cars at the Rex Mays Riverside races. In this 1969 edition, he was "only" 3rd. He led eventual winner Mario Andretti (#1) and 2nd-place finisher Al Unser (#15). (Photo Courtesy Riverside Automobile Museum)

Motorhomes had just come into vogue in the early 1980s and spectators employed them to their best use to see the action at a Cal Club race. (Photo Courtesy Riverside Automobile Museum)

The leading pack of Formula 5000s are coming at Turn 6 in a hurry in an early-1970s race. (Photo Courtesy John McCollister)

128   Lost Road Courses

Stock Car Legend Bobby Allison at Riverside

Bobby Allison reigns as the top stock car driver at Riverside over the years, taking up when Dan Gurney retired. On the short 2.62-mile road course that the stockers used, he was hard to beat. He also won the International Race of Champions (IROC) event twice there, once with a broken back, showing his versatility as well as his high pain threshold. His first race at Riverside was less than memorable; in 1965 he started 42nd and finished 29th in the *Motor Trend* 500. But he made up for it afterward. He ended up with six wins and $360,000 in winnings. Allison placed in the top five in 19 races and top 10 in 25 events. He holds the unusual distinction of winning the 1975 Winston Western 500 in an AMC Matador, one of the best performances ever anywhere for that ill-fated car.

Bobby Allison was a top finisher at Riverside for several years in the early 1980s driving his Miller Hi-Life Buick. (Photo Courtesy Riverside Automobile Museum)

1974–1976: Formula 5000

Meanwhile, Formula 5000 had done well, especially when compared to the cost to put on a USAC or CART event. Using readily available American V-8s and European open-wheeled chassis, F5000 offered fast and loud racing, which was very attractive in its first few years in the late 1960s and early 1970s. Such drivers as Mario Andretti and Brian Redman won at Riverside in cars including Lolas and Chevrons. The "L&M" years were the best; the cigarette company could really put advertising muscle behind the series. The top F5000 event at Riverside, though, was probably the 1974 race that was put into the Can-Am weekend slot when that series folded. Mario Andretti won over such luminaries as Bobby Unser and Brian Redman. The last F5000 at the track was in 1976, and the series was folded into the new single-seater Can-Am group, which, in the end, did neither group much good.

1973: Inaugural IROC

Road racing could and did draw for events other than stock cars. IROC was dreamed up at Riverside to pit the world's best drivers from all forms of car racing together in identical cars and see who came out on top. The event was started at Riverside and succeeded as well as anything else at the time. At first 12 drivers were invited for the inaugural 1973 IROC that saw everyone driving identically prepared Porsche 911 RSRs. Several tracks hosted stops in each year's IROC, which saw a variety of series champions.

Bobby Allison won that first year, further establishing stock car racers' ability on road courses. Camaros replaced Porsches and different drivers won at different tracks, in some of the best road racing ever seen. In that light, the series was a complete success, at Riverside as well as elsewhere. A nice TV contract for the series helped, too.

The enormous air intake of mid-1970s F5000 cars is shown here on the Lola T332C of Alan Jones at the 1976 F5000 race at Riverside. He took 4th and Al Unser won. (Photo Courtesy Riverside Automobile Museum)

The series was held at Riverside from 1973 through 1979 and then one more time in 1988. Illustrating how diverse the results were, winners at Riverside's IROC included Scott Pruett, Mario Andretti, Cale Yarborough, Bobby Allison, Emerson Fittipaldi, and Mark Donohue.

1977: Can-Am Revisited

Single-seater Can-Am cars came to the track in 1977 as the SCCA tried a Hail Mary to resurrect the once-popular series. This time around they simply re-bodied F5000 cars from that defunct series to make them into single-seater closed-body cars. My, how much had changed in just six years! The new series lasted 10 years and produced some very fast cars that still dominate vintage racing events today, but it was not nearly as popular as the original Can-Am series. Riverside hosted seven such events, with sponsors including Pepsi and Budweiser; it featured some good racing and heroes such as Alan Jones and Al Holbert.

1979: IMSA Success

IMSA racing came to Riverside in 1979 and the series then ran yearly at the track almost to the end. It was the country's last big sports car series and was successful for a time everywhere they raced. But at Riverside, IMSA came to the track only because the *Los Angeles Times*, after several years' absence, agreed to sponsor an IMSA race and bring back that magic name: the *Los Angeles Times* Grand Prix. Who could resist? Certainly not Les Richter, who had been slow to embrace the new series.

The 1981 Camel GT IMSA event was an especially big one; it was a stop on the World Sports Car Championship circuit. Jim Busby, in a Porsche 935 K3/80, won. All the way through 1987, the *Los Angeles Times* Grand Prix was held for IMSA cars, although the newspaper took on several partners, so the event was at times the *Los Angeles Times*/Toyota Grand Prix, the *Times*/Nissan Grand Prix, and even the *Times*/Ford Grand Prix, before bowing out in 1987 as once again simply the *Los Angeles Times* Grand Prix.

The IMSA series played out with Porsche 935s and BMWs on top in the early years, before more fearsome GTP cars took over. A Porsche won again in 1983, but from then on it was GTP cars in the winner's circle: Porsche, Lola, and Nissan. Drivers began to express the opinion that Riverside, a course built in the 1950s, was proving unsuitable for racing the high-powered IMSA cars of the late 1980s.

The last big road race at Riverside other than for stock cars was the 1987 *Los Angeles Times* IMSA. This one featured Paul Newman in a very fast Datsun Z-car; however, he did not finish due to a minor crack-up. Newman *was* an accomplished race car driver and took 3rd in a 1983 Trans-Am race at the track. A Jaguar won this final race, a fitting end even if the sleek GTP car had no resemblance to the XK Jaguars that were such a factor in the track's early days.

1980: The End is Near

The track went to some odd lengths to save itself. For example, over one 1980 weekend, it hosted bicycle, roller-skate, and running races as well as Can-Am and Trans-Am. One innovation did work: off-road racing. This increasingly popular form of motor racing seemed made for Riverside, with its combination of road course and surrounding desert landscape proving perfect for the very competitive and popular racing from that group.

A 7.6-mile course was created in the original turkey ranch lands, and off-road racing was featured at the track right until

In the 1978 International Race of Champions (IROC), Gordon Johncock leads Al Unser, Al Holbert, and Bobby Unser. But Super Tex A. J. Foyt won this one. The popular series that pitted top drivers against each other in identical production cars was conceived at Riverside and held there for several years. (Photo Courtesy John McCollister)

the end. Parnelli Jones was the best-known convert to this type of racing. His rough and tumble ways seemed to suit the highly competitive off-road racing world.

Management noticed that another open-wheeled racing series, Formula 5000, was as popular with fans and cost less to bring to the track. That series ran in a few forms through the 1980s, and could still draw crowds of more than 50,000 in the mid-1970s. Indy car racing came back to the track for the CART series in 1981, 1982, and 1983, but these events did not pull as well at Riverside as they did elsewhere. At first glance, they did appear to be getting large crowds; however, most of the 40,000-plus fans that came out in stifling August heat, each time, were there more to see an accompanying 400-mile NASCAR race. CART's open-wheeled cars and their drivers suffered in the heat and the series moved away from Riverside for good after the 1983 season. Before then, the event saw such winners as Bobby Rahal (1983) and Rick Mears, twice (1981 and 1982).

It was 1983 that saw the beginning of the end at Riverside. That year, longtime track manager Les Richer sold his share of the track to Fritz Duda, a local real estate developer. Richter had to know what would happen next. Even though Duda was interested in racing, he was still primarily a developer.

New general manager Dan Greenwood worked hard to keep the track busy, but it was only a matter of time until the opportunities presented by the area's growing population were too much to resist. Increasing noise complaints from neighbors, who had moved in long after the track was established, also did not help, unfair as those complaints may have been. The track was closed in 1989 to make room for the inevitable shopping centers and housing developments.

The last professional races were SCORE off-road rambles and a NASCAR Winston West event in 1988. Rusty Wallace

The Moreno Mall entrance sign now stands where Riverside's famed Turn 6 once was. Not a trace is left of the once-great racetrack. Photo Courtesy Judy Rudow)

won the NASCAR event, and thus became the last big-time professional driver to win a feature event at Riverside. On hand as Grand Marshal was Herschel McGriff, who, due to many wins over the years in second-tier stock car races, was actually Riverside's all-time winningest professional driver. The following year saw a few club races and the last efforts of the Skip Barber Racing School. The last laps of racing at the track were under the auspices of the Cal Club, and evacuators and bulldozers were already running in the background as the cars circled the track for the last time. Musing over his years at the racetrack, at the end, Richter acknowledged the many people who had worked to keep racing alive there. "I think that the romance of Riverside over the years was due to the hundreds of people, from different walks of life, that would step forward, work on weekends, work to try to make the raceway a better place to go see speed."

Several miles away from the old location of the track itself stands the Riverside Museum, housing many mementos of road racing at the track. In the late 2000s several popular reunions were held at the museum but now it seems to be in a state of suspended animation as the man who was the driving force behind the museum is no longer with us.

A Porsche finds that it gets lonely on the track and in the stands, during a Riverside IMSA 6-hour enduro. (Photo Courtesy John McCollister)

Today, absolutely nothing remains of the track, not even a random piece of asphalt or street named for the famous drivers and cars that raced there. A recent visit to a computer shop located between old Turn 6 and Turn 7 produced interest from a young sales clerk but no knowledge of the fact that the very ground he was standing on once was pounded by mighty Can-Am cars. The drama, excitement, pathos, and exaltation that surrounded the Riverside track and drew hundreds of thousands of people for 33 years is fading even from local memory.

Roosevelt Raceway

TOO GOOD FOR ITS OWN GOOD

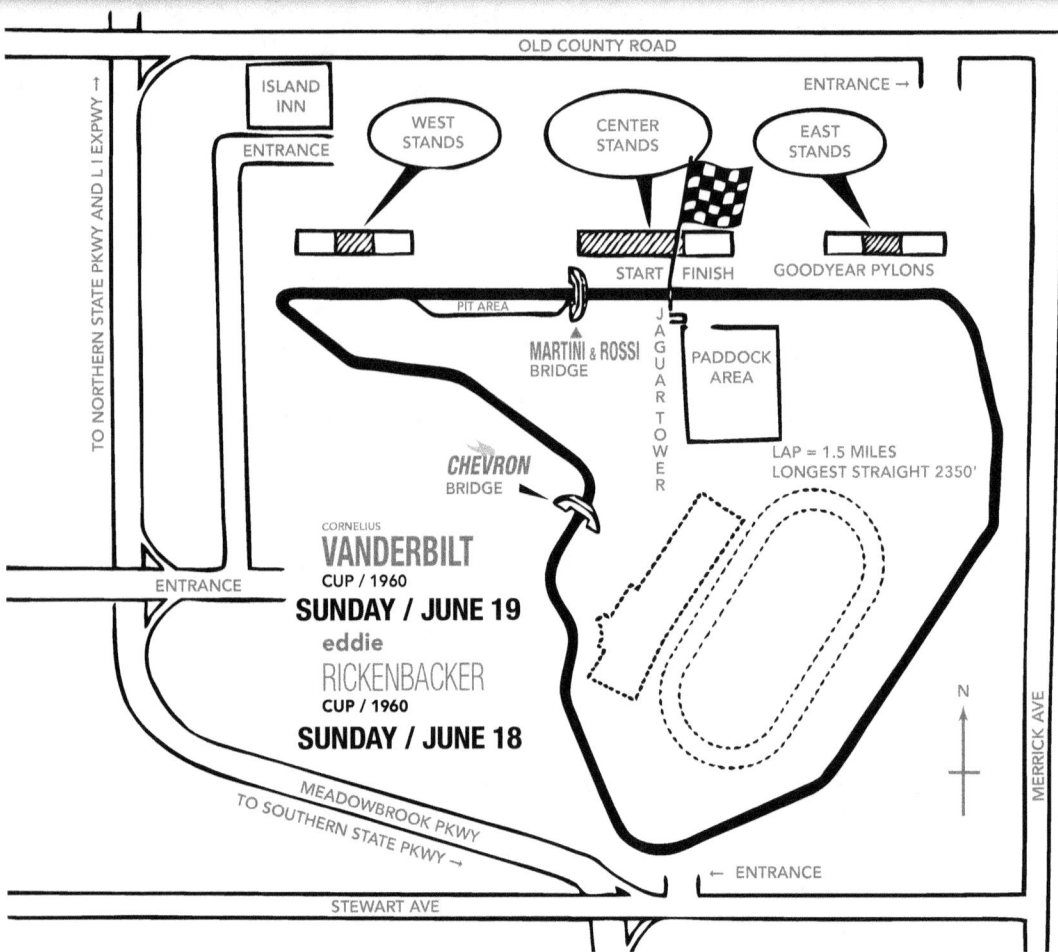

This map shows the last Roosevelt track, laid out in the old parking lot for an SCCA race weekend in 1960. (Illustration Courtesy Martin Spetz Program Collection)

With a few exceptions during the first half of the 20th Century, road racing was not a hugely popular sport in the United States. Then, in the early Depression years, it fell away entirely. The Vanderbilt Cup was an attempt to bring the sport back to prominence and the Roosevelt Raceway was built to accommodate it.

The location chosen for the track, Roosevelt Field in Westbury, New York, was best known for its airstrip from which Charles Lindbergh took off for his famous 1927 trans-Atlantic flight. Just about 30 miles from New York City, it was expected to lure big crowds of race fans from that metropolis. America's best-known hero from World War I and race driver, Captain Eddie Rickenbacker, was one of the guiding forces for the group that was bringing Roosevelt Raceway to life and the Vanderbilt Cup with it. He announced the building of the track and the holding of the Vanderbilt Cup Race in February 1936. Other prestigious and influential backers were the very wealthy George Washington Vanderbilt III, George Preston Marshall, and 1908 Vanderbilt Cup winner George Robertson.

The newly revived Vanderbilt Cup event was a 400-mile road race to be held on Columbus Day, 1936. To really create excitement it was billed as an American-European showdown, with Indy-type cars and drivers facing off against the best of Europe's Grand Prix cars and drivers. This

CHAPTER 13

Westbury, Long Island, New York
1936–1937, 1960

Facility	4 miles, 3.7 miles, 1.5 miles
Principal Events	Open and SCCA racing for the Vanderbilt Cup
Current Status	Shopping malls on property; original facility gone

"Shorty" Cantlon put in a few fast laps in his Miller for the crowd on media day. (Photo Courtesy of Nassau County Department of Parks, Recreation & Museums, Photo Archives Center)

international competition was, in fact, part of the legacy from the original Vanderbilt Cup races.

The name alone, Vanderbilt Cup, carried with it a lot of prestige, and an earlier incarnation of the race, held in the early 1900s, had been one of the few exceptions to the rule that road racing was not popular in the United States. However, that event, held on public roads on Long Island, was so out of control that it was actually lampooned in Ken Purdy's seminal book, *Kings of the Road*. The earlier Vanderbilt Cup was held six times at various Long Island locations and then, despite the huge crowds it drew, or perhaps *because* of the huge crowds it drew, moved to a new location out of state and was last held in 1918.

1936: The First Revival

A massive total purse of $60,000 (1st place alone amounted to more than $600,000 in 2016 dollars) and personal, social, and business clout attracted many of Europe's top teams and America's oval championship drivers as well. This first year the German teams stayed home, though, citing previous commitments to competing events on the continent. Americans who were familiar with the European scene would not have the chance to see the big white cars (Mercedes-Benz and Auto Union) that were dominating formula racing in Europe at the time.

One person they did see was the "Flying Mantuan," Tazio Nuvolari from Mantua, Italy. Still regarded as one of the best (if not *the* best) racing driver of all time, he drove a 4.1-liter V-12 Alfa Romeo as part of the Ferrari team. Other Alfa drivers included Giuseppe Farina, Count Brivio, and (non-team) Raymond Sommer. Bugattis were there in the hands of Brian Lewis, Jean-Pierre Wimille, and oddly enough, Indy winner Louie Meyer. Freddie McEvoy, Philippe Étancelin, and E. K. Rayson drove Maseratis.

All these European cars and drivers were used to the challenges of road racing circuits. American cars were primarily two-man speedway cars (although for this race, the riding mechanic could be left behind), dirt-track Millers, and even a stretched Offy midget. Gearboxes and brakes, so critical in road racing, were not a priority for these cars.

Part of the starting field for the 1936 Vanderbilt Cup shows the way the track was laid out so all of it would be visible from the grandstands. (Photo Courtesy of Nassau County Dept. of Parks, Recreation & Museums, Photo Archives Center)

Designing a New Course

Mark Linenthal, a prominent architect and friend of George Preston Marshall, was hired to design the course. The layout he designed was a 4-mile track with a single 3,775-foot straightaway and 16 flat corners, several of them hairpins. The surface was hard-packed sand and gravel. The founders planned to produce a truly world-class facility, with spacious and well-equipped garages, massive double-decked grandstands, a posh clubhouse, generous parking, and thoroughfares to deal with anticipated traffic. The aim was to attract the East Coast social set, not the riffraff dirt-track fans who had kept that form of motor racing alive through the Depression.

The finished track was America's first purpose-built road course, and it was designed with the intent that the 50,000 grandstand spectators could see every bit of its 4 miles. Sounds good, but in practice this meant a totally flat track and a lot of convoluted curves. Not a good design for the American machines of the day. Moreover, it was not a particularly fast track for anyone's cars.

This is the original 4-mile Roosevelt course as it was configured for the 1936 race. To make it faster, the middle swirls were removed for the 1937 edition, making it 3.7 miles around. (Photo Courtesy of Nassau County Department of Parks, Recreation & Museums, Photo Archives Center)

The 1908 Vanderbilt Cup winner George Robertson shows "Shorty" Cantlon around the new Roosevelt track during an early media day. (Photo Courtesy of Nassau County Department of Parks, Recreation & Museums, Photo Archives Center)

Indy 500 winner Wilbur Shaw, one of the American hopefuls, at speed during a race practice. The heavy two-man Indy car could not match Nuvolari's qualifying lap record of 69 mph and crashed early in the race. (Photo Courtesy of Nassau County Department of Parks, Recreation & Museums, Photo Archives Center)

The powerful Alfa-Romeo team that dominated the 1936 Vanderbilt Cup: from left, Antonio Brivio, Tazio Nuvolari (the winner), and Nino Farina. Nuvolari demonstrated his road course mastery with an easy victory. (Photo Courtesy of Nassau County Department of Parks, Recreation & Museums, Photo Archives Center)

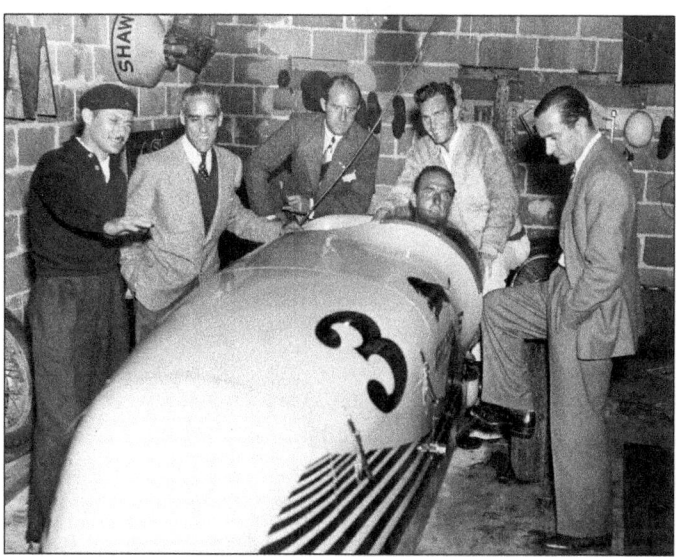

Nuvolari (2nd from left) and Brivio (far right) discuss strategy with American Wilbur Shaw, in the cockpit of the Gilmore Offenhauser Special. (Photo Courtesy of Nassau County Department of Parks, Recreation & Museums, Photo Archives Center)

Dignitaries and celebrities were given rides around the track just prior to the start of the 1936 race. (Photo Courtesy of Nassau County Department of Parks, Recreation & Museums, Photo Archives Center)

The 40,000-seat main grandstands just before they opened for the 1936 Vanderbilt Cup. As per instructions, the stands and course were built so that the entire track was visible from every seat. (Photo Courtesy of Nassau County Department of Parks, Recreation & Museums, Photo Archives Center)

Practice showed that no car, American or European, was going to be able to achieve the predicted speeds on the twisty circuit, despite its very long straightaway. Accordingly, the race distance was shorted from the planned 400 to 300 miles, so race day would not stretch on into the evening.

After two days of qualifying, a 45-car field was filled. Nuvolari was the fastest with an average lap speed of just a tick under 70 mph. Race day saw Nuvolari remain the fastest and he won by more than two minutes. American driver Billy Winn, though, stole the hearts of the crowd with a wild, sliding driving style, which kept his big American Miller dirt-track car near the top most of the way. When he retired with

One of the top American contenders, on paper at least, Babe Stapp, in the *Topping Special*, was outmanned in the final 1936 race. (Photo Courtesy of Nassau County Department of Parks, Recreation & Museums, Photo Archives Center)

Several cars that did not make the starting grid for the 1936 Vanderbilt Cup have their own unofficial race, here led by an unidentified Bugatti. (Photo Courtesy of Nassau County Department of Parks, Recreation & Museums, Photo Archives Center)

Reportedly, this is Nuvolari getting the checkered for his 1936 win, but it is hard to verify. In addition, the claimed turnout of 60,000 for the race was doubtless exaggerated. (Photo Courtesy of Nassau County Department of Parks, Recreation & Museums, Photo Archives Center)

just 10 laps to go, Wimille moved ahead of Brivio to take 2nd. Sommer was 4th, McEvoy 5th, with Rose 6th (the first American). Several photos were taken of Nuvolari in the winner's circle holding the Vanderbilt Cup, which was at least half as tall as he was.

This first race of the revived Vanderbilt Cup had created a lot of excitement, but the massive stands were far from full. About 60,000 attendees were claimed but few believed that figure. One of the goals of the organizers, to keep the riff-raff out, may have worked *too* well. Stiff admission prices kept many people of *all* social and economic strata away. Plus the New York papers pretty much universally panned the event. However, a 1937 race was promised and American drivers bought several European cars to prepare for the match, including Sommer's Alfa and Étancelin's Maserati.

1937: Enter the Big White Cars

Sure enough, the event was back on the 1937 racing calendar, scheduled for the Fourth of July weekend that year. Promoters even upped the ante: $70,000 in prize money and lap leader awards were promised, plus special financial incentives for the top-finishing American cars. However, an American driver in a European car proved to be the early sensation, as Rex Mays driving a heavily modified, ex-factory Alfa turned in the fastest practice and qualifying laps on the newly redesigned 3.7-mile course. Taking out several turns entirely no doubt added to Mays' early success, as did the addition of 67-degree banking on the final turn. He, after all, was an oval track racer. Everyone benefited from a redone, harder-packed track surface.

For this second year the German teams did show up with their big V-12s. Mercedes-Benz had their top two drivers, Rudolf Caracciola and Dick Seaman; Auto-Union brought the popular Bernd Rosemeyer and Ernst von Delius. For some reason never fully explained, race promoters had the German teams paint swastikas on their cars, something that was not done in Europe outside Germany. When the race was held, the Nazi party and swastika symbol were not yet the international pariahs they later became. Nuvolari and Farina were back, but by this time, German machines were outperforming the Alfas.

At first no one could match Mays' times, but soon the European drivers got the hang of the course. Other Americans in the field included Indy winners and 1930s racing legends

The original caption for this course photo from the 1937 event program says it all. Cars ran counterclockwise. (Photo Courtesy Martin Spetz Collection)

They don't design program covers like this these days, and more's the pity. A contemporary Alfa comes closest to resembling the car on the cover. (Photo Courtesy Martin Spetz Collection)

By 1937, Tazio Nuvolari realistically had no chance to beat the Germans, but he broke two cars trying. (Photo Courtesy of Nassau County Department of Parks, Recreation & Museums, Photo Archives Center)

The all-Conquering Auto Union and its driver Bernd Rosemeyer leave the pits for the 1937 Vanderbilt Cup races. Note the swastika, custom-painted for this event, on the side panel. German cars did not carry this symbol when racing in Europe. (Photo Courtesy the Collection of Hank Wieand Bowman and Family)

Wilbur Shaw and Mauri Rose, both in 8-cylinder Maseratis.

The more diverse international makeup of the field attracted a lot of pre-race attention, but shortly before race day, Amelia Earhart's disappearance in the Pacific was announced. It knocked the race and everything else off the front page and newscasts. Then rain fell on race day, July 3, and forced postponement to Monday, July 5 (no racing on Sundays). Again, many doubted the track's eventual claimed attendance of more than 70,000.

After President Franklin Roosevelt started the race by wire from his Hyde Park residence, the 90-lap 300-mile race was again interesting. Pre-race sentimental favorite Mays put on a great show and might have actually challenged for the lead but poor pit work cost him too much time. As it was, Rosemeyer was the early leader, but Caracciola soon passed him. The Mercedes-Benz then failed, putting the Auto Union back on top. Seaman came in 2nd with Mays 3rd. Auto Union's second car in the hands of von Delius came in 4th. Despite some repeat heroics by Billy Winn, whose sliding style again amazed Europeans, the first all-American combo was Bill Cummings in a Miller back in 7th. Nuvolari broke two cars (his and Farina's) and did not finish. The same fate took Winn out of the race.

Thus ended the brief but spectacular two-year revival of the Vanderbilt Cup on Roosevelt Raceway. Although another race was initially scheduled for Columbus Day 1938, it was soon scrubbed from the calendar. There just was not enough interest in this type of racing in the area. Two more races were held at the Roosevelt facility, an amateur road race in late 1938 and a midget race on a modified half-mile track in front of the grandstands in 1939.

1960: Last Gasp Revival

In 1960, there was a final attempt at reviving the Vanderbilt Cup at Roosevelt Raceway, or at least a version of it. Another Vanderbilt, 62-year-old Cornelius, was the connection to the glory days of the event and lent his prestige to getting it going again. The New York SCCA region used a 1.5-mile road course created from access roads and parking facilities around the harness racing field. Leveraging the prestige of the Vanderbilt Cup, the SCCA was convinced to let professional drivers into the usually all-amateur field.

However, they were all to drive the same kind of car, Formula Juniors. These cars had just been introduced to the racing world and were very popular, so it was perhaps not surprising that drivers including Indy champ Jim Rathman, Rodger Ward, the Rodríguez brothers, Jim Hall, Carroll Shelby, and Walt Hansgen all entered.

On Sunday, June 19, the Cornelius Vanderbilt Cup Race was the feature of the weekend. By SCCA regional racing standards, a large audience of more than 37,000 people was on hand. The Cup race was just 75 miles, which was really a 50-lap sprint. Even though it was a sprint race, the lack of development in the still-new Formula Junior class showed. Only 14 of the 33 starters finished as many of the cars had highly stressed small engines and delicate chassis that were not yet up to being raced hard, especially by racers such as the above-mentioned set.

Local driver Henry Carter, in a Stanguellini Formula Junior, became the first winner of the newly invigorated Vanderbilt Cup. Of the "name" drivers entered, only Pedro Rodríguez finished, and he was only 5th. However, his pit crew furiously claimed that a lap had been missed and Pedro had actually won. A confusing review of the charts did not uphold this claim, so for all time, he is recorded as having that 5th-place finish.

Other races were held that day, and winners were familiar top East Coast drivers: Walt Hansgen, Bob Grossman,

This is the only hint of the mighty racetrack that once stood where shopping malls now reign. And they only acknowledge the harness racing history. (Photo Courtesy Judy Rudow)

The majestic old grandstands once stood on this ground, but now, not a trace remains. A box office and movie theater now stand in its place. (Photo Courtesy Judy Rudow)

Charlie Kolb. That was the last hurrah for Roosevelt Raceway, but the Vanderbilt Cup race moved on to the Bridgehampton track, about 60 miles farther out on Long Island.

A Transition to Horse Racing

Between the close of the racetrack in the late 1930s and the seemingly inevitable development, the property was converted into a harness racing track, using many of the buildings and the grandstands that had been erected for motor racing. The Old Country Trotting Association opened the track in 1940. The harness track was innovative in many ways, as was its motor racing predecessor, and as population grew out from New York City, it proved to be popular through the 1980s.

It may be best known, though, for a 1963 riot that started after a controversial finish decision. The horseracing track was closed in 1988 and the old Roosevelt Raceway and surrounding property was slowly developed in the years that followed. The grandstands stood until 2002. A movie theater and at least two shopping malls now stand where the track once ranged. Like so many of the old racetrack locations I investigated, it appears that most of this development took place in the last ten years or so. Today, not a trace remains of the old racetracks.

You have to love the political incorrectness of this wall painting from Roosevelt's drivers' lounge and bar, or the fact that there even was such a facility serving alcohol, for that matter. (Photo Courtesy of Nassau County Department of Parks, Recreation & Museums, Photo Archives Center)

STARDUST INTERNATIONAL RACEWAY

DUST AND DRAMA IN THE DESERT

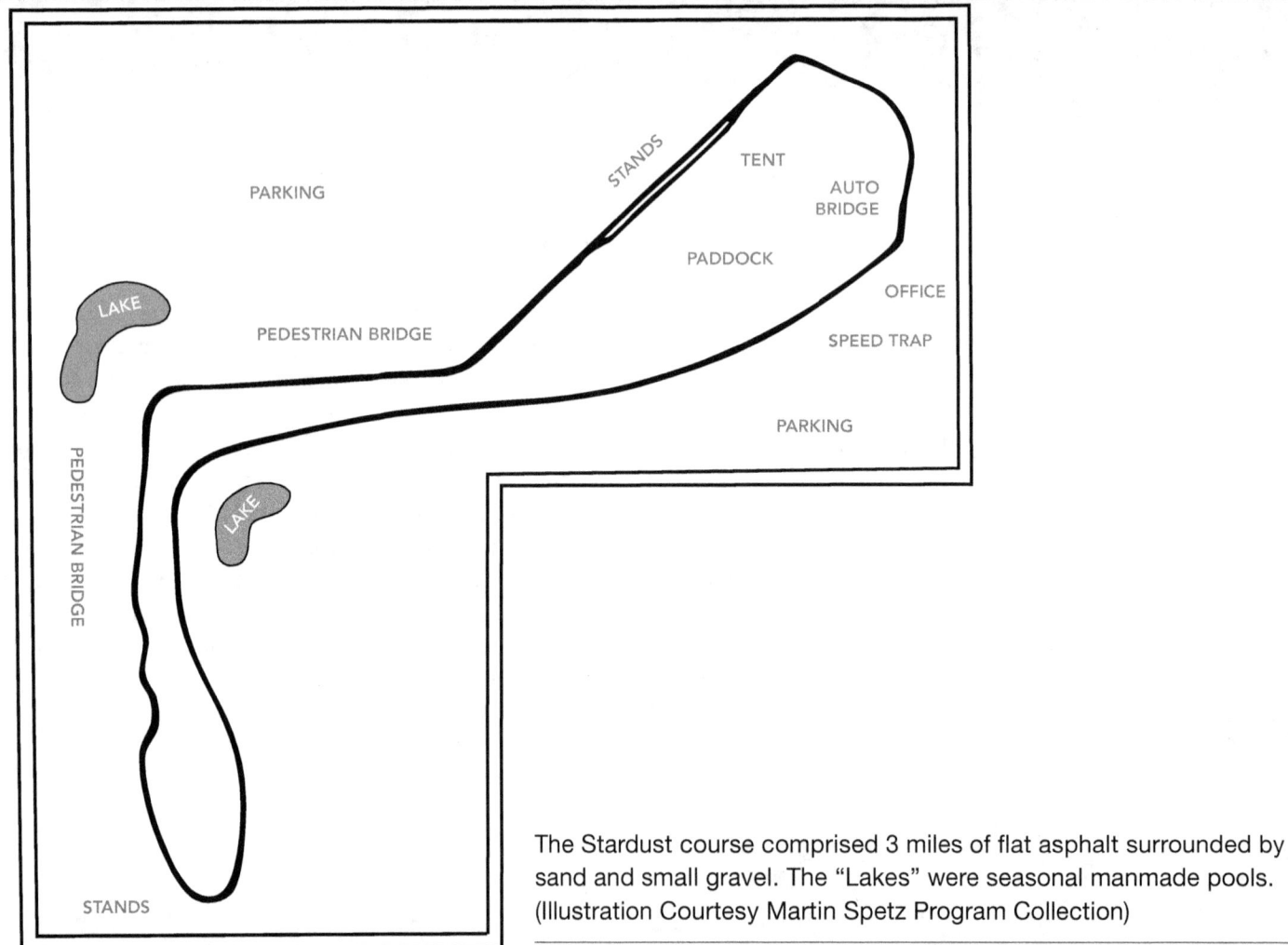

The Stardust course comprised 3 miles of flat asphalt surrounded by sand and small gravel. The "Lakes" were seasonal manmade pools. (Illustration Courtesy Martin Spetz Program Collection)

It's hard to imagine today, when Las Vegas stretches from horizon to horizon in the desert, but when Stardust International Raceway opened in Las Vegas in 1965, it was on a stretch of empty, sparse desert acreage at the end of a dusty dirt road 4 miles from the nearest settlement. In other words, far from the glitter and glamour the city offered even in the mid-1960s. Thanks to the enthusiasm of the management of the Stardust Resort and Casino, that empty stretch of land soon shook with the sounds of some of the fastest and most appealing cars of the late 1960s.

Today, shopping malls and the Spanish Trails housing development occupy the track location. Even if the track was successful in terms of attendance (it certainly was successful in terms of attracting top cars and drivers), it is doubtful that it could have withstood the pressure of development.

The Stardust Resort and Casino built the racetrack in 1965, apparently in an attempt to attract high rollers. Las Vegas sporting events were famous for attracting wealthy and glamorous people who enjoyed traveling to them, talking to their friends about them, being seen around them, but then

140   Lost Road Courses

CHAPTER 14

Las Vegas, Nevada
1965–1970

Facility 3 miles, 13 turns, asphalt, 2,400-foot straightaway
Principal Events Can-Am, Trans-Am, USRRC, USAC Champ Car
Current Status Housing developments and shopping malls; no trace of the old track remains

In the 1967 Can-Am, John Surtees leads Bruce McLaren, shown here. Surtees' Lola T70 went on to win as the McLaren had a rare DNF. (Photo Courtesy Pete Lyons)

never actually showing up for the event itself. This was fine for the hotels and casinos, of course; they wanted those high rollers to stay in the casino's gaming rooms anyway.

According to the casino's press release, none other than Stirling Moss designed the course. In reality, he did have some minimal input in the early stages, but certainly was not the primary designer. Track owners were described as the Stardust Racing Association that included officers of the Stardust Resort and Casino. Anyone familiar with the history of Las Vegas knows about the difficulty of verifying just who owned what in those days. Enough said.

Today the old track site shares the fate of Riverside, its closest major track from the old days: It has been totally overtaken by housing and shopping developments. In its day it was absolutely dry and dusty and those conditions did not endear it to anyone. But the Stardust operation had displayed a magic touch with everything they had tried, from building a PGA golf course to staging the Lido de Paris, a very popular nighttime attraction. Their iconic neon sign, so 1960s-ish, could be seen for miles and was at the time the most attention-getting sign on the strip.

Road racing had been tried at Las Vegas before, but lacked a suitable venue. An SCCA race was held at the city's McCarran Field in 1960. It was not a successful event, and no wonder when you read what Ken Miles wrote about the venue in *Competition Press*: "It is a wilderness of asphalt surrounded by limitless reaches of high desert across which winter winds roam uninhibited by anything other than tumbleweeds and the glitter towers of the Vegas strip." Unfortunately, he could have written almost the same thing about the Stardust Raceway six years later. The strip was really not all that glittery in those days anyway, but by 1965, when the Stardust was scheduled to open, it had grown considerably glitterier than in 1960. But was it ready to support high-level road racing?

The newly formed Stardust Racing Association found a cheap 800-acre section of unwanted desert land (480 of which were actually used for the track complex) in what is today a housing area bordered by Tropicana Boulevard, Rainbow Boulevard, Piedmont Boulevard, and Flamingo Road. Next, they hired a well-liked track manager, Leo Margolian, and went to work building a track. Despite the publicist's claims to the contrary, amenities at the track were few, certainly not what Las Vegas would do today... or should have done then.

Course construction began on July 25. With a flat landscape and few natural obstacles such as trees and boulders, it was able to be graded quickly and was ready, more or less, for the first race in October.

Chapter 14: Stardust International Raceway

Here is the layout for the Stardust Resort and Casino in 1965. The racetrack was several miles out of the town center in what was then trackless desert. (Photo Courtesy Las Vegas Tourism Bureau File)

1965: Racing Starts at Stardust

The first race at Stardust was a non-spectator Cal Club weekend event in mid-October 1965. The event ran smoothly and produced a nail-biting finish in the main event. Race-long leader Norm Smith spun his Porsche 904 on the last turn and was passed and ultimately beaten by a few yards by the Cheetah of Jerry Entin. The first winner of a Stardust race was Jim Parkinson in a Dolphin, who also had a close win, just 2 seconds ahead of Ed Barker's Spitfire. The fastest lap was turned by Entin, just a tick over 1:58, something for subsequent racers to shoot for. Everyone enjoyed the cocktail parties hosted by the Stardust Casino; they were far more lavish than the norm for a club race.

The Entin-won race was just a warmup, a shakedown really, and the first big race was held on November 14. Did I say "big race"? Well, if you have a race in Las Vegas, even in those days, you had better be ready for a publicity barrage, no matter how big the race really is. The Stardust provided publicity for its inaugural big event in a lavish manner indeed. A $36,700 purse was announced for this first race, to be known as the Stardust Grand Prix. The casino bought a special section in the November 27 issue of *Competition Press*, seven pages no less, extolling the virtues of the track and Las Vegas as a destination, particularly the Stardust.

Many details about the track can be gleaned from this special section. In it, the SCCA's Cal Club was given a lot of

This early Cal Club race day at the track was a shakedown for the facility. Everything looked ready to go. No Vegas-style buffet was on hand; they did have the snack coach. Jerry Entin (#55) won this race in a Cheetah. (Photo Courtesy Las Vegas Tourism Bureau File)

The Cal Club day had some interesting cars, from a VW Beetle to an XK-E to an old Ferrari. Note the long dusty access road to the left. (Photo Courtesy Las Vegas Tourism Bureau File)

credit for assisting in course layout, organization, and planning. In one article, veteran driver Hap Sharp said that there were excellent run-off areas, as well there should be in the flat, open desert. The course was a fast one, he said, and Turn 1 would prove to be the most exciting corner on the track. Overall, Sharp was enthusiastic about the course. Spectators were less enthusiastic when they arrived. Only a few bleachers were set up so people stood behind snow fencing in the dirt and dust. Restrooms were basic. Still, race spectators in the mid-1960s did not expect great amenities.

The *Competition Press* section also boasted of the entertainment that was available in Las Vegas for racers and their fans. Headliners were Wayne Newton, Dean Martin, Eddie Fisher, the Mills Brothers, even an early version of Rowan & Martin. Lots for the "high rollers" to do in addition to visiting the racetrack!

Another sidebar in the section will bring a tear to anyone's eye: a 1964 Ferrari 250 GTO with great racing provenance selling for $13,500. The 1965 Stardust GP, the section also proudly noted, was to be the last stop on the 1965 Autoweek Championship for Sports Cars, at the time "the Western Hemisphere's most important road races."

Sharp not only proved to be prescient about the track's speed, he also won Stardust's inaugural race. However, the part about the safety of the run-off areas was only partially right. The stark desert landscape looked good at first glance for run-offs, but in reality it contained a lot of dust and pea gravel, both of which could be thrown on the course in copious amounts when someone went off for any reason. With the fastest average speed for any major road race in the country up to then (106.68 mph), Sharp sped past his teammate Jim Hall's Chaparral to win 1st place in the other team Chaparral. In addition, he won the Autoweek Championship while so doing.

Threatening skies held the crowd to about 13,000, but they had the pleasure of watching a race with a talented field of drivers. It included Parnelli Jones, Charlie Hayes, Walt Hansgen, Jerry Grant, Jerry Titus, and others. The track showed its safety potential when Walt Hansgen went flying off just after Turn 1 at high speed in qualifying but simply scooted over the sand and rocks before coming to a safe, dusty, but no doubt relieved, halt. No mention was made of any gravel being thrown on the course during this escapade.

1966: Two High Rollers

In 1966, the course attracted two high rollers of the racing sort: the USRRC and the fledgling Can-Am series. The USRRC began the season (both its and the track's) and for the first time really showed the dust and rocks problem that came to plague the track. John Cannon in *Vinegaroon Special* (previ-

In the 1966 Can-Am, the Lola T70s of Paul Hawkins and George Follmer lead the Genie of Bill Eve. That's Charlie Hayes changing a tire behind them. Hawkins earned an 8th in the final but the others were DNFs. (Photo Courtesy Las Vegas Tourism Bureau File)

ously *Genie-Olds*) won the April 24 race but several drivers had troubles caused by those flying rocks. One even put local driver Buck Fulp in the hospital when it smacked him in the face.

Complaints were also heard about the narrow width of the course. *Competition Press* reporter Cam Warren reported that it was too narrow for even two motorcycles to safely ride side by side. A slight exaggeration maybe, but a narrow course meant there was less room to avoid the rocks and dust when someone went off.

The season opener for the USRRC saw many cars break down, spilling oil that mixed with the dust to make the track even more treacherous. The spectator count was small, and this time it was blamed on 90-degree heat, which the track promoters must have known would be a problem at times. The difficult conditions bit George Follmer, who slid off right away and hit a rock intended as course decoration. Donohue won easily and reported that his Sunoco Lola-Chevy was up to 170 mph on the track's long straight.

Donohue and several others were back for the season-ending Can-Am race on November 13. He and six other drivers were still in contention for the season championship, which had consisted of just six races. More than 11,000 spectators, as well as Hollywood types including Dan Blocker and James Garner, attended.

John Surtees, the popular English driver who was making a real commitment to Can-Am racing, earned the win. He jumped to a quick lead and then led every lap in his red Lola, putting on the most overwhelmingly dominant performance of the series that year. Surtees finished the race with only Bruce McLaren on the same lap, far back. The Chaparrals of Jim Hall and Phil Hill were fastest in qualifying, but both suffered body damage during the race and Hall was forced to retire, with Hill coming in mid-pack.

That race again showed the downside of Stardust's ample run-off area. Norm Smith went off and, with nothing to slow

Staying up late in the Chaparral garage, Jim Hall looks resigned while his wife (left) reads a book. As usual, they were ready the next day. (Photo Courtesy Pete Lyons)

him down, zoomed right through the spectator fence and 100 feet inside the spectator area before he could stop. Fortunately only one person was injured, but the potential danger for a high-speed off-course excursion was dramatically displayed.

The other drivers in the race were an impressive lot: Jackie Stewart, Hap Sharp, Denny Hulme, Mario Andretti, Chris Amon, Dan Gurney, and several more of that stature. One note about Andretti: to make the final starting field, he had to win the qualifying race for slower cars. It was his first win in a sports car, the first of many for this highly versatile and immensely talented driver.

1967: The Stars Come to Stardust

The 1967 season started somewhat poorly for Stardust with the USRRC race on April 23 drawing fewer than 5,000 spectators. The USRRC was slipping in popularity compared to the fledgling Trans-Am and Can-Am events but still . . . not even 5,000 to see Mark Donohue, Sam Posey, and George Follmer? Maybe they knew that the early-season event would

Denny Hulme gets ready for another day at the office: practice for the 1967 Stardust Can-Am. His engine blew in the final. (Photo Courtesy Pete Lyons)

The Chaparral heads to the start of the 1967 Can-Am, while the McLaren team gets ready in the background. (Photo Courtesy Pete Lyons)

A view of the Can-Am paddock in 1967 where pit security, garages, and other amenities seem minimal. (Photo Courtesy Las Vegas Tourism Bureau File)

It looked like it was going to be another edition of the Bruce and Denny show at the start of the 1967 Can-Am, but neither car finished due to mechanical failures. John Surtees won. (Photo Courtesy Pete Lyons)

The promotional budget for the 1968 Can-Am race was evidently so low that a stock photo from *Riverside* was used on the cover! (Photo Courtesy Riverside Automotive Museum)

Mark Donohue checks his gloves right before the green flag falls for the start of the 1968 Can-Am. The race was a disappointment for him as he stalled right away and was out. (Photo Courtesy Pete Lyons)

see a lot of attrition, as it seemed to serve as almost a shakedown weekend for many of the teams. Sure enough, only 11 of 24 starters managed to finish the race. Surface oil left over from preliminary regional races made the track slipperier than usual and even race winner Donohue spun a few times over the weekend.

Donohue and his Penske Camaro were back with the Trans-Am traveling circus in late September. It was the Las Vegas 350 and Mark won by more than a minute and a half. Las Vegas is best known for its nighttime action, and this one started at sunset and finished in the dark. Huh, what about taking the high rollers away from the gaming floors at night? It did not seem to bother the drivers much as all eyes were on the Cougars and Mustangs that were battling for the season's championship. Camaros such as Donohue's could not win the championship at this point but could make things interesting with a win when only one race was left in the season.

Mustangs were 2nd and 3rd here to help in their ultimately successful quest for the title. Trans-Am in those days would seem to be a natural great attraction for a Las Vegas–based raceway, but that was the pony car circuit's only trip to Sin City.

The Can-Am race that ended Stardust's season in 1967 was one of the most dramatic and exciting of the series that year. The Bruce and Denny show, just getting started in 1967, failed here as both Bruce McLaren and Denny Hulme broke their McLarens, leaving John Surtees to earn the win. The race began in spectacular fashion when a Turn 1 spin put several cars out of the race, many with rock-caused damage. One car spun so violently that the driver actually started going the wrong way down the track when he recovered from the spin!

The race saw a lot more attrition and Mark Donohue seemed assured of the win (it would have been his most significant to date) when the Chevy engine in his Mark 3B Lola quit with two turns (not laps, turns) to go. Surtees raced by him at that point and won in the two-year-old red Traco Chevy-powered Mk2B Lola. It was the same car that he had won with here the year before, a rare feat indeed in those days of rapid technological advances.

Jim Hall's Chaparral is *already* banged-up, and this is before the horrific 1968 crash that destroyed the car. Following close, Bruce McLaren's soon-to-be-retired car does not look a whole lot better at this point. (Photo Courtesy Pete Lyons)

1968: Can-Am Carnage

The Can-Am race had been a success and was back on the schedule for 1968. But Trans-Am was gone from the year; instead a USAC race was held at about the same time the Trans-Am had run. The USAC series was nowhere near as popular as Trans-Am but was still a prestigious event for the track. At the same time, drag racing was still going strong. If there was an indication of what was soon to happen to the Stardust track, it did not appear in print.

The USAC race, held on March 31, was a 150-mile event that attracted several top USAC Indy car drivers, but not enough of them: only 17, a thin starting field. Bobby Unser soon threw pea gravel all over Dan Gurney and put him out of the race. When accused later of purposely throwing the gravel, Unser claimed that he never went off course. You did not need to go off course at Stardust to find gravel to throw. If it was indeed done on purpose, karma did not catch up with Mr. Unser that day; he won the race over Mario Andretti.

Peter Revson sails by the Stardust grandstands in a McLaren Mk6B on his way to a DNF at the 1968 Stardust Can-Am. (Photo Courtesy Pete Lyons)

The season-ending Can-Am race that year was also the track's finale. Who would have thought it? A good field, a record spectator attendance, and Bruce McLaren setting a new lap record: 1:29.63. He and teammate Denny Hulme had already clinched the season title for their McLarens, but they were locked in a very tight battle for the Driver's Championship.

The weekend produced one of the series' all-time spectacular and scary moments when Jim Hall drove his Chaparral over a stalled Lothar Motschenbacher and demolished his car in an unforgettable 20-foot-high flip. Confusion reigned, but the track's poor spectator safety measures actually worked out to everyone's advantage this time because spectators were able to run on the course to the car and pull Hall out just as the demolished Chaparral burst into flames. Hall was seriously injured with two broken legs, abrasions, and burns, and although he raced again (but not in Can-Am), he never seemed quite the same. The Chaparral itself was so badly damaged that even what parts were left could not be used again.

The race was not without further drama, but fortunately nothing else that devastating happened. Denny Hulme won the race and the series championship as his top contender, Mark Donohue, stalled on the starting line and was not able to get going again. Mark might have considered himself lucky to be on the sideline because several cars were involved in a first-turn crash that created an immense cloud of dust that completely blanketed the track and limited visibility to near zero in some places. Several cars were damaged by the crash or the dust and had to retire or just hang in there with a dust-clogged engine or damaged body panels and run poorly all race.

The Can-Am race was accompanied by regionals and in one of them so many cars went off course and had to work their way through the loose dirt, gravel, and sand that bordered it that one wag suggested that the upcoming Stardust off-road race had started a week early.

The track used to pass right through where this intersection of Spring Valley and Rainbow are now. (Photo Courtesy Ricci Reyes)

Yes, off-road. At least two Hollywood superstars, James Garner and Steve McQueen, were into it and brought some glamour to this grubbiest form of motorsports. Drag racing and off road went on for a couple more years but the 1968 season was the last full year for the road course.

1969: It Ended All Too Soon

Fittingly, the Cal Club ran the last event at Stardust. Club racer Alan Johnson won a late-February event in 1969: the featured race for A-B Production, A-B sports racers, and A sedan. Johnson drove a Porsche 910 to the win over a strong field of Lolas, McLarens, Sting Rays, Cougars, and other Porsches. A nice event, and put on well as usual by the Cal Club, but not enough to make a difference in the way new Stardust Resort and Casino owners felt about the track. If anything would have.

The new owners at the Stardust were not interested in putting needed money into the track to upgrade both its amenities and road surface. Las Vegas was doing fine with its traditional attractions, gambling and nightlife, and the potential to pull people in via road races was no longer of much interest. Larry Horton, by then the track's manager, leased the land and ran drag racing events until 1970. Real estate developer Pardee Holmes then bought the land, pulled up the track, and built the Spring Valley community on it. The casino itself was demolished in 2007. It had become old, gawky, and bloated compared to the slick casino hotels in vogue then and now.

Las Vegas has road racing of a sort today, but it is almost an afterthought, staged in the infield of the Las Vegas Motor Speedway: a NASCAR super oval. No gravel and no dust there. The area that housed the racetrack has been developed out of all recognition by anyone who went to races there in the 1960s. Parks, green lawns, and upscale desert housing dominate the scene today.

Where there was once nothing but rock and sand in the old Stardust infield, parks and trees now grow. (Photo Courtesy Ricci Reyes)

Chapter 14: Stardust International Raceway

War Bonnet Raceway Park

THE FUTURE RECREATION, VACATION AND RACING DESTINATION

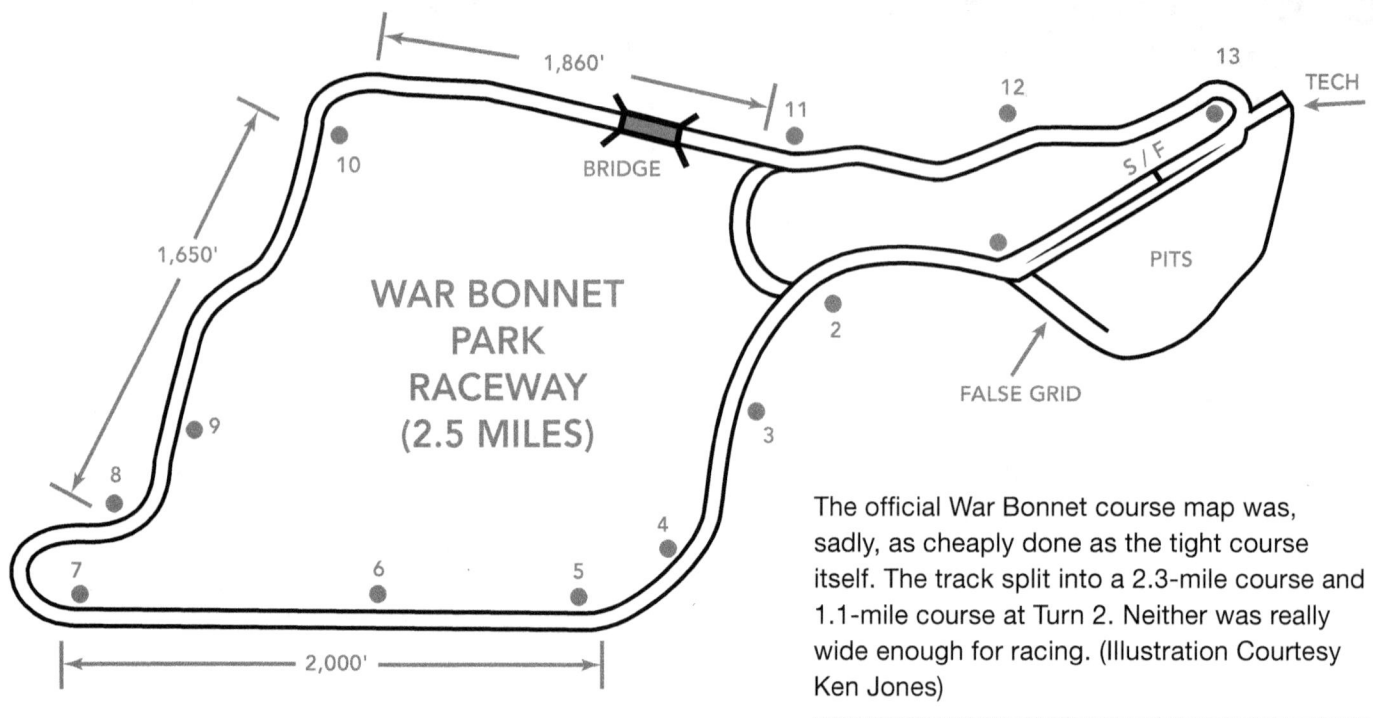

The official War Bonnet course map was, sadly, as cheaply done as the tight course itself. The track split into a 2.3-mile course and 1.1-mile course at Turn 2. Neither was really wide enough for racing. (Illustration Courtesy Ken Jones)

As a grandiose promoter, Bob Moore had hyperbole in abundance. In the late 1960s he turned his attention to the growing sport of road racing. He had a bold plan to build the "Nürburgring of the Midwest" in Oklahoma and he named it War Bonnet. Building the track was part of his plan to raise the profile of his company, Sports Diversified, Inc., from a second tier sports promotion firm and also to create one of the leading road courses in the United States.

During this era, the Tulsa, Oklahoma, area, where Moore and Sports Diversified were based, didn't see an awful lot of sports car racing. Plenty of inexpensive land was available, and he saw the opportunity to build a racetrack and a community around the track. The site chosen for all of this was next to the small town of Hannaford, a mere 20 miles from Tulsa. Accordingly, he leased the 1,100 acres of undeveloped land for the track and started building it in early 1966. Initial plans called for a 5.7-mile road course, "the longest in the country," along with shorter loops, an oval track, and a dragstrip. He chose the name "War Bonnet" to honor the area's Native American heritage. It had a nice ring to it, too.

Moore promised a $3.5-million investment in the track facilities, which would include covered pits for 100 cars with spectator boxes above, a three-story communications tower housing office space, press boxes, a sports car club meeting room, showers, locker rooms, and private boxes for visiting dignitaries. Trackside bleachers would hold 20,000 spectators and another 30,000 could be accommodated in the infield that would be reached by pedestrian and vehicle track overpasses. No one could fault Mr. Moore for thinking small! It's no wonder that the local Northeast Oklahoma SCCA region was excited and eager to cooperate.

His plans to build the "Nürburgring of the Midwest" were ambitious indeed. Records indicate that Moore was never anywhere near the real Nürburgring. The famous German track's 18-mile course and hilly, thickly forested surroundings were a far cry from anything that War Bonnet could ever become. But why not? The prose was wonderful. The reality was something else.

CHAPTER 15

Hannaford, Oklahoma
1966–1969

Facility	1.1 miles, 2.3 miles
Principal Events	SCCA, Trans-Am, Formula 5000
Current Status	Housing development and county park; most of old course remains

Springtime in Oklahoma. Sprites lead a parade as colorful on the track as off. (Photo Courtesy Robert Baron)

1966: A Road Course of Small Proportions

When the first events opened the track in late July 1966, everyone who showed up to drive, officiate, or watch found much less than promised in Moore's initial press releases and sales pitches to the local SCCA. The course was a mostly flat 1.1 miles, really just a big oval laid down among stunted oak trees, prairie grass, and scrub brush with enough wrinkles thrown in to make it a "road course." Only 100 yards or so separated the two straightaways. No buildings were in evidence, not even the three-story tower with all the attractions that was promised. And it was a minor miracle that the first weekend was even held at all.

Ken Jones, one of the people who used the track often during its short lifetime, remembers showing up the Tuesday before that opening weekend and finding nothing paved, just a road grader lazily moving a bit of dirt around the staked-out course. The situation had not improved dramatically when he showed up the next afternoon. But Bob Moore promised that all would be ready for the opener. Drivers passing by to scout it out were aghast at seeing what Jones had found, and began asking one another if the track would really open Saturday. Even late on Thursday, no pavement had been laid, although the track was completely graded by then. Paving finally began on Friday at noon and was actually completed in time for the next day's school, although Ken Jones reports that the asphalt pavement was "still warm."

Today, the remains of the track are easy to find; a surprising amount of it still exists. Unlike other developments, the community that built up around the old track did not ride roughshod over the course and leave no trace of it. Far from it. The entire circuit was incorporated into the main access road for the homes that line it.

But no one was really alarmed, or if they were they kept it mostly to themselves. They realized that the track was in its very early stages. They would no doubt be adding more facilities and completing the longer course soon. In the meantime, here was a real place to race at last.

Actor and race car driver James Garner visited War Bonnet in 1968 and took a fast lap with Don Yenko.

Chapter 15: War Bonnet Raceway Park 149

The big Oklahoma sky dwarfs two formula cars in a 1968 War Bonnet race. (Photo Courtesy Robert Baron)

The tight, narrow bridge that could barely accommodate two cars and was flooded during races has been widened considerably today. (Photo Courtesy Judy Rudow)

The calendar at War Bonnet started out slowly enough. Drivers' schools and SCCA regional races opened the track on July 24–25 and August 7–8, 1966. A local driver, Nick Nero of Prairie Village, Kansas, won both of the two regional feature races driving a very hot 427 Cobra. He went on to enjoy some national success with this car. Each school/race weekend drew more than 100 entries and, for the first time, the August event was open to spectators.

You don't make much money from regional races and drivers' schools, so War Bonnet managed to put an SCCA National on the schedule during its first year. It was scheduled for a good time, too; its October 1–2 weekend represented the last chance for Oklahoma area drivers to qualify for the SCCA Runoffs. The weekend attracted 100 entrants and a reported 5,000 spectators, although one reporter noted that they must have been well scattered around the course. He couldn't spot anywhere near that number hidden around the flat 1.1-mile course, and there wasn't anywhere to hide.

Quoted in the region's SCCA newsletter, an unidentified participant in that first weekend's school wrote about his initial impressions of the track: "Yes, the track does have a decent amount of elevation change. You really noticed it going into the last turn, which was a hairpin onto the start/finish straight. The first turn was fun and then there was what was generally considered a decreasing-radius right turn that was tricky followed by a blind, off-camber left-hand turn that was 'interesting' to say the least.

"If you went off there you'd tumble downhill toward the start/finish straight and timing and scoring. I saw a couple of cars do that. The only time there was time to even blink a bit and look at instruments was down the long front start/finish straight. Otherwise, you were extremely busy the rest of the way."

One good thing was that spectators could see almost the entire course from the infield.

1967: Expanding War Bonnet

The course, originally planned to be 5.7 miles long, was expanded in its "second phase" to 2.3 miles in time for the 1967 season. It was a far more interesting and challenging course than its 1.1-mile predecessor. It used almost all of the original course and took a meandering tour through Oklahoma countryside to add the additional 1.2 miles. One of the more unusual features was a bridge over a deep gully that had a small stream at the bottom. The bridge was barely wide enough to allow two cars to go through, gingerly, side-by-side. What would happen if two Group 7 or Trans-Am cars were barreling down the road next to each other?

Local racer Tom Parker recalls what it was like to drive the longer course in a Camaro Z-28. "Down the straight, very close to the wall, twitch the car to the right, long gentle bend to the left onto the long course, very fast downhill, four-wheel

The parking lot was often muddy, as it is for the 1968 Grand Prix of Oklahoma. (Photo Courtesy Robert Baron)

This is the low-budget program for the 1968 Trans-Am race, which was won easily by Mark Donohue. (Photo Courtesy Ken Jones)

drift up the other side at 110 mph, shift to fourth for the downhill straight, brake hard at the 200 marker, down to first for the hairpin, shift to second, turn left, shift to third, turn right and shift into fourth, see the tach rise to 6,500 rpm before the right turn onto the bridge, experience the weightless sensation as the car tops the bump right after the bridge, long left turn out onto the short course, right, blind left, brake hard for the entrance to the hairpin, down to first with the power on hard, slide out just short of the wall and hit second just under that start/finish banner."

It was hard to be mad at Bob Moore if the course was not measuring up to his promises. According to contemporary reports, he was always friendly, always smiling, and always ready to pitch in and do any hard labor necessary to make the day work. If money was needed for something urgent, he was quick to write a check. The only problem was that the check often bounced.

SCCA Grand Prix

The big race for the summer of 1967 was a June 25 stop on the SCCA's Grand Prix series, the predecessor to the Continental Cup. This was the year before the big American V-8s came into the series. Gus Hutchinson won the 130-mile race at War Bonnet, his third straight win in the series in his Lotus 41-Ford. Dr. Lou Sell was 2nd and gave Hutchinson a run for his money in the opening 20 laps of the race.

The weather never gave Moore and his backers a break. Saturday was the hottest June 23 on record at 94 degrees, then it rained the night before and on race day. Any off-course excursion either day meant an immediate bog-down in the mud that surrounded the pavement. The mile-long dirt access road also became a quagmire that backed up spectator traffic for hours. Reports from the race dwelt a lot on that access road and the mud it and the rain created.

After a couple of regional SCCA races and drivers' schools, War Bonnet had a second chance to hold a national race at almost the same time as the previous year, October 7 and 8, 1967. Big Can-Am types as well as many other interesting cars showed up. Race reports from the day show

Ken Jones drives his Formula Vee through the pits to the starting line in a wet War Bonnet event as Dick Smothers looks on. (Photo Courtesy Ken Jones)

little detail but an exciting two-car duel went on in the feature. Bud Morley, in a Can-Am Lola-Chevy, edged out Bobby Aylward's McLaren. If either car flinched at the bridge, it was not reported. Other cars in the race included a Ferrari Dino 206 driven by Lee Cutler, a Porsche 906, along with several Cobras and Corvettes.

Reports of financial problems at the track first leaked, and then flowed out. Moore was unable to meet some local financial obligations as the 1968 season drew near. But local backing was found and the track went into receivership, providing funds for the season to continue. A lot was dependent upon an upcoming national Trans-Am event's ability to draw 30,000 people, the number predicted by Moore.

1968: Trans-Am Takes to the Track

On May 12, 1968, the first and only Trans-Am race ever run in Oklahoma took place, the War Bonnet 250. Two races were scheduled: 90 laps and 207 miles for the under-2-liter cars, 110 laps and 253 miles for the Trans-Am 2-plus liters. However, not enough under-2-liter cars showed up, so everyone ran in the same 253-mile race. This turn of events was not uncommon in Trans-Am.

Mark Donohue won that race, running his Camaro for three hours "like he was on rails." He was so consistent and smooth that he looked slow, but he lapped all but three of his competitors. Parnelli Jones was the most spectacular, dirt-tracking his Mustang all the way. He actually passed Donohue a few times in the early stages of the race, turning in a new course record lap of 1:35.4 in the process.

Jones drove one of the infamous "Tunnel Port" Mustangs, the most powerful engine on the Trans-Am circuit in that, or possibly any, year. The intake ports were so large that the intake valves actually ran through the ports. Ford later dropped the engine because its lack of low-end torque created more problems than the high-end horsepower solved (Jones' "dirt-tracking" style was an attempt to keep the revs up).

Peter Revson and George Follmer, aboard the Javelins, ran up front and swapped positions frequently all afternoon while fighting for 2nd place. Jones was able to make up most of the deficit after pitting for new tires and passed Revson late in the race for 3rd, but not without controversy.

Malcolm Starr provided the ultimate excitement and started the confusion in the race by running through two fences and into the crowd at Turn 10. No one was seriously injured but the race was red flagged in the resulting confusion. When it was restarted with 40 laps still to run, Donohue was in the lead and never gave it up. The confusion started at the finish when Jones was penalized for continuing under a red flag, but after a two-hour debate he was awarded 3rd place. Certainly no doubt existed that Donohue's Camaro was the fastest car out there, whatever the special challenges presented by the War Bonnet course.

However, no confusion existed about the fact that the course and its officiating crew needed some upgrading for the next year's event. They didn't know it yet, but there would be no next year's event.

A crowd of 15,000 was reported, and this figure may have been possible considering the amount of national attention Trans-Am racing was creating that year. However, it was far short of the 30,000 that was forecast for the event. Ken Jones recalls that 15,000 might have been the correct number anyway.

But it may have been just as well because spectator safety measures were almost nonexistent. Yellow cards were nailed to trees marking the spectators' borders, and a roll of yellow tape was haphazardly strung from tree to pasture fence post. The track had no fencing, and, as a matter of fact, there never was any during the track's existence. More fans could certainly have been out there despite everything, but no doubt the days of rain that preceded Sunday's big race had dampened the enthusiasm of car racing fans and kept them home.

The 1968 Oklahoma Grand Prix was won by Dr. Lou Sell in an Eagle-Chevy. The airplanes must have been trucked in for display purposes. (Photo Courtesy Robert Baron)

Dick Smothers is shown on the War Bonnet back straight in the Oklahoma Grand Prix; he finished 10th. He raced nationally that year in the SCCA's Formula B series and never failed to attract a lot of attention. (Photo Courtesy Robert Baron)

As reported, the race was exciting and successful, but the track faced many problems during the course of the weekend that had to be resolved. The days preceding the race saw a continual downpour of rain that again turned the dirt access roads into quagmires. Reports indicate that several Trans-Am cars attempting to drive to the track were bogged down to such an extent that it took a tow truck to extricate them and their trailers. Somehow, the experienced Trans-Am team truck drivers did get their trailers and big rigs through, probably thanks to their well-honed driving skills. Once they were at the track they found a dirt pit area that also was quite muddy.

The track's surface was not up to the standards expected for an event of this caliber, so how the course was ever approved for a Trans-Am event is a mystery. Probably (sincere) course improvement promises were made, but in the end the repaving was not done. Preliminary events on Saturday were held in terrible conditions. The little stream under the bridge actually rose high enough to flood that part of the course. Dan Davis, the current publisher of *Victory Lane* magazine, remembers that in the supporting Formula Vee race, every one of the nine-car field hydroplaned and spun out at that spot on the first lap.

Despite this negative reporting, regional SCCA drivers and officials were generally pleased with the event and sadly noted that the good racing that went on was overshadowed by the reporters' apparent eagerness to latch onto the negatives of the weekend. And the weather wasn't the fault of the course or Bob Moore (although it always seemed to rain for races at War Bonnet).

The 12-page black-and-white program for the War Bonnet Trans-Am race was probably the paltriest produced for any event on that series, but it did contain some outrageous claims and promises. Moore was no doubt dealing with the financial strains and went all out to promote the track's future and convince people to (literally) buy into it. He again called War Bonnet "the Nürburgring of the Midwest." War Bonnet, he proclaimed, "will soon become the greatest raceway on the North American continent. In less than five years it will become a way of life.

"When you buy a home on War Bonnet Estates next to the course, with its soon-to-come 18-hole championship golf course and

In this shot, it really looks like a racetrack! Shift point signs are a prominent feature as formula cars round the far hairpin on the long course in a 1968 War Bonnet race. (Photo Courtesy Robert Baron)

Chapter 15: War Bonnet Raceway Park   153

Roadsters were tried on the track as a spectator pull, but they did not fare well. (Photo Courtesy Robert Baron)

other soon-to-come recreational and social amenities, you are buying much more than just a home. On Sunday you can enjoy a car race on the War Bonnet track from the comfort of your lawn or veranda. After the race go hunting on the spacious, game-filled grounds. Then a quick massage and dinner at the clubhouse and you or your guests can leave via your private plane in the facility's soon-to-come 3,000-foot airstrip."

At the same time he trumpeted these lofty plans, Moore did not have the capital to make the claims a reality. Even though there were few massages and no planes landing for the next race, the War Bonnet Grand Prix of Oklahoma hosted some pretty good racing. On June 16, the SCCA Formula series returned to War Bonnet, with the new F5000s dominating the lineup. Again, considering the track's reputation, and the narrow, tight course, it is difficult to see how the SCCA granted its sanction for an event with cars of this power. But it went off just fine.

Lou Sell, 2nd the previous year, won in an Eagle-Chevy over George Wintersteen. Sell set a lap record that will stand for all time: 1:30 flat. As always, a lot of attention was paid to Dick Smothers, racing in the series' second-tier Formula B. A lot of attention also went to an unusual supporting race, the Tulsa-based supermodifieds that had a preliminary race on the short course. A good effort was made to draw a different kind of fan. Spectators did notice, however, how slow the cars were compared to the F5000s that raced soon afterward. Local oil company Sunray DX remained a loyal sponsor and kept Bob Moore and War Bonnet going for a while longer.

Sunray put its full weight behind the Sunray DX Grand Prix, the last big race held at War Bonnet, in late 1968. It was rewarded with a lot of unanticipated publicity when movie star James Garner showed up at the track and chatted with spectators and drivers. However, his on-course activity was restricted to driving the pace car and a hot lap with overall feature race winner Don Yenko. The claimed crowd of 7,000 saw quite a race as Yenko, in his Corvette, just held on over Milt Minter in a Porsche 904.

1969: The Dream Fades

A full schedule was initially announced for the 1969 season. The reality of the situation was that by this time, Moore was reduced to living in the timing tower. Funds for maintaining the track, let alone realizing his other dreams, were obviously scarce. Two SCCA races were finally held on the basic course. Bill Moore (no relation) won the first race in an F5000 Lola T142, which was a powerful car for the tight course, especially with rain pelting down. The second event, in July, was highlighted by everyone in the pit area cramming around a TV set in the back of a pickup truck to watch the moon landing.

Later that year, Sunray, having merged with SunOil to form Sunoco, pulled its track sponsorship. That was the death knell for War Bonnet. There just weren't any more funds to keep the track open, and Moore's rubbery checks were no longer enough. For a few years, he fought developers with court actions, but they ultimately proved to be fruitless. The track closed without notice and was soon overgrown with weeds and long grasses.

For years, it remained pretty much as it had been left, with a few houses built on the portions that had been added to make it 2.3 miles. The road surface, even in the areas that contained houses, deteriorated continually and was barely drivable by the late 1990s. In the early 2000s, though, the population surrounding Tulsa had grown enough so that a real housing development was gradually built around the 1.1-mile course. A recreational complex was constructed in the infield, complete with soccer fields and tennis courts.

Most of the old track surface was at least repaved and the entire old course is still there, under new smooth asphalt. Residents use it daily but they don't have to worry about the mud, which seemed to plague every race in War Bonnet's heyday. Grass now grows on lawns in the old runoff areas and on the infield. Reunions and car shows held on the old short circuit recall the dreams that fueled War Bonnet.

Ken Lawrence and Ken Jones show the split point for the two courses. The shorter course went right, the longer Trans-Am course went to the left. (Photo Courtesy Judy Rudow)

A sharp right uphill and you are on the way to the backside of the long course. (Photo Courtesy Judy Rudow)

This is the meandering, long-course 1,650-foot back straight today. (Photo Courtesy Judy Rudow)

Ken Lawrence and Ken Jones, both of whom raced at the track, stand atop the base of the old timing tower, the only artifact that remains of the War Bonnet track today. (Photo Courtesy Judy Rudow)

WATKINS GLEN

A ROAD COURSE HISTORY NOT FORGOTTEN

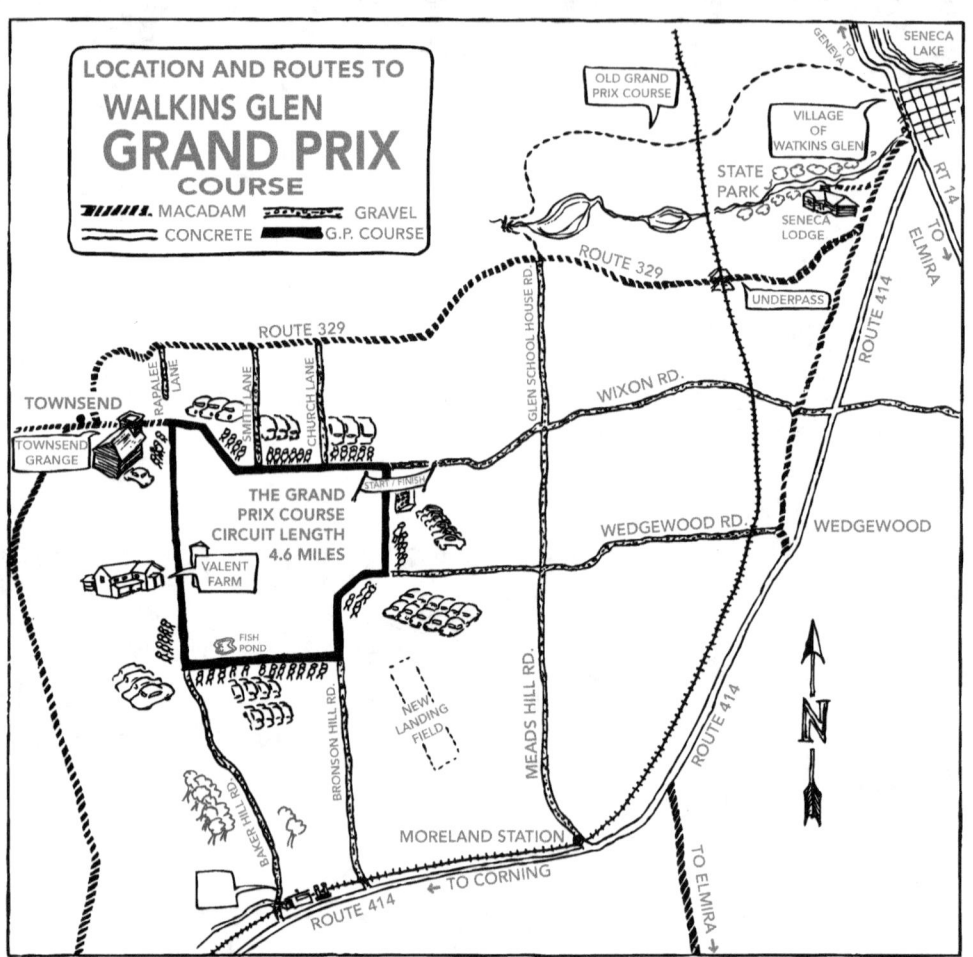

A course map of the 1953–1955 Watkins Glen course is rather cartoony. Made up of local farm roads and specially built sections, the course had nine turns. That long downhill back straight went by the Valent Farm and ended up at Townsend Corner. (Illustration Courtesy International Motor Racing Research Center)

Glen had a population of 3,000 and was (and still is) a charming small town with an old-fashioned main street, surrounded by broadleaf forests and small farms. Argetsinger convinced the city fathers that the race he was proposing would draw lots of needed tourists and attention to the town. All they had to do was to close a few streets in town and the surrounding countryside for racing and have the railroad stop trains during race hours.

Amazingly, they accomplished all of it and the race was on! The course surface consisted of asphalt, concrete, and even a few dirt road sections. The first race, scheduled for October 2, 1948, was the first road race held in North America following World War II.

These through-the-city years have been well documented, and the racing was wonderfully exciting and romantic. Top drivers from all over the country convened at Watkins Glen for the Watkins Glen Grand Prix weekend. It started with less than 100 entries; of those, at least a third were MGs. But spectators were delighted with those 100 cars, and soon were even more delighted.

In very short order, the Watkins Glen field grew to include all of the top drivers and racing teams of the day. A fascinating

If you don't know the name Watkins Glen . . . why are you reading this book? Watkins Glen holds the most unique place in American road racing history, from its postwar, through-the-streets roots to modern-day racing at the highest level. During its nearly 60 years, racing at Watkins Glen has included SCCA, USAC, NASCAR, FIA Formula 1 and sports cars, Formula 5000, Indy Cars, Trans-Am, and Can-Am.

It all started in 1948 when a young Cam Argetsinger, who had spent his idyllic boyhood summers on a lake near Watkins Glen, had the idea of bringing European-style, through-the-streets road racing to the little Upstate New York town. Set in the scenic Finger Lakes region, Watkins

CHAPTER 16

Watkins Glen, New York
1953–1955

Facility 4.6 miles, 9 turns
Principal Events SCCA, unsanctioned races
Current Status The entire course remains, some of it as part of the present configuration, some reverted to county roads

A mixed pack and a big crowd fill Townsend Corner in the 1955 Grand Prix. John Sinclair leads in a Jaguar-Cadillac Special. Right behind him is the Excalibur J Special. (Photo Courtesy John Bishop)

mix of pre- and postwar cars started out in the first couple of years, but Cunninghams, Ferraris, Allards, and the other fast cars of the early 1950s soon enhanced the field. The cars' speed and size outgrew the city course faster than the officials realized, and despite yearly safety improvements, they had to find a new location when a passing race car killed a spectator in the 1952 race. The fact that the spectator, tragically, a young boy, was in an area banned to onlookers made no difference. The venue was no longer acceptable for the bigger and faster cars that were coming to the race.

Calls in the media demanded an immediate ban on all forms of motor racing, but especially on-road courses. "The Watkins Glen Grand Prix is one of the greatest sporting events in the United States. The races demonstrate how a small community with intelligent leadership and hard work can devise an event that can attract people from all over the world," said the area's representative to the state government. It was going to be up to the community to prove him right by coming up with a new course with an emphasis on safety.

The Transition Track

The Watkins Glen course used from 1956 to today has stayed pretty much in the same location. Although the course has seen several enhancements, it remains the iconic East Coast track for the big events mentioned earlier and is as up-to-date as any racing facility in the world. Today when most people think of racing at Watkins Glen, they envision the old picturesque through-the-city course or today's state-of-the-art, purpose-built track and its surrounding modern facilities.

But there was another track, one that is almost forgotten today: a transition track that bridged the gap between the banning of through-the-streets racing and the construction of the all-new purpose-built facility that is still in use today. Used from 1953 through 1955, this track had its own attractions, hazards, and highlights, and saw some great racing. It included sections built for the race as well as some public roads. Its bones remain and, indeed, some of the public road sections are in busy everyday use.

For three years, it withstood the scrutiny and criticism of a world shocked by tragic fatalities at Indianapolis during practice and the famous 500, and especially the June 1955 Le Mans accident, in which more than 80 people were killed.

The Watkins Glen Grand Prix Corporation, a group that was formed by the Chamber of Commerce to stage the race, selected the 1953–1955 course. In an enviable never-say-die attitude, they went out to find the site for a new track where a course could be laid out that would meet everyone's standards. The course they came up with was in an area known as Upper Dix, at the top of a hill in farmland a little southwest of the center of Watkins Glen.

Early Watkins Glen racing favorites George Weaver and Bill Milliken helped select and prepare the roads that made up the new course. They came up with a 4.6-mile basically boxy-shaped course, a series of right-hand turns with a couple of squiggles thrown in. A few old farmhouses from longtime Watkins Glen families stood not too far from the side of the roads. The new portions of the track that were somewhat hastily built included some connecting roads, the pits, the start/finish line stretch, and a few bleachers. Snow fencing was installed around the course.

Probably the most thrilling feature was an exceptionally long straightaway across the fields from the start/finish area; it was more than a mile long and all downhill. Speeds of more than 150 mph were reported on this long straight, and it ended with a 90-degree right-hand turn across from the Townsend grange building. Small cars topped out about halfway down the straightaway; big cars had to be very careful when braking because they were sure to take a good, hot rubbing from having to slow so much to safely make the corner.

The SCCA refused to sanction the first race, but it still drew a good enough crowd of spectators and racers to ensure the Watkins Glen Grand Prix Corporation that they were on the right track (pun intended). Even though photos show a course still without adequate spectator protection (by today's or even late-1950s standards), it went off without incident and the SCCA sanctioned the 1954 race.

During the first year, 1953, only three races were offered: the Seneca Cup for all modified comers, the Queen Catherine for all cars 1,500 cc and under, and the Grand Prix for everyone else.

During 1954 and 1955, five major races were offered as part of the Grand Prix weekend: the Seneca Cup Race for cars of an unrestricted category, the Collier Brothers Memorial Trophy for production MGs only, the Glen Trophy Race for production sports cars of all classes except production MGs, the Queen Catherine Cup for modified cars of 1,500 cc and under, and the Watkins Glen Grand Prix for modified cars of 1,500 cc and over.

1953: A Shaky But Promising Start

The 1953 race did not have SCCA sanction and the national club made some effort to discourage people from competing. It had been put together too hastily, they reasoned, and they were fearful about safety. They need not have worried. A relatively small but interesting field of 100 cars resulted. The 1953 race, held on September 19, saw an emphasis on spectator control, as you'd expect. Photos from the race show spectators standing three and four deep behind snow fencing in heavy clothing because the weather became unseasonably cool and crisp.

Argetsinger and others in charge of putting together the new course and its facilities had done a first-class job on safety, especially with communications systems, which were state-of-the-art for the time. Three workers manned each of the 31 flag stations, each in constant communication with the start/finish area. Ample emergency vehicles were on hand, and thankfully they were not needed, at least during that first year.

The safety and well-being of the local farmers whose fields were next to the track and in some cases used for spectator viewing areas was not forgotten, either. Spectators, the event program admonished, were not to enter the farm buildings or trample on their unpicked crops; this was harvest season after all! Dodging piles of the inevitable cow manure was left to the individual spectator's discretion.

In the Seneca Cup, a diverse field included Formula 1 Maseratis all the way down to the little Formula 3 cars. Phil Cade, driving a Maserati with a 5.6-liter Chrysler engine, led much of the race, only to be beaten in a nifty move by M. R. J. Wyllie in the last turn. Wyllie was one of the pioneers of the sport and a leading advocate for safety measures in sports car racing. He must have put his approval on the weekend. Wyllie, driving a factory-modified Jaguar XK-120, may have been a safety advocate but he pushed his way by Cade in the last turn to win by about 20 yards.

Bill Sadler's Hillman Minx Special and the MG of David Bryson have just arrived in the paddock the day before the 1953 Grand Prix. (Photo Courtesy Bill Sadler)

This shot from the 1953 race speaks volumes. Note the old-school helmet, the upright driving posture, and the basic preparation of the car, a modified Hillman Minx. This was Bill Sadler's first race at the Glen. (Photo Courtesy Bill Sadler)

The Queen Catherine Cup Race was an exciting contest between two OSCAs that were constantly trading places. But Henry Wessells, one of the OSCA drivers, had engine trouble. That allowed George Moffett to assume the lead and take the win. This race saw the only accident of the day when Phil Coles rolled his Singer on the last corner. Even though on-course reaction was swift, no other cars were near enough to suffer any damage and no one, including Cole, was hurt.

The Grand Prix saw Walt Hansgen win one of his earliest big races, in a Hansgen Jaguar Special of his own design and build. The talented Hansgen was an ace mechanic as well as an accomplished driver. He dueled almost race-long with the Allards of George Harris and Delevan Lee. Hansgen seemed to have the race in hand, but he developed fuel starvation problems a few hundred yards from the finish line on the last lap. He limped across the line to win over Harris by a scant two car lengths.

Drivers were not altogether pleased with the new course. Visibility was not great and run-off areas were insufficient; a few were bordered with telephone poles and drainage ditches. That long straightaway intimidated some. Still, everyone was glad that racing at Watkins Glen was going ahead.

1954: The Sophomore Season

After the promising but somewhat shaky 1953 start, the 1954 race showed that racing at Watkins Glen was back, and in overwhelming fashion, with entries from 220 cars. The SCCA must have been glad they took this one on; it was a record entry for an SCCA event. These cars were an impressive lot, too, and driven by most of the top East Coast drivers of the era. The entry list included eight Ferraris, a number of Cunninghams, several Allards J2Xs, assorted OSCAs, a Kurtis-Cad, and many production cars.

The Saturday, September 18, races were kicked off by a cannon shot that, according to reports, was absolutely ear deafening and certainly got the attention of the 200,000 people on hand for the races. Spectators absolutely crammed every available place to eat, sleep, and (in many cases) even stand in the little town the night before the races. The first three races were 11 laps each.

For the second year in a row, M. R. J. Wyllie won the Seneca Cup for cars in the "unrestricted" category. The crowd's favorite, though, was a little F3 Cooper, which was among the leaders for quite a while before its lack of displacement caught up with it and it fell back. Allards and specials followed Wyllie in.

The Collier Brothers event for MGs saw a great field of 32 cars. The TD of Gus Ehrman barely won it, less than one second ahead of Ralph Durbin's TF and three other TFs. In those days, such marque races were actually among bone-stock production cars; driver skill was the deciding factor.

The new Glen Trophy Race for production cars other than MGs was next and Dick Perrin, to no one's surprise, won in a Jaguar XK-120, with George Constantine and Warren Smith next, also in Jaguars. Constantine was to become a major force in East Coast racing over the next few years. The semifinal Queen Catherine Cup (16 laps) was again dominated by OSCAs. Frank Bott, from Illinois, won this one. The Stanguellinis and Siatas in this race at least impressed the crowd with their looks.

The Grand Prix race shaped up as a battle between the Cunninghams and Ferraris. The brutally fast Cunninghams were, of course, built and raced by the Briggs Cunningham

These are some of the cars that raced in 1953, from the 1954 program.

team and featured Chrysler V-8 engines. The sleek Ferraris were establishing a winning tradition in the United States. Both teams featured top drivers. Bill Spear and Jim Kimberly were the top Ferrari drivers; Sherwood Johnson and Phil Walters were the best for Cunningham.

Spear led for the first half of the race. But then he famously made eye contact with Walters as they entered Townsend Corner side-by-side and he dropped back. Then, the bumps on the course led to mechanical failure and Walters won, almost

Allan Patterson is at the 1954 race in a Cad-Allard, a popular early-years car at Glen races. (Photo Courtesy John Bishop)

From the 1954 race, Dick Irish, in an early Ferrari, leads Sherwood Johnson's Cunningham CR-4 on County Route 16 headed toward the last turn. (Photo Courtesy John Bishop)

A mishap at Townsend Corner involves several production cars. Identifiable (left to right) are a TR2 in the hands of Bob Salzgaber, a Porsche driven by Art Bunker, a Healy already abandoned by Ed Glowacke, and a Jaguar driven by Hugh Sutherland. (Photo Courtesy John Bishop)

unopposed. It was a popular Cunningham win. Kimberly brought his Ferrari in 2nd. Onlookers noted that the heavy Cunninghams had less trouble with the bumpy course and even seemed to handle better in the rain, at least on this course.

A two-engined Porsche Special, with two superchargers, driven by noted unlimited hydroplane driver Lou Fageol, also raced that weekend. Fageol, evidently comfortable in wet conditions thanks to his boat-racing background, dug a new course for himself in the mud on the outside of each turn and used it to the surprise and bewilderment of his fellow drivers. However effective this technique was, he came in only 10th.

The race was again a success on the course: no injuries or bad incidents. Rain halfway through the final had not dampened anyone's spirits. It was nothing but onward and upward for the Watkins Glen Grand Prix weekend on the new course.

1955: Swan Song at the Middle Track

The 1955 race showed that the new course, like its predecessor, did not have the ability to accommodate the newer, more powerful cars. Also, the course surface was simply breaking up, particularly in the first turn and at Townsend Corner. Drivers complained that the fearsome long downhill straight was made worse by a rough, washboard-like surface.

The Jaguar D-Types and Mercedes-Benz 300SLs, among others, piqued excitement for the weekend. M. R. J. Wyllie won the Seneca Cup for the third straight year, this time in a C-Jaguar. Such wins gave him further credibility when he worked to increase safety measures in the SCCA. The first 300SL to run at the Glen was in this race, in the hands of Dan Boylan. He came in a strong 2nd after starting near the back of the pack. Only one nasty flip occurred, but the driver sustained only minor injuries.

Someone let an HRG and a few VWs sneak into the supposedly all-MG Collier Brothers Memorial Race, making it more of an under-1,500-cc event (but without Porsches). Still, MGs took the first three places; Oakleigh Robinson took the checkered flag in his TF less than 3/10 of a second ahead of Henry Willard in an older TC. It was noted that in this race especially, many of the small cars simply over-revved their engines on the long straight and, as a result, broke down.

The Glen Trophy Race was where Mercedes-Benz really shone; it was the cars' second appearance at the track on the same day. The 300SLs took the top two places in the hands of Paul O'Shea and Ed Hugus. The best that the formerly all-conquering Jags could do was a 3rd place in the hands of Dick Thompson. O'Shea was gaining quite a reputation as a Mercedes-Benz ace while Thompson may have been biding his time before stepping into his first Corvette. The next year saw the great Thompson–O'Shea duels that were a highlight of the 1950s.

This famous painting of the 1954 race is displayed as a wall mural in downtown Watkins Glen. It shows Bill Spear and Phil Walters heading toward Townsend Corner in the 1954 Grand Prix. (Painting by Robert Gillespie, glenspeed.com to see more)

The pits for the 1955 race were crowded and hectic, but work had to be done, as here on Bill Sadler's *Sadler Special*, which took 18th in the Queen Catherine Cup race that year. (Photo Courtesy Bill Sadler)

The start of the 1955 Start Seneca Cup sees Bob Bucher in a rebodied Cad-Allard (#29) along with Phil Cade's Maserati (#7) and John Plaisted's Cheetah (#222). (Photo Courtesy Gus Iacozili Collection)

In the 1955 Seneca Cup Race, George Rabe drove a historic Riley-Ford, *Ardent Alligator*, that won the 1949 Grand Prix with Miles Collier driving. By 1955, it was no longer competitive and came in 30th. (Photo Courtesy Gus Iacozili Collection)

This year, another perennial favorite, OSCA, did not win the Queen Catherine Cup. Briggs Cunningham's car suffered mechanical failure while in the lead, which allowed Porsche 550s to come in 1st and 2nd. Years later, Bill Weldon's winning 550 is still often listed in race results as a Simca Special, as it was in the event program. However, it was most assuredly a Porsche 550. In a photo finish, Weldon was over the line by just half a car length in front of Art Bunker's 550.

This race is also notable because it was the last appearance of Bill Sadler's small-bore *Sadler Special*. The following year, he returned in a new big-bore *Sadler Special* that stunned the racing world by winning the initial Glen Grand Prix over the usual fierce opposition of foreign and domestic superstars.

In the 1955 Collier Brothers Memorial Trophy, the TD driven by Harry Logan, Jr. (#158) leads the Oakleigh Robinson race-winning TF (#116). (Photo Courtesy Gus Iacozili Collection)

The final race of the middle course, and one might even say of the "old days" at Watkins Glen, was the Grand Prix. It drew the usual fine field, but this time the race was no contest. Sherwood Johnson drove a Cunningham team D-Jaguar to victory. At the beginning, Bill Spear, another Glen veteran,

The 1955 Glen Trophy Race sees two drivers who were to be frequent rivals in years to come. Dick Thompson is in the Jaguar XK-140 MC (#112) and Paul O'Shea is driving the race-winning Mercedes-Benz 300SL (#18). (Photo Courtesy Gus Iacozili Collection)

Addison Austin came in 10th in the Glen Trophy Race, driving the first Corvette to race at the Glen. (Photo Courtesy Gus Iacozili Collection)

Bill Sadler in the *Sadler Special* (#128) leads a practice session at the 1955 Queen Catherine Cup. Next to him is Joe Giubardo, *MG Special*, followed by a bevy of Porsche 550s, including the Queen Catherine Cup winner of Bill Weldon (#103). (Photo Courtesy Bill Sadler)

At the start of the 1955 Grand Prix are Duncan Black, Ferrari 4.5 liter (#44); Sherwood Johnston, Jaguar D (#60); John Bennett, Maserati 300S (#59); and Bill Lloyd, Maserati 300S (#16). (Photo Courtesy Gus Iacozili Collection)

Sherwood Johnston was the 1955 Grand Prix winner in a Cunningham-sponsored D-Jaguar. (Photo Courtesy Gus Iacozili Collection)

In the 1955 Grand Prix, Charles Moran, Jr. screams by in a Cunningham C4R. Even though the car was outdated, he still managed a creditable 7th. (Photo Courtesy Gus Iacozili Collection)

162   Lost Road Courses

A bemused crowd sees 1955 Grand Prix Race winner Sherwood Johnston shake hands with car owner Briggs Cunningham. (Photo Courtesy Gus Iacozili Collection)

1956: The Final Course

The Le Mans accident had horrified the whole world, and again brought racing under intense scrutiny. By the end of 1955, the clamor was overwhelming for banning road racing, if not entirely, then certainly on public roads. Watkins Glens' city fathers decided to keep the popular race weekend going, but knew that a purpose-built circuit was necessary. They would no longer use public roads, and as a result, the safety of both spectators and drivers could be better controlled. The city rallied behind the cause and sold individual shares to citizens to help raise money for a new track.

The new circuit was used for the first time for the 1956 Grand Prix weekend, and from then on, the course allowed for races to be scheduled throughout the year. NASCAR even came onboard. The international Formula Libre races held in the late 1950s attracted the best European drivers, Formula 1 arrived in the early 1960s, and the track was on its way to becoming the international icon it is today.

Plenty has been written about those years, but the middle course has been more or less neglected and consigned to always being the least mentioned in modern articles on racing at the Glen.

Today, the Glen still celebrates its great racing history with a vintage-racing weekend with citywide events and vintage racing at the new track. The Argetsinger family–led International Motor Racing Research Center is headquartered in Watkins Glen and conducts research on the Glen's own events as well as racing around the world. They don't have to go far to research the facility that is still a favorite of racing fans everywhere, whether it is the first, the middle, or the present course in Watkins Glen.

challenged Johnson for several laps; in the end, his Maserati 300 could not match the D-Jag's acceleration. Bill Lloyd, in another Maserati, was 3rd; he never really challenged for the top spot.

The rough pavement slowed the average race speed considerably to 83.3 mph. Also contributing to the slower times was the fact that as the hot day wore on, the pavement softened significantly. One driver remarked that it was like driving on marshmallows. When the weekend was over, everyone was speculating that the course surface would have to be redone before next year's race. But bigger changes than a resurfacing were in store.

The fearsome Townsend Corner looks harmless today. At this point, the fastest cars in the 1953–1955 races would have been reaching top speed, in some cases over 150 mph. (Photo Courtesy Judy Rudow)

This is the site of the start/finish line of the 1953–1955 course today, showing portions of the present facility. (Photo Courtesy Judy Rudow)

WESTWOOD MOTORSPORTS PARK

WET, WICKED AND TWISTY

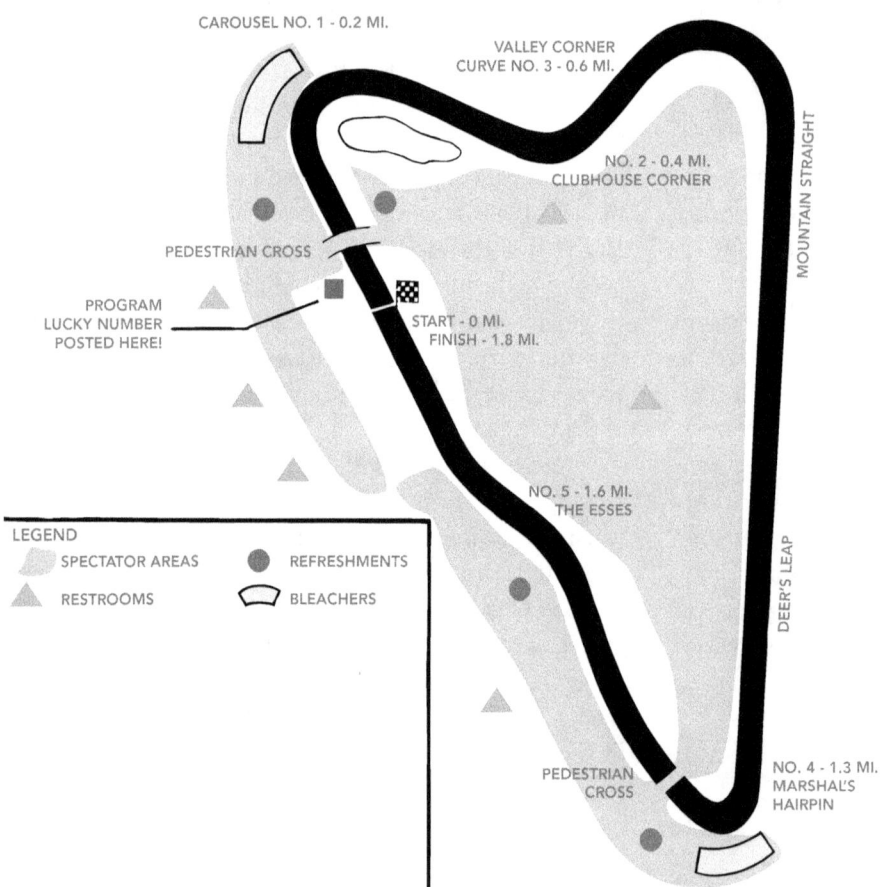

Westwood, when fully realized in the late 1980s, looked very similar to its first weekend in 1959. The main differences: bleachers, pedestrian bridges, and the number of restrooms. (Illustration Courtesy John Randall)

Furthest from the mainstream of road racing were two Western Canadian tracks: Edmonton and Westwood. Both had their share of top races and attracted leading cars and drivers of the day, Edmonton admittedly more so. But Westwood had the longer life, the more interesting history, and saw such great drivers as Jerry Grant, Pete Lovely, Eppie Wietzes, Bob McLean, and Michael Andretti make their marks there.

Many North American tracks were constructed in out-of-the-way, even desolate, places. But none were constructed in a more out of the way place with less capital investment than Westwood. No other track was constructed to such an extent by the sweat of its future racers, who were exhorted to go to such lengths as to "quit drinking" to come up with the money needed to build the track.

The Sports Car Club of British Columbia (SCCBC) had used an old regional airport at Abbotsford, British Columbia, as its home track for several years. But in 1958, airport management notified the club that the track was too valuable to accommodate sports car racing and was needed for commercial air travel. To continue racing, the club would have to find a new facility. Simply finding a new airport course would not be a real solution, because as at Abbotsford, airports all over the country (and continent) were rapidly closing to non-aviation activities. Building its own facility was the club's only practical answer. If it were even practical.

A potential site for a new course was located in a remote logged-off area next to an old gravel pit north of the little British Columbia town of Coquitlam. Although other areas might have an open-desert or wind-swept plains site that would need little clearing for a road circuit to be laid down, wet and woodsy British Columbia was different. But the proposed site was an easy 20-mile drive from the bustling young metropolis of Vancouver, a city full of rabid racing fans and racers.

The February 1958 issue of the SCCBC's club magazine, *Pit Pass*, laid it out: $50,000 was needed for final clearing of the land, paving the course, and putting in an access

CHAPTER 17

Coquitlam, British Columbia, Canada
1959–1990

Facility	1.8 miles, 5 turns, average 26 feet wide
Principal Events	Pepsi Pro, Player's Pacific, Trans-Am, Formula Atlantic
Current Status	Housing development; only traces of the track remain

A consortium of enthusiasts determined to develop a racetrack for the region built Westwood. The construction crew, actually SCCBC members, begins to clear the land at the new Westwood facility in this 1959 photo. For months, weekends and two weekday nights were devoted to clearing land and preparing for paving. (Photo Courtesy SCCBC Archive)

road. This $50,000 would let them start without more than "basic facilities" and did not include the cost of the land itself, which was being rented from the provincial government in British Columbia for a "nominal fee." The $50,000 would all have to come from individual sales of debentures. Club Vice President Claire Wilson, writing in *Pit Pass*, urged members to buy those debentures, even if it meant personal hardship. "Squeeze out those extra pennies! Stop smoking! Stop drinking! Take the bus!"

The official debenture sales brochure provided specifics, including a description of the 480-acre facility, named therein as Westwood. It was named after Minister of Recreation Earl Westwood, whose assistance in securing the government's lease for the site had been vital. Huge stumps, gnarly roots, tough scrubby trees, shallow ponds, and glacial rocks covered the area. On the plus side, a good base of gravel existed directly beneath the topsoil, ideal for laying the planned 2-mile blacktopped circuit. The entire cost of the project was estimated to be $82,000, with the club kicking in $32,000 of its own funds on top of the $50,000 to be raised by the debenture sales.

Debenture sales proved to be strong enough (liquor sales no doubt plunged in British Columbia during the same period) and construction was started on the Westwood facility during the winter of 1958.

Needless to say, building a racetrack for just $82,000 is mind-boggling by today's standards, no matter how many club members volunteered to help. That's right, club members. Many of the same guys who had bought debentures now showed up to build the track by the sweat of their brow, digging outhouses, hauling away rocks, and cutting down trees. Family members were often part of the work crews, starting the family feel that was to be part of the charm of Westwood.

Work sessions were held regularly, rain or shine, on Tuesday and Thursday evenings and over weekends. It took six months during the winter of 1958–1959, an amazingly short amount of time considering the budget, to get the job done. The track was finally completed at a cost of $180,000. Two of the major contractors helped float the funds, which were eventually paid back by the club.

The original plan was for a track of 2.4 miles, but it ended up at 1.8 miles long and 26 feet wide. No formal blueprint for the circuit appears to have been drafted; rough sketches exist, but to an extent, the course was simply made up as the clearing proceeded. Even the famous (or infamous) Deer's Leap hill on the backstretch was not planned. The contractor simply refused to flatten the 75-foot rise that was on the backstretch for what he was being paid for his services.

This photo, taken during the short, 1.8-mile track's first weekend shows the beautiful surroundings that appeared on a sunny day. Unfortunately, there were few of these days. (Photo Courtesy SCCBC Archive)

1959: The First Race, Finally

The club had hoped to hold the first race in April 1959. Even with everyone's best efforts with pick, ax, and shovel, the inaugural date was moved to May, then June 7. Then, abnormally heavy rains and boggy grounds caused a delay in hard-surfacing the circuit. Even a slated June 28 debut was canceled.

Finally the course opened for racing on July 26, 1959. The field featured fewer than 100 cars, mostly local. More entries from the States might have come, but the scheduling fluctuations at Westwood had led many drivers to make other plans. One American, Pete Lovely, established the first lap record: 1:26, 75.6 mph in his Lotus 15. He was quoted as saying that the circuit was similar to Monaco, where he had raced with the Lotus F1 team earlier that year. Pete certainly was talking about the course, not the surroundings, when he made that comparison. The land-locked Westwood site was about as far from the Mediterranean harbor-side setting at Monaco as it could be. Rugged mountains and thick forests surrounded the British Columbia circuit. On a nice day it was as beautiful as any course in the world, Monaco included.

Beautiful but dangerous. The beautiful (when sunny), challenging course was the most hazardous of any in the Northwest, by far. Ironically, it all started with Mike Balfe, one of the leaders in the drive for construction, who was taken to a local hospital with a concussion and bruises after his TR3 rolled over three times on a circuit curve. Another driver flipped his MGA during the second race but escaped uninjured.

Hazards aside, and this was motor racing after all, SCCBC members had every right to feel intensely proud of the circuit made possible largely through their own labors and funds.

Rains Come and Come

Unfortunately, after the blue-sky-filled opening weekend, it often rained at Westwood, gaining it the nickname *Wet*wood. To make things worse, just plain dirt covered most of the areas surrounding the track and where spectators stood. When it rained, these areas became muddy quagmires. Over the years, some grass grew in these areas, but for the first several seasons, muddy shoes and tires were frequent souvenirs of a race weekend at Westwood.

The early timing tower at Westwood was a trailer unit used previously at Abbotsford. Drivers' wives and girlfriends took care of the timing stations. (Photo Courtesy SCCBC Archive)

A Driver's View of Westwood

In the first issue of *Pit Pass*, the local club's newsletter, a participant in Westwood's first weekend described the course from a driver's perspective.

"At the start/finish line across from the pits there is ample room for drivers to pull off and for Le Mans starts. The course then runs slightly uphill for a few dozen yards then goes into a sweeping left bend, which develops into the Carousel, a 14-degree banked, semi-circular right-hand turn.

"As cars accelerate out of the Carousel, the road is slightly uphill; it then slopes suddenly and simultaneously goes into a sharp left, almost camber-less corner: the Clubhouse corner.

"After the Clubhouse, the track falls steeply for about a fifth of a mile to the 'Valley Corner' curve, a right-hander that tunnels the cars onto the straightaway. This straight is about a half-mile long; it rises to a spot called Deer's Leap then drops as the cars reach the Hairpin.

Cars approach the hairpin at top speeds and must slow to about 30 to take the corner. This tricky turn starts level, and then goes uphill as it proceeds. Still uphill for a quarter of a mile, the course winds through the Esses, the only flat-out curves on the track. A short straight runs from the Esses back to the start/finish line."

John Randall, in his Brabham, approaches the Carousel Turn, one of Westwood's most challenging and iconic features. (Photo Courtesy John Randall)

Deer's Leap and the Carousel in particular provided a lot of white-knuckled excitement and more than their share of bent metal at Westwood.

To go with the dirt/mud, many small- to medium-sized boulders were strewn about the infield (this was glacial fill, after all) and an off-course excursion could result in a nasty dent in the fender or the loss of an oil pan. This was one hazard that never really went away in the entire 32-year history of the track. Even though grass eventually grew over them, this only made them harder to see and thus more dangerous.

The First Race

The first race of the first Westwood racing weekend went fittingly enough to one of the course's volunteer construction workers, Tom Meehan, who won the mixed-breed sprint event in a Cooper-Porsche. The feature saw Frank Becker's 2-liter Ferrari come in first, followed by Jim Rattenbury in his D Jaguar, while a 3-liter Testa Rosa Ferrari driven by George Keck came in 3rd. These three had quite a tussle, to the delight of the crowd.

Becker's smaller Ferrari seemed to have just the right blend of power and nimble handling for the tight and tricky circuit. His two pursuers were notably faster on the straights. This formula for winning at Westwood was basically unchanged over the years; it was a course where a big horsepower advantage did not ensure a victory.

From a spectator's viewpoint, the course was great, with banked areas providing excellent viewing. For the first race and first few years of competition, amenities were Spartan, especially bathrooms, or the lack of them. Pit toilets were the

One of Westwood's hazards that never really went away was glacier rocks. They took out many an oil pan, as with this Maserati 2000. (Photo Courtesy Tom Meehan Collection)

Bob McLean was one of the most successful and popular Western Canadian drivers of the 1960s. Here, in a 1962 Westwood race, he temporarily leads Pete Lovely. He won often at Westwood and elsewhere, but was tragically killed in an accident at Sebring. (Photo Courtesy Pete Lovely Estate)

norm. The facility had very much of a primitive, hand-built-out-of-wilderness feel to it. Which it was, after all.

Not being able to race for months had left the SCCBC group with a lot of pent-up desire. This showed as races were scheduled almost every other weekend to the end of that first year. This pattern continued for years; there was no lack of enthusiasm for putting on and competing in races at Westwood.

Lap times continued to drop. George Keck drove a Ferrari TR that, many years later, was worth more than $10 million. In the middle of a torrid race with Lovely, Keck broke Lovely's record when he turned a 1:23.67 lap time.

Highlights through the Years

Track development continued during the 1960 season but at a slow pace. Westwood had originally scheduled March 27 as the opener, but the event was canceled. The facility, still in very raw shape, was awash in mud after a series of especially heavy rains. So an Easter Sunday opening was scheduled and had a successful event, mainly marked by the first of many spectacular airborn crashes at the circuit as Seattle's Bill Toews went flying in a Porsche Special.

Deer's Leap was the culprit as it was so many other times. Toews' description of the event, quoted in local papers the next day, is probably typical of what others said after a similar experience at the same place in later years. "Jim Rattenbury and I had just come to the crest of Deer Leap and I was just moving to overtake him. All of a sudden *Whosh!* Up I went. It was like I'd snagged a parachute. When I hit, I thought I was under control again, but over I went. I don't remember how many times."

Attendance of 5,000 to 10,000 spectators was common for even the most mundane race at Westwood during those early years. They came to see local heroes including Jim Rattenbury in a D-Jaguar, G. B. Sterne in a perennial Morgan, Arleigh Pilkey in a Lotus of some sort, and especially budding star Bob McLean, who started out in an MGA and soon moved to Formula Junior and up. Top regional drivers who entered routinely included Seattle's Jerry Grant and Pete Lovely, as well as Yakima, Washington's Lew Florence. The racing schedule at Westwood started out full and remained that way for the entire 32 years of its existence.

Westwood hosted grassroots racing at its best. Small-bore cars line up for a Le Mans start on a wet Westwood afternoon. It often rained, and a racing day in the 1960s usually concluded with two Le Mans start races, one for over-1,600- and one for under-1,600-cc cars. (Photo Courtesy Tom Johnston)

"Almost spooky" said track announcer Vince Howlett of the atrocious conditions for the 1967 Pepsi Pro event. Here, John Randall leads eventual winner Ross de St. Croix. (Photo Courtesy Vince Howlett Collection)

For instance, both the 1960 and 1990 seasons saw 10 races being held. Races varied over the years from the local conference and club affairs to big-time Formula Atlantic and Trans-Am events. Spectator turnout remained strong, too, all through the circuit's three decades, despite the popular media's increasing fascination with professional sports.

Track management, surprisingly enough, was never a full-time occupation. It fell instead to the current president of the SCCBC. Bob and Hilda Randall shared the duties of that position for several years at the same time that their son John won many races there in a Brabham BT-5. Pete Jardot, the longest-serving president, had the unfortunate responsibility of overseeing the closure of the track during its last days.

During the 1950s, Le Mans-type starts were popular throughout the racing world; they dwindled in popularity rapidly as the 1960s started. However, they never went away at Westwood. All except the biggest feature race weekends in the 1960s began with Le Mans starts; sometimes two, one for smaller- and one for larger-bore cars. These hectic starts sometimes resulted in incidents such as the one in 1961 when two local drivers, Terry Nilsson and Lyle Forsgren, collided during the Le Mans dash to their cars, picked themselves up, and jumped into each other's vehicles!

My father had a very long running start. In one instance, he lost his key behind the seats upon entering his car. After the run across the track he embarrassed himself and his teenage son because he had to kneel down outside the car and fumble behind the cushions for the key while the rest of the field rumbled away in the distance.

Four Westwood late-1960s regulars share the track on a typically wet and dark day: the Rattenbury Special, Milt Davis in a 911, John Randall in a Brabham BT5, and G. B. Sterne in a Morgan. It's difficult to identify the race weekend; Westwood offered a dozen or more a year. (Photo Courtesy John Randall)

Westwood's Marquee Races

Westwood typically held two major events during each season. These races, named after their sponsors, were usually the Player's Pacific in the spring and the Pepsi Pro events in the fall. Different types of cars competed in these big races over the years, sports racers to formula. The season often ended with endurance events of up to 10 hours long, although 7 hours was the most typical distance. Although the endurance

Don Jenson (Burnett Mk 2) chases Bill Cupp (Genie) in an early-1970s Westwood race being held in all-too-typical wet conditions. (Photo Courtesy John Randall)

The start of the 1967 Player's Pacific race sees frequent Westwood winner Lew Florence leading in a Genie, followed by race winner Bill Amick driving a McLaren and Stan Burnett with a Burnett Special. (Photo Courtesy Ron Miller)

Pepsi Pro

Western Canada's Pepsi bottlers sponsored the Pepsi event, and it attracted top Northwest drivers as well as cross-Canada heroes, such as Eppie Wietzes. Initially the feature event of a Pepsi weekend was for Group 6 (Can-Am type) cars. These events saw cars and drivers just a step below those being featured in the Can-Am circuit, such as Genies, Cobras, and Ford GT40s. The Pepsi Pro for sports cars was staged from 1965 through 1969 and saw such top drivers as California's Chuck Parsons and Oregon's Monte Shelton winning the feature. The Pepsi Pro moved from being sports car dominated to featuring formula cars in the early 1970s. The last Pepsi Pro event at Westwood was in 1974.

races attracted mainly local drivers (not to mention what must have been a very dedicated crew of workers; these events often being held in dismal late-fall weather conditions), events such as the Pepsi Pro and Player's Pacific had more universal appeal.

A noteworthy early Pepsi Pro event was the 1966 edition. The biggest Westwood race of the season, as far as prize money went ($7,500), it was held on October 1 and settled the Canadian Drivers' championship for the year. Ross de St. Croix

Westwood began featuring Formula cars in the 1970s. Sharing the front row in this 1970 Pepsi Pro are Eppie Wietzes, McLaren Mk10B and Bill Brack, Lotus 70. Wietzes won his 3rd big title at the track in this race. (Photo Courtesy Murray Chambers)

You'd think that stock cars would be too big and clumsy for the Westwood track, but here they are in an early-1970s race. (Photo Courtesy Gerry Lomas)

Even as the area around it was being developed and the popularity of road racing declined, big crowds continued to come out to Westwood in the 1970s. (Photo Courtesy Gerry Lomas)

In a 1980 Trans-Am race, Rick Stark is about to overtake the damaged car of Greg Nichols. Both men are in C3 Corvettes. (Photo Courtesy Brent Martin)

beat Eppie Wietzes in the two-heat event to take both the race and season crowns over Wietzes, who came in 2nd in both areas. Wietzes drove the same GT-40 he had campaigned extensively for a couple of years; de St. Croix drove a McLaren-Chevy.

The races were held in typical hard Westwood rain and de St. Croix stood ankle-deep in water as he received his victor's spoils at the start/finish area. At least two top cars were almost destroyed in puddle-caused spin/crashes, and several other contenders could not handle the wet and gloomy conditions that track announcer Vince Howlett described as "almost spooky." Photos from the race indicate that this was not hyperbole.

The Pepsi series ushered in the domination of open-wheeled formula cars as the track's most popular group with its 1969 Formula A race. The Canadian Formula A series was not as big as Formula A or F5000 was in the United States. Nevertheless, it attracted some top drivers, including Eppie Wietzes, Horst Kroll, and Bill Brack. Formulas B and Formula Ford headlined in the 1969–1974 editions of the Pepsi Pro. The sponsor bowed out after the 1974 season.

Player's Pacific

The Player's Pacific had a much longer run. From the first event in 1962, the English tobacco company known for its sponsorship of the Lotus F1 team in the 1970s sponsored headliner events at the track most seasons through the last year. As with the Pepsi event, organizers frequently tried to place the date of their event near a big event south of the Canadian border to attract top drivers who were participating in such events as a USRRC weekend at Seattle's Pacific Raceways. But the weekend could stand on its own merits, especially when it became part of the early Canadian national championship for road racing and then when it went on to be a scoring part of formula car circuits.

The Player's Pacific eventually attracted such top drivers as Keke Rosberg and Dan Marvin. The Player's began by featuring Group 6 sports car main events and switched its focus to single-seater formula cars in the 1970s, as happened with the Pepsi event. Western Canadian fans seemed to love formula car racing. Formula Ford was the featured marque of the

Tom Johnston raced and sponsored cars at Westwood in the 1970s, and became its historian 30 years later. Here, his Johnston FA (#3), driven by Ross Bentley, leads Bruce Shaughnessy's Lola (#21). (Photo Courtesy Brent Martin)

Trans-Am Porsches come down the back straight over Deer's Leap. Lush greenery has finally grown over the rocks that lined the course. (Photo Courtesy Robert Barg)

Mixed formulas became a regular thing at Westwood in the 1980s. Here, Bob McGregor, in the winning March 78B Formula Atlantic (#17), leads three Formula Fords into the hairpin turn. (Photo Courtesy Brent Martin)

early 1970s Pepsi Pro events, and Formula B was the feature of early 1970s Player's, followed by the ferocious Formula Atlantics starting in 1974 under the auspices of the Canadian Auto Sports Committee (CASC).

Formula Atlantic

Formula Atlantic became the biggest draw of the course during the 1980s; the popular series, which sometimes went under different names but featured the same cars, drew the largest crowds ever seen at Westwood. Such stars as Gilles Villeneuve, Keke Rosberg, and Michael Andretti competed at Westwood. Local favorites who could hang with the top dogs of the day included Frank Allers and Andy Mahood in formula cars and Tony Morris in stock cars.

To no one's surprise, a Formula Atlantic car eventually set the ultimate track record at Westwood. Although in the early days a sub-1:00 lap would have been all but inconceivable, it was achieved and stands today as the never-to-be-broken 58.75. Michael Andretti in a Ralt RT4 Cosworth Atlantic car turned this astonishing time during a 1983 qualifying. Only one other driver ever dipped under 1:00 at Westwood, Hiro Matsushita in an Formula Atlantic Swift DB-4, who did 59.705 in a 1989 Player's Pacific race.

NASCAR, Trans-Am and Club Racing

NASCAR held Winston West and Western Grand National series races at Westwood, and the biggest races were run in the mid-1970s. Well-known American NASCAR drivers were not on hand, so regional drivers won. The American-made iron made quite a favorable impression on locals as these large cars navigated the tricky course.

Trans-Am racing came to Westwood more than once; however, the much-loved original series missed the Canadian course. The later Trans-Am incarnation of the mid-1970s held several events there, though, and attracted top names, such as Peter Gregg, Ludwig Heimrath, and John Paul.

Club racing of course continued, and in one of the last races at the track, Lawrence Howlett turned in a 1:26 lap in a Honda Civic, no less. This was the same time turned in 30 years earlier as a lap record by Pete Lovely in a Lotus 15, dramatically showing the development of cars during the track's 32 seasons.

The Final Years

Rumors began to circulate that the track was facing some unforeseen difficulties. But racing went on. The most traditional club race of course was the inevitable endurance event, still held at the end of the season. Over the years, the organizers grew a bit wiser and ended the season earlier in the fall, thus reducing the chance that the Enduro would be run in the deplorable conditions that the track was famous for (and some stalwart SCCBC members no doubt secretly enjoyed).

In fact, the last event at the track was indeed the endurance race, a seven-hour affair held on October 8, 1990. Everyone present was quite aware that this was the track's swan song, and much sorrow was expressed as the popular track closed its gates forever. Professional drivers Ross and Gord Bentley were the last winners at the track in that event, driving their own Bentley B Sports Racer.

Westwood did not suffer a quick and dramatic decline and closure as did other tracks; rather, it simply started to fade. It was such a popular and challenging course with strong local support and it eventually slipped into mundane existence as a housing development. It was not simply because the track was becoming run down, as is often the case, and was just not worth preserving. In 1980 a group of SCCBC members formed an organization called Gateway Productions to improve the Westwood track and attract bigger racing groups. The group invested $60,000 on fencing, tree clearing, widening the track, and general cleanup, and these improvements were definitely noticeable.

A few years later, faced with the probability of the track being lost, a few other members contributed to make safety and access improvements, simply to make its last memories good ones. The track was still serviceable and attracting decent crowds and quality race cars. But the lure of the tax base it could produce if developed for housing was too strong an incentive for local government. They had their chance when the original lease, so hopefully signed in 1959, was up.

With fanfare, the last races were run in 1990 and the track was bulldozed to make way for golf courses and upscale homes. It was enough to make the remaining SCCBC drivers take up drinking once again.

Michael Andretti (#43) set the all-time Westwood course record driving a Ralt in the 1983 Formula Atlantic race. He won the race, too. Here, Josele Garza (#25) and Dan Marvin (#7) flank him. (Photo Courtesy Brent Martin)

The famed and feared Deer's Leap as it appears today: part of a quiet residential neighborhood. (Photo Courtesy Tom Johnston Collection)

Men who raced at Westwood gather together at the current course location. What remains of the Carousel Turn is in the background. (Photo Courtesy Martin Rudow)

EPILOGUE

The last exhaust notes have long since faded away from the tracks featured in *Lost Road Courses*. For a long time these tracks were remembered only in old racing magazines, rarely-seen private photo collections from people who were there, or when someone stumbled across a part of an old racetrack such as Meadowdale or Marlboro.

But now they, or at least the cars that raced on them, have received a second life.

Vintage racing came on like gangbusters in the 1990s, and car aficionados started buying classic race cars that ran on defunct historic tracks, such as Riverside and Bridgehampton. Just an "old race car" rusting away in the corner of a barn or garage quickly became a valued vintage racer as interest in racing cars from the 1950s, 1960s, and 1970s soared. Modern racetracks, such as Laguna Seca and Road America, found that their most popular road course events were vintage races. Watkins Glen shut down the town again to hold vintage racing festivals.

At the same time vintage racing grew in popularity, the stories of the old days of road racing came into demand too. Many books have now been written about the great cars, races, and drivers of the era. Mark Donahue, Walt Hansgen, and Dave MacDonald have been the subject of books and major magazine articles detailing their exciting careers. Dan Gurney, Phil Hill, Parnelli Jones, Carroll Shelby, and others were, and still are, celebrated featured guests at vintage racing events. Today you can see many of the actual cars that appear in this book back out there on the track in vintage events.

As for the tracks themselves, none seem poised for similar revival. Only Greenwood and Marlboro remain relatively complete, and their surfaces and support facilities have crumbled or disappeared entirely. The same forces that combined to hasten their original departures are present to an even greater degree: the need for land development, complaints about noise and traffic congestion on race days, the need to reinvest in crumbling road surfaces, and fading interest in road racing. It is more likely that those few courses that still exist will too soon disappear entirely. However, this book presents a sojourn back to the glory days of these tracks. When Gurney, Donahue, Unser, Jones, Foyt, and many other legendary drivers waged battle in Trans-Am, Indy Car, Can-Am, Formula 1 and stocks cars.

Tracks, such as Riverside, War Bonnet, Augusta, Continental Divide, and the like, have left an enduring legacy. These tracks set the stage for top drivers supported by the best teams to drive some of the most innovative and fastest cars. And often the fans, who attended these races, witnessed some of the most thrilling and fiercest racing of the era. And although the tracks no longer host races and in most cases do not exist, these tracks often contributed to the development of safety procedures at other tracks, and those other tracks learned about facility management, race promotion, and many other factors that contribute to long-term success.

They should be remembered and celebrated for being colorful, exciting, and sometimes dangerous arenas. They were simply and gloriously the result of the dreams of men and women whose reach exceeded their grasp. The memories they created for those lucky enough to be there (and even for those who followed them closely from afar) are still held dear.

Facing Page: The field prepares for the start of the 1955 Watkins Glen Grand Prix. Farm buildings loom in the background as a late-afternoon hazy sun illuminates the landscape. Duncan Black (Ferrari 4.5) and Sherwood Johnston (D-Type Jaguar) sit on the front row; onlookers, course officials, photographers, and pit crew personnel obscure the rest of the field. Johnston handily won on this course, but its configuration only lasted three short years at the Glen. (Photo Courtesy International Motor Racing Research Center, Gus Iacozili Collection)

Additional books that may interest you...

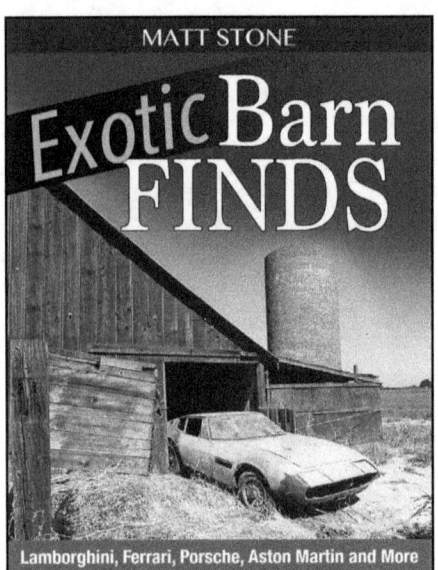

EXOTIC BARN FINDS *by Matt Stone* Veteran author and historian tells the story of more than 25 barn finds. The unique twist? Rather than the usual prewar or muscle car era product out of Detroit, these cars are all beloved imported sports cars of a bygone era. Think Ferrari, Lamborghini, Jaguar, Aston-Martin, Porsche, Maserati, Alfa Romeo, and others. There is even a Jay Leno-found 300SL Gullwing in the mix! Although there is no shortage of "barn find" tales surfacing these days, no collection covers exclusively the imported sports car icons that have become household names from an era past. All the tales are told with full detail on how they were found and why they are special. Softbound, 8.5 x 11 inches, 144 pages, 350 color photos. *Item # CT541*

MOTORAMA: GM's Legendary Show & Concept Cars *by David Temple* Motorama expert and experienced author David Temple has comprehensively researched the show, the cars, and the personalities to create a fascinating story with new photos of these magnificent cars. Temple goes into detail on the body, frame, engine, drivetrain, and special features of each showcase model. He has also retraced the ownership histories of some of these cars. This book features fascinating period photography of Motorama cars at the show, in development, and at different locales. No other automotive show rivaled the extravagant and elaborate Motorama for stunning productions and awe-inspiring cars. Hardbound, 8.5 x 11 inches, 192 pages, 400 color and b/w photos. *Item # CT533*

DAVID KIMBLE'S CUTAWAYS *by David Kimble* This book reveals the secrets, techniques, procedures, and the dedication to craft that is required to produce these amazing illustrations. Kimble covers the step-by-step procedures while producing fresh artwork for this book featuring a McLaren Can-Am car as well as a vintage Harley-Davidson. Although the procedures covered here are unique to Kimble, and pretty much a pipe dream to mere mortals, this title provides an inside look into how he does it. Also included are the stories and tales of how it all started, traveling the world to illustrate cars, behind the scenes with manufacturers, the Corvette years, as well as a gallery of many illustrations. Never before has David Kimble shared the procedures for bringing these beautiful technical illustrations to life. Hardbound, 11 x 8.5 inches, 192 pages, 210 color images. *Item # CT535*

LOST DRAG STRIPS II: More Ghosts of Quarter-Miles Past *by Scotty Gosson* This book picks up where the best-selling first volume left off, covering even more tracks with archival photos of racing in the tracks' heyday and coverage of the notable cars that ran there. This volume also includes some of the tracks that survived, those that fought off the economic demons and the urban sprawl and that against all odds, continue to operate today. Softbound, 8.5 x 11 inches, 176 pages, 265 photos. *Item #CT550*

Check out our website:

CarTechBooks.com

✓ Find our newest books before anyone else

✓ Get weekly tech tips from our experts

✓ Get your ride or project featured on our homepage!

**Exclusive Promotions and Giveaways on Facebook
Like us to WIN! Facebook.com/CarTechBooks**

www.cartechbooks.com or 1-800-551-4754

www.ingramcontent.com/pod-product-compliance
Lightning Source LLC
LaVergne TN
LVHW081534060526
838200LV00048B/2081